TABLE OF CONTENTS

STUDY GUIDE

Jane P. Sheldon, Ph.D.
University of Michigan-Dearborn

Psychology: Core Conce~~pts~~

Philip G. Zimbardo
Stanford University

Robert L. Johnson
Umpqua Community College

Vivian McCann
Portland Community College

PEARSON

Boston Columbus Indianapolis New York San Francisco Upper Saddle River
Amsterdam Cape Town Dubai London Madrid Milan Munich Paris Montréal Toronto
Delhi Mexico City São Paulo Sydney Hong Kong Seoul Singapore Taipei Tokyo

PEARSON

10 9 8 7 6 5 4 3 2 1

ISBN 10: 0-205-25299-0
ISBN 13: 978-0-205-25299-2

PREFACE

This Student Study Guide is designed to help you explore the world of psychology. Psychology has applications to many aspects of your life; it can help you be a better student, a more productive employee, and a more successful parent. This study guide will assist you as you read, conceptualize, and synthesize the material in the text.

Each Chapter includes the following sections:

> **Before You Read . . . Term Identification**
> This section contains a list of key terms from the chapter along with a page reference for each term. The best way to use this list is to make flashcards or, even better, develop mnemonics (memory strategies) to help you remember the different concepts and terms. Use the definitions in the margins of the textbook chapter for help.

> **Lecture Assistant**
> This outline is meant for you to bring to class to help you take notes. Information is organized for you so that you can spend less time writing and more time listening to lecture and synthesizing material. It is also a great place to begin studying the chapter content!

> **As You Read . . . Practice Activities**
> These sections include questions and other activities designed to help you comprehend the material and apply the concepts to your life. There are numerous exercises that are designed to engage you in actively processing the material, and Web links have been included so that you can further explore many of the topics. You will find complete answer keys for these activities and exercises in the Appendix.

> **After You Read . . . Practice Tests**
> These sections are designed to help you review what you have learned and discover whether you need to further study any of the material. A series of practice tests and a comprehensive review test give you practice in test taking and help you to review what you know. Answers for these tests are found in the Appendix.

> I hope you will find this Student Study Guide a helpful ancillary in your study of psychology and that you find that study an exciting and rewarding journey.

Acknowledgments

This Student Study Guide was not a solitary undertaking. Several people assisted me as I prepared this work. Specifically, I thank:

* The authors of this text, Philip G. Zimbardo, Robert L. Johnson, and Vivian McCann, for writing a textbook that students find readable and interesting. I am grateful to have had a small part in creating such a wonderful resource.

* My editor at Pearson, Kerri Hart-Morris, for her insights, feedback, and patience.

* Bob Wolf, for his unending encouragement, understanding, and support.

Jane P. Sheldon, Ph.D.
Professor of Psychology
University of Michigan-Dearborn

CHAPTER 1
Mind, Behavior, and Psychological Science

Before You Read... Term Identification

Make flashcards using the following terms or, even better, develop mnemonics (memory strategies) to help you remember the different concepts and terms. Use the definitions in the margins of this chapter for help. Numbers refer to page numbers in the textbook.

applied psychologists (5)
behavioral perspective (17)
behaviorism (16)
biological perspective (12)
case study (31)
cognitive perspective (16)
confirmation bias (8)
control group (27)
correlational study (28)
critical thinking skills (7)
cross-cultural psychologists (20)
culture (20)
data (26)
dependent variable (27)
developmental perspective (19)
double-blind study (32)
emotional bias (8)
empirical investigation (24)
expectancy bias (31)
experimental group (27)
evolutionary psychology (13)
experimental psychologists (5)
functionalism (15)
humanistic psychology (18)
hypothesis (24)
independent variable (27)

informed consent (32)
introspection (14)
naturalistic observation (30)
necker cube (16)
negative correlation (29)
neuroscience (13)
operational definitions (24)
placebo (32)
positive correlation (28)
pseudo-psychology (7)
psychiatry (6)
psychoanalysis (19)
psychodynamic psychology (17)
psychology (4)
random assignment (28)
replicate (26)
scientific method (24)
sociocultural perspective (19)
structuralism (14)
survey (30)
teachers of psychology (5)
theory (24)
trait and temperament psychology (18)
whole-person perspectives (18)
zero correlation (29)

Lecture Assistant *for Chapter 1*

Tear this outline out and bring it with you to class in order to facilitate your note taking.
Spend more time listening to the lecture and less time writing!

Chapter Opening Problem: How would you test the claim that sugar makes children hyperactive?

1.1 WHAT IS PSYCHOLOGY—AND WHAT IS IT NOT?

- *Psychoanalysis =*

- *Psychology* (from "psyche," the ancient Greek word for "mind") =

  Core Concept 1.1 *(What is the broad definition of psychology?)* =

A) Psychology: It's More than You Think

1) Three Ways of Doing Psychology:

- *Experimental Psychologists =*

- *Teachers of Psychology =*

- *Applied Psychologists =*

2) Applied Psychological Specialties (their names and what the practitioners do):

a) _____

b) _____

c) _____

d) _____

e) _____

f) _____

B) Psychology Is Not Psychiatry

C) Thinking Critically about Psychology and Pseudo-Psychology

- *Pseudo-psychology =*

1) <u>Six Critical Thinking Skills:</u>

   a)

   b)

   c)
- *Anecdotal Evidence =*

   d)
- *Emotional Bias =*

- *Confirmation Bias =*

   e)

   f)

D) Thinking Critically about the Chapter Problem

E) Psychology Matters: Using Psychology to Learn Psychology

- *Cognitive Map (Concept Map) =*

1.2 WHAT ARE PSYCHOLOGY'S SIX MAIN PERSPECTIVES?

Core Concept 1.2 =

A) Separation of Mind and Body and the Modern Biological Perspective

- René Descartes =

1) <u>The Modern Biological Perspective</u> =

2) <u>Two Variations on the Biological Theme</u> =

- *Neuroscience =*

- *Evolutionary Psychology =*

    ○   *Natural Selection =*

B) The Founding of Scientific Psychology and the Modern Cognitive Perspective

1) <u>Wilhelm Wundt</u> =

- *Periodic table* =

2) <u>Introspecting for the Elements of Conscious Experience</u> =

- *Reaction time* =

- *Introspection* =

3) <u>Wundt's Legacy: Structuralism</u> =

- Edward Bradford Titchener =

- *Structuralism* =

4) <u>James and the Function of Mind and Behavior</u> =

- William James =

- *Functionalism* =

5) <u>The Modern Cognitive Perspective</u> =

- *Cognition* =

C) The Behavioral Perspective: Focusing on Observable Behavior =

- *Behaviorists* =

- John B. Watson =

- *Behaviorism* =

- B. F. Skinner =

- *Behavioral perspective* =

D) The Whole-Person Perspectives: Psychodynamic, Humanistic, Trait, & Temperament

- Freud *and psychoanalytic theory* =

1) <u>Psychodynamic Psychology</u> =

- *Psychoanalysis =*

- *Whole-person perspectives =*

2) <u>Humanistic Psychology</u> =

3) <u>Trait and Temperament Psychology</u> =

E) The Developmental Perspective: Changes Arising from Nature and Nurture =

- *Nature =*

- *Nurture =*

F) The Sociocultural Perspective: The Individual in Context =

- *Culture =*

- *Cross-cultural psychologists =*

G) The Changing Face of Psychology =

- Mary Whiton Calkins =

H) Psychology Matters: Psychology as a Major

- *Educational requirements =*

- *Types of jobs =*

1.3 HOW DO PSYCHOLOGISTS DEVELOP NEW KNOWLEDGE?

A) Core Concept 1.3 =

- *Scientific method =*

- *Empirical investigation =*

- *Theory =*

B) Four Steps in the Scientific Method:

1) Step 1 =

- *Hypothesis =*

- *Operational definitions =*

2) Step 2 =

- *Data*

3) Step 3 =

4) Step 4 =

- *Replicate =*

C) Five Types of Psychological Research:

1) Experiments =

- *Independent variable =*

- *Dependent variable =*

- *Experimental group =*

- *Control group =*

- *Random assignment =*

2) Correlational Studies =

- *Positive correlation =*

- *Negative correlation =*

- *Zero correlation =*

3) Surveys =

- *Social desirability bias =*

4) <u>Naturalistic Observations</u> =

5) <u>Case Studies</u> =

D) Controlling Biases in Psychological Research

Even the Rat Was White =

- *Expectancy bias* =

- *Placebo* =

- *Double-blind study* =

E) Ethical Issues in Psychological Research

- Ethical Principles of Psychologists and Code of Conduct (2002) =

- *Informed consent* =

- *Deception* =

- *Animal studies* =

F) Psychology Matters: The Perils of Pseudo-Psychology

G) Critical Thinking Applied: Facilitated Communication

- *Autism* =

ADDITIONAL NOTES

What Is Psychology—and What Is It Not?

1. *Fill in the blanks with the correct information.*

   The ancient Greek word "psyche" means _____ and the suffix

   "ology" means _____; therefore, "psychology" literally means

   _____.

2. In what ways is the definition of "psychology" you gave in question #1 similar to and different from the broader Core Concept definition explained in the text?

3. What does it mean that psychology covers both "internal" and "external" factors?

Psychology: It's More than You Think

4. According to the textbook, what are the three main categories of psychologists?

   A. _____   B. _____   C. _____

5. *Fill in each blank with the category of psychologist that makes the statement correct.*

   A. Of the three broad categories of psychologists, _____ psychologists constitute the smallest group.

   B. The majority of _____ psychologists work at a college or university, where most also teach.

   C. Psychologists who work in clinics or hospitals are most likely to be _____ psychologists.

   D. _____ at community colleges generally are not required to do research.

   E. Another name for _____ psychologists is research psychologists.

6. Your text describes six of the most common applied psychology specialties. *In the blanks provided, name the type of applied psychologist you would consult if you experienced the circumstances described below.*

    A. A family member has been showing signs of serious depression.

    _____

    B. You want to design effective programs to teach the public to conserve energy.

    _____

    C. You are confused by the results of your child's standardized academic achievement tests. _____

    D. You are a lawyer who needs help with jury selection.

    _____

    E. You are the vice president at a company that has been experiencing a very high turnover rate for the past year. _____

    F. You are a competitive soccer player who experiences high anxiety before big matches.

    _____

7. To learn much more about different careers in psychology, visit this site:
http://www.psywww.com/careers/websites.htm

Psychology Is Not Psychiatry

8. *Indicate whether each statement is True (T) or False (F) by circling the appropriate letter after the statement.*

A. Psychiatrists cannot prescribe medication.	T F
B. Most psychologists treat mental disorders.	T F
C. Psychiatrists always have a Doctor of Medicine (MD) degree.	T F
D. Psychiatrists can prescribe medication but they cannot perform other medical procedures.	T F
E. Psychiatry is the science of mental processes and behavior.	T F
F. Graduate training in psychology usually emphasizes research methods.	T F
G. Most psychiatrists use a medical perspective with their patients.	T F
H. Psychiatry is a broader field of study than psychology.	T F

9. Differentiate between psychologists and psychiatrists in terms of training and what they typically do.

PSYCHOLOGISTS	VS.	PSYCHIATRISTS

Psychology Matters:
Thinking Critically about Psychology and Pseudo-Psychology

10. Define "pseudo-psychology."

11. Give at least three examples of pseudo-psychology that are discussed in the text.

A. _____

B. _____

C. _____

12. The authors of your textbook list several critical thinking skills they want you to develop. What are the six questions the authors believe you should ask yourself when you confront new ideas?

A. _____

B. _____

C. _____

D. _____

E. _____

F. _____

13. *For each example below, tell which of the six critical thinking questions are most applicable and explain why.*

    A. In a TV ad for "fat-burning" pills, a man who has taken the pills states that he lost forty pounds in one month. In addition, a physician states that she recommends the pills to her patients who are trying to lose weight.

Critical Thinking Questions: _____

_____

_____

_____

    B. Your friend returns from a visit to a psychic and excitedly tells you how accurate the psychic's knowledge of his past and present experiences was. He says that because the psychic knew so much about his past and present, he's sure that her predictions about his future are going to come true.

Critical Thinking Questions: _____

_____

_____

_____

    C. You read an Internet article that says kids who go on shooting sprees at school and kill their classmates all have been victims of bullying. The authors of the article, a high-school principal and vice principal, point out that at their school, they've had no violence of any kind because they developed and instituted an anti-bullying program in their school. They offer to give workshops about their program to other school personnel for a minimal fee.

Critical Thinking Questions: _____

_____

_____

_____

14. Why should we be wary of anecdotal evidence?

15. Define "confirmation bias" and explain how it can negatively affect critical thinking.

16. *Fill in the blanks with the correct terms.*

    A. Paying attention to information that is consistent with our beliefs while ignoring information that is contrary to our beliefs is the _____.

    B. Evidence based on just a few people's experiences is known as _____ evidence.

    C. The tendency to make judgments based more on attitudes and feelings than on rational thoughts is known as _____.

17. To engage in critical thinking and explore pseudo-psychology further, visit the *James Randi Educational Foundation* at the following site:

                http://www.randi.org

James Randi used to be known as The Amazing Randi, a successful magician. Using his knowledge of illusions, deception, and magic tricks, he formed his organization to teach the public critical-thinking skills and to expose, using the scientific method, individuals who are purposefully using pseudo-psychology to take advantage of others.

Psychology Matters: Using Psychology to Learn Psychology

18. What is a "cognitive map"?

What Are Psychology's Six Main Perspectives?

19. About 2,500 years ago, what beliefs in the following societies laid the foundations for psychology?

    A. Greek society _____

    _____

B. Asian society _____

_____

C. African society _____

_____

20. According to the text, what were the two main influences on the development of Western psychology as a science?

    A. _____   B. _____

21. In Medieval Europe, why did the Church actively discourage exploration of human nature?

22. Name the six modern perspectives in psychology.

    A. _____   D. _____

    B. _____   E. _____

    C. _____   F. _____

Separation of Mind and Body and the Modern Biological Perspective

23. In the seventeenth century, what radical concept related to psychology did René Descartes propose? What were scientists able to discover because of Descartes' ideas?

24. *Fill in the blanks with the correct information.*

    The biological view has strong roots in _____ and _____ . The field of _____ combines biological psychology, biology, neurology, and other fields interested in brain processes. _____ psychology is a variation on the biological perspective. It is based on the work of _____ . It suggests that our characteristics come from the process of _____ .

The Founding of Scientific Psychology and the Modern Cognitive Perspective

25. *In the space provided next to each approach or perspective, write the names of the individuals associated with that concept. More than one name can be used for each.*

    NAMES: John Dewey, William James, Edward Titchener, Wilhelm Wundt

A. Introspection _____

B. Functionalism _____

C. Structuralism _____

D. Progressive education _____

26. *Match each term to its most appropriate definition or description by writing the letter of the term in the space next to the description. Terms can be used more than once.*

TERMS
A. Functionalism   B. Introspection   C. Structuralism

DESCRIPTIONS
_____ Devoted to revealing the components of the mind
_____ Tied to applied psychology
_____ Wundt is the "father" of this
_____ Devoted to understanding how and why the mind works
_____ Subjective rather than objective
_____ Describing one's own perceptions and emotions

27. What role did chemistry's periodic table play in the development of psychology?

28. For a wonderful, fascinating biography of William James, visit this website:
     http://www.des.emory.edu/mfp/jphotos.html

29. What does the modern cognitive perspective emphasize?

The Behavioral Perspective: Rejection of Introspection and a Focus on Observable Behavior

30. Why did John B. Watson, B. F. Skinner, and other behaviorists believe that the mind should not be the focus of study in psychology?

31. Briefly explain the behavioral perspective.

32. A great, easy-to-read biography of John B. Watson can be found at:
    http://facweb.furman.edu/~einstein/watson/watson1.htm

The Whole-Person Perspectives: Psychodynamic, Humanistic, Trait, & Temperament

33. What is the difference between a *psychoanalyst* and a *psychologist*?

34. *Match each term to its most appropriate definition or description by writing the letter of the term in the space next to the description (one letter per space). Terms may be used more than once.*

TERMS
A. Psychodynamic psychology   C. Humanistic psychology
B. Psychoanalysis   D. Trait & temperament psychology

DESCRIPTIONS
_____ Emphasizes the idea that the mind can be unconscious
_____ Emphasizes human beings' free will
_____ Includes the idea that unconscious energies motivate people's behavior
_____ Uses free association and the analysis of dreams
_____ Emphasizes stable personality differences between people
_____ Focuses on the positive aspects of human nature
_____ Usually used by physicians with a specialty in psychiatry and special advanced
       training

35. What are the Big Five, and what theory incorporates this concept?

The Developmental Perspective: Changes Arising from Nature and Nurture

36. According to the text, the main idea that defines the developmental perspective is:

_____

_____

The Sociocultural Perspective: The Individual in Context

37. What are cross-cultural psychologists, and what bias in psychology are they trying to counter?

38. Define "culture."

Section Summary

39. Complete the table below. For each of the perspectives, identify any subcategories and then tell what processes would be emphasized by a psychologist associated with the general perspective.

Perspective & Subcategories	Emphasized Processes
A. Biological	
B. Cognitive	
C. Behavioral	
D. Whole-Person	
E. Developmental	
F. Sociocultural	

The Changing Face of Psychology

40. Who was Mary Whiton Calkins? _____

41. The following site about Mary Whiton Calkins presents a terrific overview of her life:

42. *Indicate whether each statement is True (T) or False (F) by circling the appropriate letter after the statement.*

    A. Currently, about 50 percent of the doctorates in psychology are awarded to women.   T F

    B. In 1950, the American Psychological Association elected its first female president.   T F

    C. In 1906, only 20 percent of American psychologists were women.   T F

43. An excellent website devoted to the history of women in psychology and in related fields is one by Dr. Linda Woolf of Webster University and her students: http://www.webster.edu/~woolflm/women.html

44. For a detailed timeline of the inclusion of African Americans in U.S. psychology, visit the following American Psychological Association (APA) site: http://www.apa.org/pi/oema/resources/african-american-psychology.pdf

Psychology Matters: Psychology as a Major

45. *Indicate whether each statement is True (T) or False (F) by circling the appropriate letter after the statement.*

    A. In most states, a license to practice psychology requires a doctoral degree and a supervised internship.   T F

    B. Most college or university teaching jobs require at least a master's degree.   T F

    C. In many states, master's-level psychologists in private practice are not allowed to advertise themselves as "psychologists."   T F

46. NEED A BREAK?
To get a better understanding of the field of psychology, visit MyPsychLab.

How Do Psychologists Develop New Knowledge?

47. Explain the main way(s) that pseudo-psychology differs from psychology.

48. *Fill in the blanks with the correct terms.*

   A. A testable explanation for a set of facts or observations is known as a scientific

   _____.

   B. The _____ is a way to put ideas to an objective pass-fail
      test.

   C. _____ involves collecting objective information using
      careful measurements based on direct experience.

   D. In science, a _____ is <u>not</u> just a guess or speculation.

49. According to the text, a good theory has what two attributes?

   A. _____   B. _____

Four Steps of the Scientific Method

50. Name the four steps of the scientific method and describe what happens in each one.

Step of Scientific Method	What Happens
A.	
B.	
C.	
D.	

51. *Match each term with its description by placing the letter corresponding to the term in the
    space next to its description.*

TERMS
A. Replicate   D. Control group   G. Operational definitions
B. Dependent variable   E. Data   H. Experimental group
C. Hypothesis   F. Independent variable   I. Random assignment

20

DESCRIPTIONS

_____ Individuals in a controlled test who do not receive the treatment

_____ A statement predicting the outcome of a study

_____ The measured outcome of an experiment

_____ Pieces of information gathered in a study

_____ Individuals are divided into groups by chance alone

_____ Individuals in a controlled test who receive the treatment

_____ The factor that the researcher varies

_____ Objective descriptions of concepts that are involved in a scientific study

_____ A control for bias usually done by someone besides the researcher who did the original study

52. Why is it crucial that a research hypothesis be falsifiable?

Table 1.3: What Questions Can the Scientific Method _Not_ Answer?

53. What kinds of questions is science unable to answer?

54. *In the following example, identify the different parts of the study.*

Dr. Vargas is interested in seeing whether a new method of teaching psychology is better than his usual lecture method. He teaches one class using traditional lecture. He teaches the other using a discussion method. At the end of the term, he tests both classes to see which gets higher scores on the final exam.

A. Independent variable =

B. Dependent variable =

C. Control group =

D. Experimental group =

55. In the above example, what very important aspect of a controlled experiment is missing? Why might this omission be a problem in the study?

56. *Underline the word(s) in parentheses that will make each statement correct. (Both options may be correct!)*

A. A testable prediction is known as a (theory/hypothesis).

B. Controlled experiments need to have (operational definitions/an independent variable).

C. Researchers may use (replication/an experimental group) to discover whether the results of a study are accurate.

D. The outcome data of an experiment are the (independent variable/dependent variable).

E. To try to make certain there are no pre-existing differences between groups in an experiment, researchers use (replication/random assignment).

F. A researcher decides to measure intelligence by obtaining participants' scores on an intelligence test. Therefore, those test scores are the researchers' (independent variable/operational definition).

Five Types of Psychological Research

57. In the table below, name the five types of psychological research, briefly describe them, and tell any limitations of each.

Type of Research	Brief Description	Limitations
A.		
B.		
C.		
D.		
E.		

58. *Indicate whether each statement is True (T) or False (F) by circling the appropriate letter after the statement.*

   A. Naturalistic observations are the best scientific method to use to assess cause-and-effect relationships.   T F

   B. When there is no relationship between two variables, this is called a negative correlation.   T F

   C. Experiments allow the researcher more control over variables than any other research method.   T F

   D. A positive correlation indicates that an increase in one variable causes an increase in another variable.   T F

   E. A correlation coefficient of −0.80 indicates a very weak correlation.   T F

   F. Asking research participants questions is called the survey method.   T F

   G. The "clinical method" is also known as the experimental method.   T F

   H. Observing people in their usual surroundings and recording their behaviors is the research method referred to as case study.   T F

59. *Fill in the blanks with the correct information.*

   A _____ statistic summarizes the relationship between two variables. A _____ means there is no relationship between the variables. A _____ means that the variables change in the same direction (i.e., either both increase or both decrease). In a _____, one variable increases as the other decreases.

Controlling Biases in Psychological Research

60. *Underline the word(s) in parentheses that will make each statement correct. (Both options may be correct!)*

   A. If a researcher allows his or her expectations to affect the outcome of a study, this is referred to as (emotional/expectancy) bias.

   B. A (placebo study/double-blind study) is an experimental procedure in which neither the researcher nor the participants know who is in the experimental group and who is in the control group.

C. A way to get rid of expectancy bias in a study is to use a (correlational study/double-blind study).

D. Robert Guthrie's book, *Even the Rat Was White*, pointed out ways in which (expectancy bias/emotional bias) has long been a problem in psychological research.

E. A sham "drug" used in drug studies is often called a (placebo/sugar pill).

F. (Peer criticism/Replication) can help reduce bias in scientific research.

G. Researchers' biases can affect the way they (interpret results/design a study).

61. Visit the following website and participate in one of the many online studies being conducted by researchers from a variety of different universities!
http://psych.hanover.edu/research/exponnet.html

62. How does a double-blind study help reduce bias? Whose biases are reduced?

63. *Fill in the empty boxes of the concept map below.*

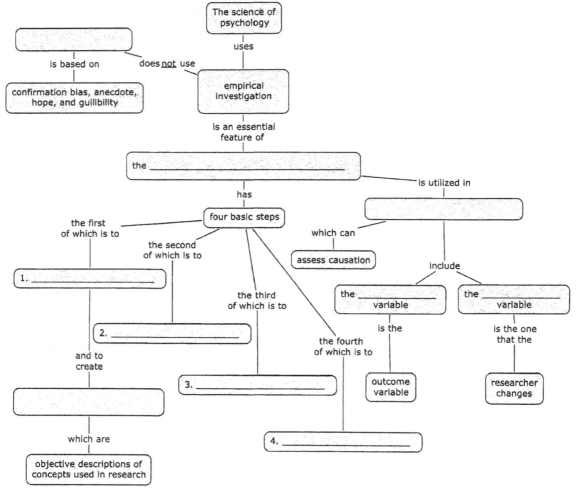

64. For each of the following vignettes, identify the best type(s) of research design for investigating the issue described. For each study, about which source(s) of research bias would you be most concerned?

TYPES OF DESIGNS		SOURCES OF BIAS
Experiment	Case study	Emotional bias
Correlational	Naturalistic observation	Confirmation bias
Survey		Expectancy bias

A. Researchers want to investigate claims made by a company that a supplement will increase weight loss threefold without causing physical problems.
    Design(s) chosen:
    Possible source(s) of bias:

B. Managers at a manufacturing firm are concerned about high turnover and low morale. They engage the consulting services of two industrial-organizational psychologists to find out what is going on in the departments with the worst records over the past three months.
    Design(s) chosen:
    Possible source(s) of bias:

C. Child development specialists want to test the assertion that preschool-aged children who are in daycare more than twenty hours per week have more behavioral problems than those who are not in daycare at all.
    Design(s) chosen:
    Possible source(s) of bias:

D. An insurance company wants to gather information about safety-related behaviors of teenaged drivers in a region of the country where there has been a huge number of fatal accidents with teen drivers.
    Design(s) chosen:
    Possible source(s) of bias:

E. A team of biological psychologists and medical doctors want to know how development is affected in patients under the age of four who have had an entire hemisphere of their brain removed in order to control their seizures.
    Design(s) chosen:
    Possible source(s) of bias:

Ethical Issues in Psychological Research

65. According to the American Psychological Association's *Ethical Principles of Psychologist and Code of Conduct*, what two main ethical obligations do researchers have when dealing with research participants?

   A. _____   B. _____

66. *Fill in the blanks with the correct information.*

   A. In order to insure ethical practices, most research institutions have watchdog committees, called _____, which oversee research.

   B. Persons who have participated in research involving deception must be _____ after the study to make sure they suffer no lasting ill effects.

   C. APA ethical guidelines state that under most circumstances, participation in research should be _____ and _____.

   D. _____ insures that participants are apprised of the procedures of research, as well as any potential dangers, so that they can choose to opt out if desired.

67. Why might researchers need to use deception in a psychology study? What ethical safeguards are in place to protect participants in such studies?

68. What ethical guidelines are in place for animal research?

69. *Explore two outstanding professional organizations for psychologists (and for all others interested in psychology):*

   The American Psychological Association (APA) is one of the most prominent organizations in the country for psychologists. Visit its website at:
   http://www.apa.org

   The Association for Psychological Science (APS) is a professional organization that promotes scientific research in all fields of psychology. Visit:
   http://www.psychologicalscience.org

Psychology Matters: The Perils of Pseudo-Psychology

70. Give a specific example that shows why pseudo-psychology can be harmful.

Critical Thinking Applied: Facilitated Communication

71. *Underline the word(s) in parentheses that will make each statement correct. (Both options may be correct!)*

   A. "Facilitated communication" was a technique used with individuals who have (mental retardation/autism).

   B. It is a (substantiated/unfounded) belief that individuals with autism have untapped language abilities that can be accessed with help.

   C. (Anecdotal/Scientific) evidence showed that, when facilitators knew the questions posed to the autistic children, the children's answers made sense.

   D. Scientific research showed that when facilitators did not know the questions posed to the autistic children, the children's answers (made sense/did not make sense).

72. What lessons about critical thinking can we take away from the issue of facilitated communication?

PRACTICE TEST #1

1. Psychology is best defined as the scientific study of _____.
   A. human and animal behavior
   B. behavior and mental disturbance
   C. behavior and mental processes
   D. human behavior and animal instincts

2. Which of the following psychological perspectives is most closely associated with the study of attending, thinking, knowing, and remembering?
   A. behaviorist   B. cognitive   C. psychoanalytic   D. biological

3. _____ was the philosopher who asserted that the mind and body are separate.
   A. Aristotle   B. Plato   C. Descartes   D. Darwin

4. _____ is the practice of asking people to report their mental experience.
   A. Insight   B. Structuralism   C. Extrospection   D. Introspection

5. _____ focus on understanding the elements of consciousness.
   A. Structuralists
   B. Functionalists
   C. Evolutionists
   D. Behaviorists

6. Which of the following psychological perspectives assumes that human behavior is best explained by unconscious conflicts?
   A. behaviorist
   B. cognitive
   C. psychodynamic
   D. humanistic

7. Which of the following psychological perspectives assumes that humans are intrinsically motivated to reach their full potential?
   A. behaviorist
   B. cognitive
   C. psychodynamic
   D. humanistic

8. Rena is a business executive who wants to increase worker productivity and communication, so she consults a(n) _____ psychologist.
   A. I/O   B. engineering   C. sports   D. clinical

9. Lindsay is a psychiatrist. She completed which of the following degrees?
   A. MD   B. PhD   C. EdD   D. PsyD

10. Dr. Jordan predicts that there is a relationship between the amount of chocolate a child eats and the hyperactivity level of the child. This prediction is a _____.
    A. theory   B. variable   C. hypothesis   D. paradigm

PRACTICE TEST #2

1. Jamal has had chronic pain since an accident. In desperation, he feels he has found relief in a mixture of seaweed and prune juice. He swears by this treatment, although he has seen many articles warning that it is a fraud. He could best be described as having a(n) _____ bias.
   A. expectancy   B. observer   C. confirmation   D. placebo

2. Steve is a psychologist who believes that behavior is controlled by events in the environment that happen after the behavior. He is most likely to be a(n) _____ psychologist.
   A. cognitive   B. evolutionary   C. behavioral   D. psychodynamic

3. Ted is seeing a humanistic psychologist for therapy. Ted's psychologist most likely focuses on _____.
   A. striving for growth and developing potential
   B. how Ted's environment has shaped his behavior
   C. cultural guidelines that shaped Ted's personality
   D. the conflict between personal desires and social restrictions

4. What best differentiates scientific psychology from pseudo-psychology?
   A. scientific psychology's focus on the natural rather than the social world
   B. scientific psychology's method of testing ideas against objective observations
   C. scientific psychology's absolute certainty of its findings
   D. scientific psychology's more widespread public acceptance

5. In an experiment, the variable that is manipulated is called the _____ variable.
   A. control   B. independent   C. dependent   D. confounding

6. Dr. Rodriguez wants to find out whether studying to music helps learning. She randomly assigns male and female students to two groups. One group studies while listening to music and the other studies without listening to any music. Both groups have similar grade point averages. She then compares the groups' scores on the final exam. In this study, the independent variable is _____.
   A. the gender of the students   C. whether or not the students listen to music
   B. grade point averages   D. students' scores on the final exam

7. Dr. Rodriguez wants to find out whether studying to music helps learning. She randomly assigns male and female students to two groups. One group studies while listening to music and the other studies without listening to any music. Both groups have similar grade point averages. She then compares the groups' scores on the final exam. In this study, the dependent variable is _____.
   A. the gender of the students   C. whether or not the students listen to music
   B. grade point averages   D. students' scores on the final exam

8. In a correlational study, the researcher is unable to exercise any control over the variables. Thus, correlation does not imply _____.
   A. the result   B. a relationship   C. causation   D. description

9. Professor Li is interested in studying children's social behaviors. To do this, he visits a preschool and carefully monitors and records the children's behavior. Professor Li is engaged in what type of research?
   A. survey research   C. case study
   B. naturalistic observation   D. experimental research

10. Dr. McMurphy has a client who has an unusual combination of disorders and life circumstances. Dr. McMurphy conducts an in-depth study of her client. She is engaged in what type of research?
    A. survey research   C. case study
    B. naturalistic observation   D. experimental research

PRACTICE TEST #3

1. Which of the following psychological perspectives is most closely associated with the study of external events in the environment?
   A. cognitive   B. behaviorism   C. biological   D. psychoanalytic

2. The primary focus in the _____ approach to psychology is to study _____.
   A. psychodynamic; unconscious mental conflicts
   B. humanistic; the overt expression of inner motives
   C. biological; mental mechanisms and adaptive functioning
   D. cognitive; the environmental causes and consequences of behavior

3. The moderate relationship between SAT scores and college grades is an example of a _____ correlation.
   A. positive   B. zero   C. negative   D. academic

4. All of the following are whole-person perspectives EXCEPT _____.
   A. humanistic psychology   C. cognitive psychology
   B. psychodynamic psychology   D. trait and temperament psychology

5. According to the APA ethical guidelines for research, what should psychologists avoid doing?
   A. using animals in experiments
   B. deceiving participants in experiments
   C. debriefing subjects after an experiment
   D. requiring participation in an experiment

6. John B. Watson was the first behaviorist. The behaviorist who followed Watson was _____.
   A. B. F. Skinner   C. Abraham Maslow
   B. William James   D. Sigmund Freud

7. The psychologist most associated with psychodynamic psychology is _____.
   A. B. F. Skinner   C. Carl Rogers
   B. William James   D. Sigmund Freud

8. What type of research design would be used to study whether happy people are healthier than unhappy people?
   A. correlational   C. behavioral
   B. experimental   D. sociocultural

9. The type of bias that leads people to pay attention only to information consistent with their own beliefs while ignoring information contrary to their beliefs is called _____ bias.
   A. expectancy   B. emotional   C. hindsight   D. confirmation

10. The _____ officially approves research done by psychologists at most universities.
    A. watchdog committee
    B. research committee
    C. institutional review board
    D. research review board

COMPREHENSIVE REVIEW TEST

1. In an effort to prevent participants in an experiment from trying to figure out what the researchers are studying (and thus biasing the results), psychologists sometimes _____.
   A. get written promises to answer honestly
   B. keep all information about the participant secret
   C. keep the true purpose from the participants
   D. make up a fake reason for conducting the study

2. The developmental perspective in psychology emphasizes _____.
   A. changes as we age   C. unconscious motivations
   B. biochemical processes   D. rewards in the environment

3. Alicia wants to understand peer pressure among adolescents, so she goes to a popular mall and carefully watches the activities and interactions of a group of adolescents. Alicia is using _____.
   A. self-report measures   C. conditioning
   B. introspection   D. naturalistic observation

4. Which historical school of psychology believed that mental processes could be best understood in terms of their adaptive purpose?
   A. structuralism   C. functionalism
   B. behaviorism   D. humanism

5. All of the following are operational definitions of happiness EXCEPT _____.
   A. the number of smiles in one hour   C. a person's joyful mood
   B. a rating on a happiness scale   D. a score on a happiness test

6. Rupert wants to learn whether men or women are better drivers. To determine this, he decides that he will measure driving ability by examining the number of tickets that people have received. Thus, he is using the number of tickets as _____.
   A. the control group   C. an independent variable
   B. the theory of good driving   D. an operational definition

7. Random assignment to conditions is essential in which of the following types of research?
   A. correlational   C. survey
   B. naturalistic observation   D. experimentation

8. A psychologist who studies how hormones affect a person's behavior is using the _____ approach.
   A. functional   B. structural   C. biological   D. evolutionary

9. The first laboratory in psychology was founded by _____.
   A. Ivan Pavlov   C. Wilhelm Wundt
   B. William James   D. Charles Darwin

10. Ivan is working with a company to help improve worker productivity. Ivan is most likely a(n) _____ psychologist.
    A. structural   B. environmental   C. forensic   D. I/O

11. The prediction that a researcher makes about the variables in a study is called a _____.
    A. theory   B. hypothesis   C. variable   D. correlation

12. The word "psyche" comes from the Greek word for _____.
    A. brain   B. study   C. mind   D. behavior

13. In true experiments, people are randomly divided into groups. Why is this done?
    A. to get a diverse, representative sample of people to participate in the experiment
    B. to find out whether there are correlations between groups
    C. to gain control over the research so that it can become a correlational study
    D. to try to make sure the groups are comparable before the treatment is given

14. If researchers find a positive correlation between the number of psychology courses completed and self-esteem level, this means that _____.
    A. people who take a lot of psychology courses also tend to have high self-esteem
    B. taking a lot of psychology courses causes an increase in people's self-esteem
    C. having high self-esteem makes people take a lot of psychology courses
    D. the higher people's self-esteem, the fewer psychology courses they take

15. William James is most associated with the _____ perspective in psychology.
    A. functionalist   C. historical
    B. biological   D. neurological

CRITICAL THINKING ESSAYS

1. Your friend reads an article about how playing video games can cause children to develop hyperactivity and how these games can cause cognitive damage. Because you have learned about the scientific method and the ways in which psychology studies such questions, what would you tell your friend about the article she read? What would you tell her to ask before getting rid of her son's video game system?

2. Discuss some of the ways in which psychologists and other scientists distinguish between science and pseudoscience. Why do you think pseudoscientific beliefs are so persistent in the face of the disconfirming evidence that has been produced?

3. In what ways are the six main perspectives of psychology similar and different?

CHAPTER 2
Biopsychology, Neuroscience, and Human Nature

Before You Read . . . Term Identification

Make flashcards using the following terms or, even better, develop mnemonics (memory strategies) to help you remember the different concepts and terms. Use the definitions in the margins of this chapter for help. Numbers refer to page numbers in the textbook.

action potential (52)
agonists (61)
all-or-none principle (53)
amygdala (68)
antagonists (61)
association cortex (73)
autonomic nervous system (57)
axon (52)
biopsychology (42)
brain stem (65)
cerebellum (66)
cerebral cortex (69)
cerebral dominance (73)
cerebral hemispheres (68)
corpus callosum (68)
central nervous system (56)
chromosome (46)
contralateral pathways (57)
CT scanning (computerized tomography) (64)
dendrite (51)
dna (deoxyribonucleic acid) (46)
electroencephalograph (EEG) (63)
endocrine system (58)
evolution (43)
fMRI (functional magnetic resonance imaging) (64)
frontal lobes (69)
gene (46)
genome (46)
genotype (45)
glial cell (55)
hippocampus (67)
hormones (59)
hypothalamus (68)
interneuron (51)
limbic system (66)

medulla (66)
mirror neuron (70)
motor cortex (69)
motor neuron (50)
MRI (magnetic resonance imaging) (64)
natural selection (44)
nervous system (56)
neural pathways (61)
neuron (50)
neurotransmitter (53)
occipital lobes (72)
parasympathetic division (58)
parietal lobes (72)
peripheral nervous system (57)
PET scanning (positron emission tomography) (64)
phenotype (45)
pituitary gland (60)
plasticity (55)
pons (66)
reflex (56)
resting potential (52)
reticular formation (66)
reuptake (53)
sensory neuron (50)
sex chromosomes (46)
soma (52)
somatic nervous system (57)
somatosensory cortex (72)
sympathetic division (57)
synapse (53)
synaptic transmission (53)
temporal lobes (72)
terminal buttons (53)
thalamus (66)
visual cortex (72)

Lecture Assistant *for Chapter 2*

Tear this outline out and bring it with you to class in order to facilitate your note taking.
Spend more time listening to the lecture and less time writing!

Chapter Opening Problem: Why does Jill's experience teach us about how our brain is organized and about its amazing ability to adapt?

- *Biopsychology =*

2.1 HOW ARE GENES AND BEHAVIOR LINKED?

Core Concept 2.1 =

- *Evolution =*

A) Evolution and Natural Selection

1) <u>The Evidence That Convinced Darwin</u> =

- *Natural selection =*

2) <u>Application to Psychology</u>:

- *Phobias =*

- *Nature-nurture debate =*

B) Genetics and Inheritance

- *Genotype =*

- *Phenotype =*

1) <u>Chromosomes, Genes, and DNA:</u>

- *Genome =*

- *DNA =*

- *Genes =*

- *Chromosomes =*

- *Sex chromosomes =*

2) <u>Genetic Explanations for Psychological Processes</u> =

3) "Race" and Human Variation =

C) Psychology Matters: Choosing Your Children's Genes

2.2 HOW DOES THE BODY COMMUNICATE INTERNALLY?

Core Concept 2.2 =

A) The Neuron: Building Block of the Nervous System

1) Types of Neurons:

- *Sensory neurons (afferent neurons)* =

- *Motor neurons (efferent neurons)* =

- *Interneurons* =

2) How Neurons Work:

- *Dendrites* =

- *Soma* =
  - *Excitatory* =

  - *Inhibitory* =

- *Axon* =

3) The Action Potential:

- *Resting potential* =

- *Action Potential* =

- *All-or-none principle* =

4) Synaptic Transmission =

- *Synapse* =

  - *Synaptic gap (synaptic Ccleft)* =

- *Terminal buttons =*

- *Synaptic transmission =*

5) Neurotransmitters =

   - *Vesicles =*

   - *Reuptake =*

6) Synchronous Firing =

7) Plasticity =

8) Brain Implants =

9) Glial Cells: A Support Group for Neurons =

   - *Glial Cells =*

      - *Myelin sheath =*

B) The Nervous System

1) The Central Nervous System (CNS) =

   - *Reflexes =*

   - *Contralateral pathways =*

2) The Peripheral Nervous System (PNS) =

   - *Nerves =*

   - *Somatic division of the PNS (somatic nervous system) =*

   - *Autonomic division of the PNS (autonomic nervous system) =*

      - *Sympathetic division =*

      - *Parasympathetic division =*

3) Male and Female Brains =

C) The Endocrine System

- *Hormones =*

1) How Does the Endocrine System Respond in a Crisis?

- *Epinephrine (adrenalin) =*

2) What Controls the Endocrine System?

- *Pituitary gland ("master gland") =*

D) Psychology Matters: How Psychoactive Drugs Affect the Nervous System

- *Psychoactive drugs =*

1) Agonists and Antagonists =

- *Agonists =*

- *Antagonists =*

2) Why Side Effects?

- *Neural pathways =*

2.3 HOW DOES THE BRAIN PRODUCE BEHAVIOR AND MENTAL PROCESSES?

- *Phineas Gage =*

Core Concept 2.3 =

A) Windows on the Brain

1) Sensing Brain Waves with the EEG =

- *Electroencephalograph (EEG) =*

- *Brain waves =*

2) Mapping the Brain with Electric Probes =

3) Computerized Brain Scans =

- *CT scanning (computerized tomography) =*

- *PET scanning (positron emission tomography) =*

- *MRI (magnetic resonance imaging) =*

- *fMRI (functional magnetic resonance imaging) =*

4) <u>Which Scanning Method Is Best?</u> =

B) Three Layers of the Brain

- *Brain stem =*

1) <u>The Brain Stem and Its Neighbors</u> =

- *Medulla =*

- *Pons =*

- *Reticular Formation =*

- *Thalamus =*

- *Cerebellum =*

2) <u>The Limbic System: Emotions, Memories, and More</u> =

- *Limbic system =*

The Hippocampus and Memory =

- *Hippocampus =*

  o H. M.: The Man Whose Hippocampus Was Surgically Removed =

The Amygdala and Emotion =

- *Amygdala =*

Pleasure and the Limbic System =

The Hypothalamus and Control over Emotion =

- *Hypothalamus* =

3) The Cerebral Cortex: The Brain's Thinking Cap =

- *Cerebral hemispheres* =

- *Corpus callosum* =

- *Cerebral cortex* =

C) Lobes of the Cerebral Cortex =

  o *Phrenology* =

1) The Frontal Lobes =

  o *Prefrontal cortex* =

- *Motor cortex* =

  o *Homunculus* =

- *Mirror neurons* =

  The Left Frontal Lobe's Role in Speech =

  o *Broca's area* =

2) The Parietal Lobes =

- *Somatosensory cortex* =

3) The Temporal Lobes =

- *Auditory cortex* =

  o *Wernicke's area* =

4) The Occipital Lobes =

- *Visual cortex* =

D) The Association Cortex =

E) The Cooperative Brain =

F) Cerebral Dominance =

1) Language and Communication =

2) Different Processing Styles =

3) Some People Are Different—But That's Normal =

- *Transcranial magnetic stimulation (TMS)* =

4) Male and Female Brains =

5) The Strange and Fascinating Case of the Split Brain =

6) Two Consciousnesses =

- *Duality of consciousness* =

- *Confederation of minds* =

7) What's It to *You?* =

G) Psychology Matters: Using Psychology To Learn Psychology =

H) Critical Thinking Applied: Left Brain vs. Right Brain =

1. *Indicate whether each statement is True (T) or False (F) by circling the appropriate letter after the statement.*

    A. The human brain weighs about five pounds.   T F

    B. A human brain contains about 100 million brain cells.   T F

    C. Biopsychologists study the interaction of biology, mental processes, and behavior.   T F

How Are Genes and Behavior Linked?

2. *Fill in the blank with the correct term.*

The process by which succeeding generations of organisms change as they adapt to changing environments is called _____.

Evolution and Natural Selection

3. *Fill in the blanks with the correct information.*

Charles Darwin ultimately decided on a career in biology, although he had previously trained for careers in both _____ and _____. He served aboard a British research ship named _____, which was commissioned to survey the coastline of _____. After extensive study of plants and animals, Darwin concluded that all creatures, including humans, share a _____. The evidence that convinced him of this conclusion included that fact that there is _____ among individuals within the same species; this could give some individuals a reproductive and survival advantage over others. Thus, the process of _____ would favor those individuals best adapted to the environment, allowing them to survive and reproduce. Darwin wrote a book in 1859 about his studies and conclusions and titled the book

_____.

4. In what ways do the processes of adaptation and evolution help make sense of various psychological phenomena? Give examples.

Genetics and Inheritance

5. *Fill in the blanks with the correct information.*

A. _____ are structures made up of long, coiled strands of DNA.

B. The specific genetic code that makes you different from anyone else is called your _____ .

C. Although people are all very different, _____ percent of our genetic material is the same.

D. One's physical characteristics—influenced by but not totally due to one's genes—are referred to as one's _____ .

E. A segment of the DNA strand is a _____ .

F. In almost every cell of the human body, there are _____ chromosomes.

G. A person receives _____ chromosomes from his or her biological father.

H. DNA stands for the term _____ .

I. Genes are composed of tiny molecules called _____ .

J. The normal pair of sex chromosomes for a female is _____ and for a male is _____ .

K. The genetic code uses _____ nucleotides.

L. The complete package of human DNA contains about _____ genes.

M. Down syndrome is caused by an extra chromosome _____ .

N. Biological research shows that "race" is a _____ defined term.

O. A _____ is the complete set of genetic information contained in a cell.

6. The ethical, legal, and social issues related to genetic science are being discussed and studied intensely. To find out about research on these topics—as well as the social policy and legal issues being discussed, investigated, and acted upon—visit the following website:
   http://www.ornl.gov/sci/techresources/Human_Genome/elsi/elsi.shtml

How does the Body Communicate Internally?

7. What are the body's two main communication systems?

    A. _____

    B. _____

8. What coordinates the body's two communication systems?

9. *Fill in the blanks with the correct terms.*

    The body's first internal communication system to respond to external stimuli is the

_____. The "building block" of this fast-acting system is the

_____. The slower-acting system is called the _____. The

chemicals used by this slower-acting system are known as _____.

The Neuron: Building Block of the Nervous System

10. *In the table below, name the three types of neurons and explain what each kind does.*

Type of Neuron	What It Does
A.	
B.	
C.	

11. *Label the four main parts of the neuron in the spaces provided.*

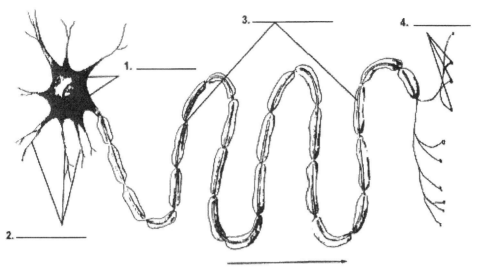

Direction of communications

12. *Match each term with its description by placing the letter corresponding to the term in the space next to its description.*

TERMS

A. Efferent neurons   E. Soma   I. Resting potential
B. Afferent neurons   F. Axon   J. All-or-none principle
C. Action potential   G. Dendrites   K. Neurotransmitters
D. Terminal buttons   H. Synaptic gap   L. Glial cells

DESCRIPTIONS

_____ They contain vesicles of chemicals.
_____ A temporarily reversed charge in the ions
_____ They carry information from the brain & spinal cord to the muscles, organs, & glands.
_____ The part of the neuron that receives messages from other neurons
_____ When the ions in the axon give it a negative electrical charge
_____ The part of the neuron that contains its chromosomes
_____ They form the myelin sheath.
_____ They carry information from the senses to the brain and spinal cord.
_____ The nerve cell either fires or it doesn't.
_____ The transmitter fiber of the neuron
_____ The chemical messengers contained in the end of the axon
_____ The chemical messengers flow across it.

13. *Underline the word(s) in parentheses that will make each statement correct. (Both options within parentheses may be correct!)*

    A. Messages received by a neuron can be (excitatory/inhibitory).

    B. Dendrites pass their messages directly on to the (soma/axon).

    C. The (axon/cell body) assesses all the messages received by the neuron.

    D. The axon gets the electrical energy it needs to fire from (charged chemicals/ions).

    E. The electrical message changing into a chemical message that then flows across the gap between neurons is called the (synaptic transmission/action potential).

    F. The typical negative electrical charge within the axon is its (resting/action) potential.

    G. Each ruptured vesicle releases about (5,000/500,000) neurotransmitter molecules.

    H. During the action potential (positive/negative) ions rapidly enter the (axon/soma).

14. *Indicate whether each statement is True (T) or False (F) by circling the appropriate letter after the statement.*

    A. Synaptic transmission refers to the relaying of information across the synapse by means of hormones.   T F

    B. Neurotransmitters are contained in vesicles in the terminal buttons.   T F

    C. An imbalance in acetylcholine is associated with Alzheimer's disease.   T F

    D. Synapses occur between neurons, as well as between neurons and the muscles or glands they serve.   T F

    E. When the all-or-none response goes out of control and very large numbers of neurons fire too easily, this can result in dementia.   T F

    F. Reuptake refers to the process in which unused neurotransmitters are broken down by special enzymes.   T F

    G. GABA regulates the sense of pleasure and reward.   T F.

    H. The most prevalent inhibitory neurotransmitter in the CNS is glutamate.   T F

15. Explain the process of "reuptake."

16. What are the names of the seven important neurotransmitters discussed in Table 2.1?

_____ _____ _____

_____ _____ _____ _____

17. *Match each neurotransmitter with its normal function, with problems associated with its imbalance, and/or with substances that affect its action. (Some options are used more than once.)*

NEUROTRANSMITTER

A. GABA	C. Dopamine	E. Serotonin	G. Acetylcholine
B. Glutamate	D. Endorphins	F. Norepinephrine	

FUNCTION, PROBLEMS, AND/OR SUBSTANCES THAT AFFECT IT

_____ Regulates sleep, dreaming, sexual behavior, mood, pain, appetite, and aggression
_____ Controls heart rate, sleep, stress, sexual responsiveness, vigilance, and appetite
_____ Control pain and produce pleasurable sensations
_____ Opiates—such as heroin, morphine, opium, and methadone—affect its action.
_____ Individuals with schizophrenia or Parkinson's disease have an imbalance in it.
_____ The primary excitatory neurotransmitter in the CNS
_____ Botulism toxin, black widow spider venom, and nicotine affect its action.
_____ Individuals with anxiety or epilepsy have an imbalance in it.

18. What are five different functions of the glial cells?

A. _____

B. _____

C. _____

D. _____

E. _____

19. *Indicate whether each statement is True (T) or False (F) by circling the appropriate letter after the statement.*

A. All neurons communicate using chemical messages called neurotransmitters.　　T F

B. The idea of computerized "brain implants" is fiction, not fact.　　T F

C. Forming new synapses and experiencing changes in dendrites are both forms of plasticity.　　T F

D. Glial cells "glue" the neurons together.　　T F

20. The following website has a quick quiz on basic neural functioning. You can test your own knowledge of the neuron (and then explore other, related sites).
http://psych.hanover.edu/Krantz/neural/struct3.html

21. *Fill in the blank boxes of this concept map.*

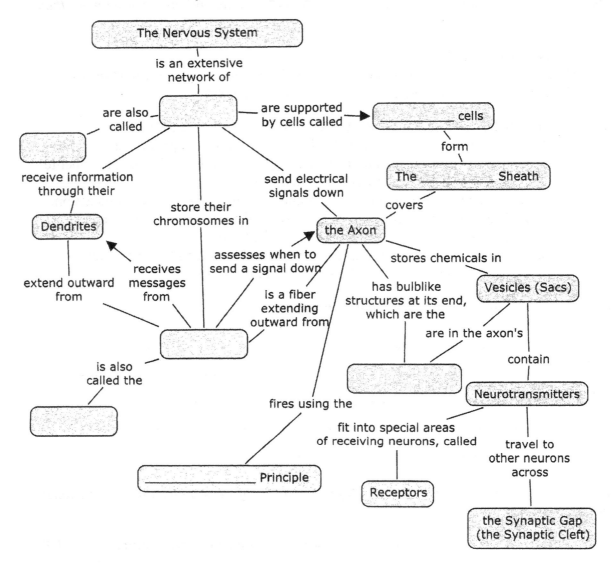

The Nervous System

22. In the spaces provided, describe a description of each nervous system and explain its functions.

Nervous System	Description	Functions
A. Central Nervous System		
B. Peripheral Nervous System		
C. Somatic Nervous System		
D. Autonomic Nervous System		
E. Sympathetic Division		
F. Parasympathetic Division		

23. Explain what "contralateral pathways" are.

24. Visit this wonderful, interactive site! Eric H. Chudler, Ph.D, created this site for children—but it has a wealth of information and is extremely helpful to college students, too, due to its demonstrations, interactions, quizzes, and superb explanations of difficult concepts.

http://faculty.washington.edu/chudler/introb.html

25. *Fill in the blanks in this concept map.*

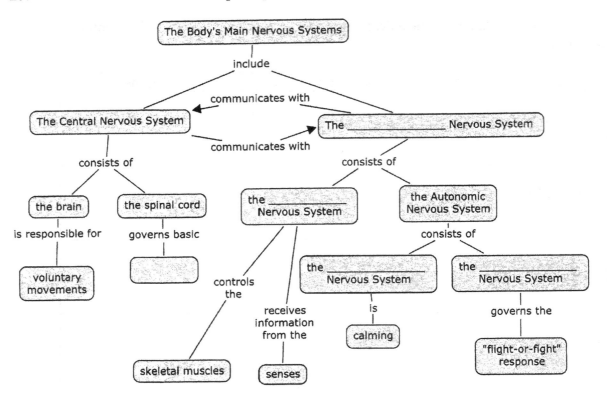

The Endocrine System

26. *Match each endocrine gland with the function of its hormones by placing the letter corresponding to the endocrine gland in the space next to its hormones' functions. (Some options are used more than once.)*

ENDOCRINE GLANDS
   A. Pituitary   C. Ovaries and testes E. Thyroid
   B. Adrenal glands   D. Parathyroids   F. Pancreas

FUNCTIONS OF THE HORMONES
   _____ Regulate calcium levels in the body
   _____ Regulate metabolism and physical growth
   _____ Stimulate body growth and regulate the conservation of water in the body
   _____ Regulate the fight-or-flight response and sexual desire
   _____ Influence development of sexual characteristics
   _____ Regulate glucose levels
   _____ Oversee the rest of the endocrine system
   _____ Regulate breast milk production and secretion

27. *Fill in the blanks with the correct information.*

In the endocrine system, the chemicals used for communication are called

_____ . In the nervous system, the chemicals are called _____ .

The master gland, or the _____ , keeps the functions of the endocrine system

under control. It is controlled by the _____ .

Psychology Matters: How Psychoactive Drugs Affect the Nervous System

28. In terms of psychoactive drugs, what are "agonists" and "antagonists"?

29. What are "neural pathways" and how do they relate to the unwanted side effects of drugs?

How Does the Brain Produce Behavior and Mental Processes?

30. Who was Phineas Gage and why is he important to the study of the brain?

Windows on the Brain

31. *Describe the six different methods listed in your textbook that scientists use to study the brain. Include the strengths and weaknesses of each method.*

Method and Description	Strengths	Weaknesses
A.		
B.		
C.		
D.		
E.		
F.		

32. NEED A BREAK?
To get a better understanding of biopsychology, neuroscience, and the brain, visit MyPsychLab.

Three Layers of the Brain

33. The three layers of the brain are the:

A. _____ B. _____ C. _____

34. What important function does the brain stem play in terms of sensory and motor pathways?

35. Name three brain structures contained in the brain stem.

36. What is the limbic system? What are three brain structures in this system?

37. *Match each term with its description by placing the letter corresponding to the term in the space next to its description. Terms can be used more than once!*

TERMS
A. Medulla   C. Thalamus   E. Cerebellum   G. Amygdala
B. Pons   D. Reticular formation   F. Hippocampus   H. Hypothalamus

DESCRIPTIONS
_____ Surgically removed in the man named H. M.
_____ Regulates breathing, heart rate, and blood pressure
_____ Helps keep a series of events in order
_____ Receives information from the senses and sends it to the appropriate processing areas of the brain
_____ Regulates sleep and dreaming cycles
_____ A pair of football-shaped structures on top of the brain stem
_____ Is the link between the nervous system and the endocrine system
_____ Involved in keeping the brain awake, alert, and paying attention
_____ Involved in storing information in long-term memory
_____ Involved in the brain's reward circuits, such as the hunger, thirst, and sex drives
_____ A bridge connecting the brain stem to the cerebellum
_____ Located under the back of the cerebral hemispheres
_____ Involved in making coordinated movements
_____ Involved in fear and aggression
_____ A bundle of nerve cells that forms the core of the brain stem
_____ Involved in monitoring the blood

38. *Label each structure of the brain in this image next to its specific letter.*

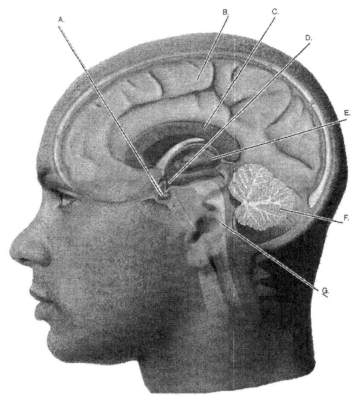

The Cerebral Cortex: The Brain's Thinking Cap

39. How do the cerebral cortex, cerebral hemispheres, and corpus callosum interrelate?

Lobes of the Cerebral Cortex

40. *Complete the following paragraph with information about the lobes in the brain.*

There are _____ lobes in each hemisphere of the brain. The _____ lobes are responsible for higher mental functions such as planning and decision-making, and they also contain the _____ cortex, which is responsible for moving muscles. The _____ lobes run along the top of the brain. The _____ cortex is part of this lobe and it specializes in the sense of _____. The _____ lobes are where our visual functions mainly reside. The _____ lobes contain the _____ cortex, which is involved in our ability to hear.

41. Explain what "mirror neurons" are, where they are located, what functions they serve, and how they may relate to certain psychological disorders.

42. *Based on the descriptions provided below, decide the probable lobe of the brain in which damage occurred. If you can be more specific in terms of which hemisphere or what area within the lobes, include that information.*

DESCRIPTIONS	DAMAGED LOBE
A. Ted cannot talk since his serious car accident.	_____
B. Because of a tumor, Miguel has significant problems understanding language.	_____
C. Ali has had trouble understanding people's emotions since crashing his motorcycle.	_____
D. Danella doesn't recognize any face, including her own, since her stroke.	_____
E. A gunshot wound has changed Mimi's personality.	_____
F. Jeff's left arm is paralyzed after his stroke.	_____
G. Tatiana's brain tumor has negatively affected her spatial ability.	_____
H. Ingrid's brain infection has caused her to lose all feeling in her right leg.	_____
I. After a fall from a building, Tomo is unable to see.	_____

43. Explain what the "association cortex" is.

Cerebral Dominance

44. *Identify the hemisphere where the functions are primarily controlled (in most people) by writing R (right) or L (left) in the blank next to the function.*

A. _____Language understanding
B. _____Speech production
C. _____Spatial orientation
D. _____Interpreting the emotional responses of other people
E. _____ Musical ability
F. _____ Regulating one's own positive emotions
G. _____ Regulating one's own negative emotions
H. _____ Processing in an analytical, sequential fashion
I. _____ Processing in a more holistic and emotional style

45. What is "cerebral dominance," and in what way is the term often misunderstood?

46. *Indicate whether each statement about split-brain individuals is True (T) or False (F) by circling the appropriate letter after the statement.*

   A. In split-brain patients, the corpus callosum is cut in order to prevent continuous epileptic seizures. T F

   B. Because of the split-brain surgery, the person's left and right eyes get different information. T F

   C. In split-brain patients, each hemisphere of the brain communicates with the same side of the body. T F

   D. Only in split-brain patients does information from the left visual field go to the right visual cortex. T F

   E. If split-brain patients see an object flashed in their right visual field, they will most likely be able to say what it was. T F

   F. When split-brain people see an object in their left visual field, they will likely be able to draw it with their right hand. T F

   G. Split-brain patients sometimes demonstrate a duality of consciousness. T F

   H. "Confederation of minds" is generally used to describe split-brain patients, but not other people. T F

47. To find out more about the two hemispheres of the brain, including split-brain research, visit Dr. Eric H. Chudler's site. He created this site for children, but it has a wealth of information and is extremely helpful to college students, too. http://faculty.washington.edu/chudler/split.html

48. Read a short biography of Roger Sperry—Nobel Prize winner for his research on the split brain—that was written by his colleague, Joseph E. Bogen, M.D. http://www.its.caltech.edu/~jbogen/text/amerphil.html

Psychology Matters: Using Psychology to Learn Psychology

49. According to this chapter, what might help you better learn and remember this material?

Critical Thinking Applied: Left Brain vs. Right Brain

50. Why is it inaccurate to classify people as "left-brained" or "right-brained"?

PRACTICE TEST #1

1. Cells that form the myelin sheath are called _____ cells.
   A. nerve   B. glial   C. GABA   D. soma

2. Genotype is to _____ as phenotype is to _____.
   A. genetic make-up; habitat conditions
   B. genetic make-up; recognizable features
   C. natural selection; environmental pressures
   D. selective breeding; evolution

3. Humans have _____ pairs of chromosomes.
   A. 23   B. 25   C. 26   D. 21

4. The chemical messengers in the endocrine system are called _____.
   A. hormones   B. interneurons   C. neurons   D. neurotransmitters

5. Organisms gradually adapt over time to their environments through the process of _____.
   A. restructuring   B. plasticity   C. assimilation   D. evolution

6. A picture of a spoon is flashed in the left visual field of a split-brain patient and a picture of a fork in the right visual field. The split-brain person should be able to _____.
   A. point to the spoon with his or her left hand
   B. point to the fork with either hand
   C. say that a spoon was seen
   D. point to the spoon with either hand

7. Humans have approximately _____ genes.
   A. 300,000   B. 50,000   C. 100,000   D. 30,000

8. You don't like cold showers, and so you stick your hand under the water before jumping into the shower. The message about temperature is carried to your brain by _____.
   A. interneurons   B. afferent neurons   C. motor neurons   D. efferent neurons

9. The part of the neuron that receives incoming messages is the _____.
   A. dendrite   B. soma   C. axon   D. terminal button

10. The ability of neurons to change—that is, to make new connections and strengthen old ones—is called _____.
    A. restructuring   B. plasticity   C. assimilation   D. evolution

PRACTICE TEST #2

1. The order in which neurons conduct a signal is from _____.
   A. axon to soma to synapse to dendrite   C. dendrite to soma to axon to synapse
   B. axon to dendrite to soma to synapse   D. dendrite to synapse to axon to soma

2. Which of the following is primarily under voluntary control?
   A. autonomic nervous system   C. sympathetic nervous system
   B. somatic nervous system   D. parasympathetic nervous system

3. The cerebellum is used primarily for _____, while the medulla is primarily used for_____.
   A. thinking; hearing   C. motor coordination; breathing
   B. posture; cognition   D. emotion; motor coordination

4. If you can see the turkey at Thanksgiving, it is because of the _____ division of the nervous system.
   A. autonomic   B. somatic   C. parasympathetic   D. sympathetic

5. If you go through a haunted house on Halloween and get goose bumps, you can thank your _____ nervous system.
   A. autonomic   B. somatic   C. parasympathetic   D. sympathetic

6. Structures of the limbic system include the _____.
   A. hippocampus, amygdala, and hypothalamus
   B. thalamus, hypothalamus, and medulla
   C. amygdala, pons and RAS
   D. cerebellum, medulla, and hippocampus

7. The hormone that is responsible for sustaining the "fight-or-flight" response is _____.
   A. dopamine   B. acetylcholine   C. epinephrine D. insulin

8. The left hemisphere in most people's brains _____.
   A. processes information in a holistic manner
   B. is better at pattern recognition
   C. is where most language and speech processing takes place
   D. is better at understanding simple commands

9. Which of the following is primarily associated with maintaining basic life functions?
   A. brain stem   B. limbic system   C. cerebrum   D. occipital lobes

10. Drugs such as nicotine that mimic neurotransmitters are called _____.
    A. anatagonists   C. impersonators
    B. faux neurotransmitters   D. agonists

PRACTICE TEST #3

1. The part of the brain that was affected in Phineas Gage's accident that changed his personality was the _____.
   A. frontal lobe   B. occipital lobe   C. parietal lobe   D. brain stem

2. Scientists study the brain by measuring brain waves using a(n) _____.
   A. EEG   B. MRI machine   C. CT scan   D. fMRI machine

3. If you stimulated Mike's amygdala, you should get ready to _____.
   A. give him something to eat   C. block a punch
   B. teach him about neurons   D. help him get ready for a date.

4. Structures of the brainstem include the _____.
   A. amygdala, pons, and pituitary
   B. medulla, pons, and reticular formation
   C. thalamus, hypothalamus, and medulla
   D. cerebellum, medulla, and hippocampus

5. If sending a current through the electrode you implanted in a rat's brain causes the rat to press a bar in its cage to get food pellets, you placed the electrode in the rat's _____.
   A. hippocampus   B. amygdala   C. frontal lobe   D. hypothalamus

6. Sleep and the dreaming cycles are regulated by the _____.
   A. medulla   B. pons   C. thalamus   D. hypothalamus

7. When you become wide awake while reading an exciting story, your _____ is at work.
   A. medulla   C. reticular formation
   B. pons   D. thalamus

8. If you are trying to keep the list of all of the brain parts in order, your _____ is implicated in this activity.
   A. cerebellum   B. medulla   C. pons   D. thalamus

9. The _____ is most associated with emotions.
   A. medulla   C. limbic system
   B. reticular formation   D. thalamus

10. Your grandmother has trouble remembering new information. What part of her brain is no longer working as well as it should?
   A. pons   B. hippocampus   C. medulla   D. thalamus

COMPREHENSIVE REVIEW TEST

1. The peripheral nervous system is comprised of which two subdivisions?
   A. the autonomic nervous system and the sympathetic division
   B. the autonomic nervous system and the central nervous system
   C. the somatic nervous system and the autonomic nervous system
   D. the somatic nervous system and the sympathetic division

2. Richard had a stroke, now he can no longer remember any new information. The stroke most likely damaged his _____.
   A. occipital lobes   C. hippocampus
   B. reticular formation   D. thalamus

3. Shondra was in a car accident and injured her head. Now she has a great deal of trouble organizing and prioritizing and she is often quite impulsive. She most likely injured the _____ lobes of her cerebral cortex.
   A. occipital   B. frontal   C. parietal   D. temporal

4. For most people, the brain's right hemisphere _____.
   A. processes information in a holistic manner
   B. is where face recognition occurs
   C. is where most logical processing occurs
   D. is where most language is processed

5. The word "apple" is flashed on the left side of a screen, and the word "strawberry" is flashed on the right side of the screen. Andrea, whose corpus callosum has been cut, would most likely be able to _____.
   A. say that she saw the apple   C. draw the strawberry using her left hand
   B. draw the apple using either hand   D. draw the apple using her left hand

6. "Fight-or-flight" behavior is associated with what part of the nervous system?
   A. the parasympathetic division   C. the sympathetic division
   B. motor neurons   D. the somatic nervous system

7. Which is an example of a parasympathetic response?
   A. getting ready to take an exam   C. breathing slowly to get to sleep
   B. running on a treadmill   D. watching a horror movie

8. The _____ sends messages from your senses to the appropriate processing areas in the brain.
   A. thalamus   B. hypothalamus   C. limbic system   D. medulla

9. Phrenology was correct about _____.
   A. voluntary movement   C. specialization of hemispheres
   B. localization of function   D. neuronal firing

10. All of the following are parts of the endocrine system EXCEPT the _____.
    A. pancreas　　　B. amygdala　　　C. thyroid　　　D. pituitary

11. Sarah had an automobile accident in which she hit her head. The doctors said that she injured her cerebellum. She is now most likely to have difficulty _____.
    A. feeling really happy　　　C. understanding what others are saying
    B. reading her history book　　　D. sitting up straight

12 The area of the brain responsible for producing speech is called _____, after the doctor who first discovered the particular area.
    A. Brady's area　　B. Gage's area　　　C. Tan's area　　　D. Broca's area

13. The left hemisphere is generally considered more _____ than the right hemisphere.
    A. specialized　　B. developed　　　C. creative　　　D. analytical

14. Manuel has a tumor in his brain that has caused him to have outbursts of aggression. What brain structure is most likely involved?
    A. amygdala　　　B. hippocampus　　　C. pons　　　D. medulla

15. Dendrites relay their messages directly to the _____.
    A. axon　　　B. soma　　　C. synapse　　　D. receptors

CRITICAL THINKING ESSAYS

1. You are involved in a strenuous game of soccer and have been playing for twenty-five minutes. Before that, you and some teammates were on the sidelines yelling feedback back and forth. At one point, two players on the other team purposefully and spitefully foul one of your teammates, so you angrily yell at them to stop.

   Discuss what structures in your brain and nervous systems are particularly active and what functions they are serving.

2. Why, in a psychology class, are you learning about how neurons function? Why is this relevant?

3. Your friends tell you that they just found out that psychologists have created "split-brain people," and that such split-brain individuals have two separate brains that cannot communicate with each other. Your friends want to know what's going on!

   What accurate information can you give your friends about split-brain patients?

CHAPTER 3
Sensation and Perception

Before You Read . . . Term Identification

Make flashcards using the following terms or, even better, develop mnemonics (memory strategies) to help you remember the different concepts and terms. Use the definitions in the margins of this chapter for help. Numbers refer to page numbers in the textbook.

absolute threshold (91)
afterimages (99)
ambiguous figures (115)
amplitude (101)
basilar membrane (102)
binding problem (113)
binocular cues (123)
blind spot (96)
blindsight (112)
bottom-up processing (113)
brightness (98)
change blindness (114)
cochlea (102)
color (98)
color blindness (100)
cones (96)
closure (119)
difference threshold (92)
electromagnetic spectrum (98)
feature detectors (112)
figure (118)
fovea (96)
frequency (101)
gate-control theory (109)
gestalt psychology (118)
ground (118)
gustation (106)
illusion (114)
inattentional blindness (114)
kinesthetic sense (105)
law of common fate (121)
law of continuity (121)
law of Prägnanz (121)
law of proximity (120)
law of similarity (120)

laws of perceptual grouping (120)
learning-based inference (121)
loudness (103)
monocular cues (124)
olfaction (105)
opponent-process theory (99)
optic nerve (96)
percept (112)
perception (89)
perceptual constancy (113)
perceptual set (121)
pheromones (105)
photoreceptors (95)
pitch (102)
placebo (110)
placebo effect (110)
retina (95)
rods (95)
sensation (88)
sensory adaptation (93)
signal detection theory (93)
skin senses (108)
subliminal perception (126)
synesthesia (108)
timbre (103)
top-down processing (113)
transduction (90)
trichromatic theory (99)
tympanic membrane (101)
vestibular sense (105)
visible spectrum (98)
Weber's law (92)
what pathway (112)
where pathway (112)

Lecture Assistant *for Chapter 3*

Tear this outline out and bring it with you to class in order to facilitate your note taking.
Spend more time listening to the lecture and less time writing!

Chapter Opening Problem: Is there any way to tell whether the world we "see" in our minds is the same as the external world—and whether we see things as most others do?

- *Sensation =*

- *Perception =*

3.1 HOW DOES STIMULATION BECOME SENSATION?

Core Concept 3.1 =

A) Transduction: Changing Stimulation to Sensation

   o *Sensory receptors =*

- *Transduction =*

B) Thresholds: The Boundaries of Sensation

- *Absolute threshold =*

- *Difference threshold (just noticeable difference) =*

- *Weber's law =*

C) Signal Detection Theory

- *Signal detection theory =*

D) Psychology Matters: Sensory Adaptation

   o *Change detectors =*

- *Sensory adaptation =*

3.2 HOW ARE THE SENSES ALIKE? HOW ARE THEY DIFFERENT?

Core Concept 3.2 =

A) Vision: How the Nervous System Processes Light

1) The Anatomy of Visual Sensation =

- *Retina =*

- *Photoreceptors =*

- *Rods =*

- *Cones =*

- *Fovea =*

    ○ *Bipolar cells =*

    ○ *Ganglion cells =*

- *Optic nerve =*

- *Blind spot =*

2) Processing Visual Sensation in the Brain =

    ○ *Visual cortex =*

a) How the Visual System Creates Brightness =

- *Brightness =*

b) How the Visual System Creates Color =

- *Color (hue) =*

- *Electromagnetic spectrum =*

- *Visible spectrum =*

c) <u>Two Ways of Sensing Color</u> =

- *Trichromatic theory* =

- *Opponent-process theory* =

  o *Afterimages* =

d) <u>Color Blindness</u> =

- *Color blindness* =

B) Hearing: If a Tree Falls in the Forest...

1) <u>The Physics of Sound: How Sound Waves Are Produced</u> =

- *Frequency* =

- *Amplitude* =

2) <u>Sensing Sounds: How We Hear Sound Waves</u>

   <u>Four Steps:</u>

   a) _____

      o *Pinna* =

      - *Tympanic membrane (ear drum)* =

      o *Hammer* =

      o *Anvil* =

      o *Stirrup* =

      - *Cochlea* =

   b) _____

      - *Basilar membrane* =

   c) _____

d) _____

      o *Auditory nerve =*

3) <u>Psychological Qualities of Sound: How We Distinguish One Sound from Another</u> =

    a) <u>Sensations of Pitch</u> =

       • *Pitch =*

        o *Place theory =*

        o *Frequency theory =*

    b) <u>Sensations of Loudness</u> =

       • *Loudness =*

    c) <u>Sensations of Timbre</u> =

       • *Timbre =*

4) <u>Hearing Loss</u> =

5) <u>How Are Auditory and Visual Sensations Alike?</u>

C) How the Other Senses Are Like Vision and Hearing

    1) <u>Position and Movement</u> =

       • *Vestibular sense =*

        o *Semicircular canals =*

       • *Kinesthetic sense =*

    2) <u>Smell (Olfaction)</u> =

       • *Pheromones =*

    a) <u>The Biology of Olfaction</u> =

        o *Olfactory bulbs =*

    b) <u>The Psychology of Smell</u> =

3) <u>Taste (Gustation)</u> =

    o   *Umami* =

    o   *Taste buds* =

    o   *Papillae* =

   a) <u>Developmental Changes in Taste</u> =

   b) <u>Supertasters</u> =

4) <u>The Skin Senses</u> =

D) Synesthesia: Sensations across the Senses

E) Psychology Matters: The Sense and Experience of Pain

   1) <u>Pain Receptors</u> =

    o   *Nociceptors* =

   2) <u>A Pain in the Brain</u> =

   3) <u>Phantom Limbs</u> =

   4) <u>The Gate Control Theory</u> =

    •   *Gate control theory* =

   5) <u>Dealing with Pain</u> =

    a) <u>Analgesics</u> =

    b) <u>Psychological Techniques for Pain Control</u> =

      •   *Placebo* =

- *Placebo effect* =

c) Controlling *Psychological* Pain with Analgesics =

6) Pain Tolerance =

3.3 WHAT IS THE RELATIONSHIP BETWEEN SENSATION AND PERCEPTION?

Core Concept 3.3 =

- *Percept* =

A) Perceptual Processing: Finding Meaning in Sensation

1) The What and Where Pathways in the Brain =

- *What pathway* =

- *Where pathway* =

- *Blindsight* =

2) Feature Detectors =

- *Feature detectors* =

- *Binding problem* =

2) Top-Down and Bottom-Up Processing =

- *Top-down processing* =

- *Bottom-up processing* =

3) Perceptual Constancies =

- *Perceptual constancy* =

  ○ *Color constancy* =

  ○ *Size constancy* =

  ○ *Shape constancy* =

4) <u>Inattentional Blindness and Change Blindness</u> =

- *Inattentional blindness* =

- *Change blindness* =

B) Perceptual Ambiguity and Distortion

1) <u>What Illusions Tell Us about Sensation and Perception</u> =

- *Illusion* =

- *Ambiguous figures* =

    ○ *Müller-Lyer illusion* =

2) <u>Illusions in the Context of Culture</u> =

3) <u>Applying the Lessons of Illusions</u> =

C) Theoretical Explanations for Perception =

1) <u>Perceptual Organization: The Gestalt Theory</u> =

- *Gestalt psychology* =

a) <u>Figure and Ground</u> =

- *Figure* =

- *Ground* =

b) <u>Closure: Filling in the Blanks</u> =

    ○ *Subjective contours* =

- *Closure =*

c) The Gestalt Laws of Perceptual Grouping =

- *Laws of perceptual grouping =*

- *Law of similarity =*

- *Law of proximity =*

- *Law of continuity =*

- *Law of common fate =*

- *Law of Prägnanz (minimal principle of perception) =*

2) Learning-Based Inference: The *Nurture* of Perception =

- *Learning-based inference =*

a) Context and Expectations =

b) Perceptual Set =

c) Cultural Influences on Perception =

3) Depth Perception: Nature or Nurture?

o *Visual cliff =*

a) Binocular Cues =

o *Binocular convergence =*

- ○ *Retinal disparity* =

b) <u>Monocular Cues</u> =

- ○ *Relative size* =

- ○ *Linear perspective* =

- ○ *Light and shadow* =

- ○ *Interposition* =

- ○ *Relative motion* =

- ○ *Atmospheric perspective* =

D) Seeing and Believing =

E) Psychology Matters: Using Psychology to Learn Psychology =

F) Critical Thinking Applied: Subliminal Perception and Subliminal Persuasion =

- • *Subliminal perception* =

1. Differentiate between "sensation" and "perception."

2. Explain what the text authors mean when they state that "the brain senses the world indirectly."

How Does Stimulation Become Sensation?

Transduction: Changing Stimulation to Sensation

3. *Indicate whether each statement is True (T) or False (F) by circling the appropriate letter after the statement.*

    A. The sensory receptors convert electrochemical signals into physical energy.   T F

    B. Sensations only occur once the neural signals reach the cerebral cortex.   T F

    C. Sense receptors are specialized neurons.   T F

    D. Physical stimuli from the external world progress to the cerebral cortex.   T F

    E. Transduction is the process of converting physical energy into neural messages.   T F

Thresholds: The Boundaries of Sensation

4. *Fill in the blanks with correct information about the senses.*

       The amount of stimulation needed for a stimulus to be detected is known as the

_____ threshold. The smallest physical change between 2 stimuli that you

can reliably detect 50 percent of the time is called the _____ threshold. The

minimal amount of change that is recognizable is also called the _____. The

theory that the JND is proportional to the intensity of the stimulus is called

_____. The line of inquiry that includes assessing the thresholds for

different types of stimulation is known as _____.

5. *Underline the word(s) in parentheses that will make each statement correct. (Both options may be correct!)*

A. The difference threshold is always large when the stimulus intensity is (low/high).

B. A specific person's absolute threshold for a given stimulus (can/cannot) change.

C. Humans are built to detect (constancies/changes) in stimulation.

D. Audrey can detect the slight dimming of the lights in the classroom, but Ross doesn't think the light intensity has changed at all. Audrey has a (lower/higher) (absolute/difference) threshold than Ross does.

Signal Detection Theory

6. According to signal detection theory, sensation depends on what three factors?

A. _____ B. _____ C. _____

7. Explain why signal detection theory is more accurate than classical psychophysics.

Psychology Matters: Sensory Adaptation

8. Define "sensory adaptation" and then explain how this relates to the inadvisability of studying while listening to your favorite music.

How Are the Senses Alike? And How Are They Different?

9. In your own words, write the core concept regarding the functioning of the senses.

Vision: How the Nervous System Processes Light

10. *Fill in the blanks with the correct terms concerning vision.*

Light-sensitive cells found in the _____ are called photoreceptors. There are two types of receptor cells: _____ distinguish between intensities of light and _____ enable us to distinguish between colors. The _____ is a small region that gives us our sharpest vision. Where the _____ exits the eye is the _____.

11. *Label the eye diagram below with the names of its structure. Number 5 is already done.*

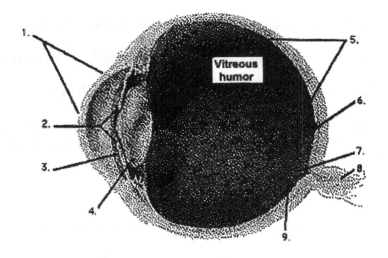

1. _____ 2. _____ 3. _____ 4. _____ 5. <u>vitreous humor</u>

6. _____ 7. _____ 8. _____ 9. _____

12. *Match each term with its best description(s) by placing the letter corresponding to the term in the space next to its description. (Terms may be used more than once.)*

TERMS
   A. Ganglion cells   D. Rods   G. Cones
   B. Retina   E. Blind spot   H. Optic nerve
   C. Bipolar cells   F. Fovea   I. Lens

DESCRIPTIONS
   _____ Cells concentrated in the fovea
   _____ Detect low intensities of light at night
   _____ Caused by optic nerve leaving the eye
   _____ Focuses light
   _____ Area in the center of the retina
   _____ Their axons make up the optic nerve.
   _____ Detect colors
   _____ Contains photoreceptors
   _____ Collect impulses from photoreceptors and send impulses on to other cells
   _____ Transports visual information to the brain
   _____ Retinal area of sharpest vision
   _____ There are approximately 125 million of them.
   _____ Turns the image upside down and left-to-right on the retina

13. *Indicate whether each statement is True (T) or False (F) by circling the appropriate letter after the statement.*

A. The retina takes two-dimensional patterns and turns them into three-dimensional patterns.   T F

B. The amplitude of light determines the sensation of brightness.   T F

C. Humans are capable of distinguishing about 5 million different hues.   T F

D. Males are more likely than females to have color blindness.   T F

E. Visible light is located near the middle of the electromagnetic spectrum.   T F

F. Within the visible spectrum, longer wavelengths correspond to sensations of blue.   T F

G. The opponent-process theory explains what happens in the cones.   T F

H. The opponent-process theory explains negative afterimages.   T F

I. The trichromatic theory explains what happens in the bipolar cells and beyond.   T F

J. The three types of cones correspond to the sensations of blue, red, and yellow.   T F

K. Most color blindness involves a problem in distinguishing red from green.   T F

L. Blacks are more likely than whites to have color blindness.   T F

Hearing: If a Tree Falls in the Forest...

14. *Fill in the blanks with the correct terms concerning the process of hearing.*

In order for hearing to occur, vibrating air molecules enter the _____ and strike the eardrum, or _____, an important structure that transmits the vibrations to three tiny bones: the _____, _____ and _____. These bones, located in the _____ ear, send the vibrations on to the primary sense organ of hearing, the _____, which is located in the _____ ear. This coiled structure is filled with fluid, which is set into wave motion that causes the _____ to vibrate. It is at this point that the vibrations are transduced by the _____ cells, becoming neural activity and traveling down the _____ to the auditory cortex.

77

15. Identify the three psychological qualities of sounds and tell what each is determined by.

Psychological Quality	Determined By
A.	
B.	
C.	

16. *Indicate whether each statement is True (T) or False (F) by circling the appropriate letter after the statement.*

    A. The eardrum is also known as the pinna.   T F

    B. The amplitude of sound waves is measured in hertz.   T F

    C. Place theory and frequency theory explain hearing sounds from 500 to 900 Hz.   T F

    D. Sounds between 1,000 and 5,000 Hz correspond to human speech.   T F

    E. Prolonged exposure to sounds that are 90 decibels will produce hearing loss.   T F

17. Distinguish between the place theory and frequency theory of pitch.

    A. Place Theory _____

    _____

    B. Frequency Theory _____

    _____

How the Other Senses Are Like Vision and Hearing

18. *Indicate whether each statement is True (T) or False (F) by circling the appropriate letter after the statement.*

    A. Nasal receptors sense the shape of odor molecules.   T F

    B. Information from all the senses is relayed through the thalamus.   T F

    C. Compared to adults, infants have heightened taste sensitivity.   T F

    D. Receptor cells for both taste and smell can be replaced.   T F

19. What are "pheromones?"

20. There are other senses in addition to vision and hearing. In the following table, explain what each sense does and identify the body/brain parts involved with that sense.

Sense	What It Does	Involved Body/Brain Parts
A. Vestibular		
B. Kinesthetic		
C. Olfaction		
D. Gustation		
E. Skin Senses		

21. What is a "supertaster"? How do they differ from non-supertasters?

Synesthesia: Sensations across the Senses

22. What is "synesthesia" and what appears to cause it?

Psychology Matters: The Sense and Experience of Pain

23. *Fill in the blanks with correct information about pain.*

In the skin there are _____, which are specialized nerve cells that sense pain. The _____ theory of pain explains why pain can be blocked by drugs or competing stimuli. _____ processing of pain is shown by the _____ effect, in which people's beliefs can reduce pain. Such processing is also shown by _____ sensations, in which people with amputations still "feel" sensations from the amputated body part.

24. *Underline the word(s) in parentheses that will make each statement correct. (Both options may be correct!)*

   A. To be deemed effective, a drug must prove itself stronger than (a placebo/an analgesic).

   B. There are (two/four) distinct brain areas that have primary roles in processing pain signals.

   C. (Aspirin/Morphine) suppresses pain messages in the spinal cord and brain.

   D. People highly sensitive to pain show more activation in their (thalamus/anterior cingulate cortex) than people with high pain thresholds.

   E. In fMRI research, acetaminophen has been shown to reduce activation in brain areas associated with (social rejection/physical pain).

25. Dr. C. George Boeree created this web site for his General Psychology course. It is a quick and entertaining tour of the seven senses.
   http://webspace.ship.edu/cgboer/senses.html

26. NEED A BREAK?
   To get a better understanding of sensation and perception, visit MyPsychLab.

What Is the Relationship Between Sensation and Perception?

Perceptual Processing: Finding Meaning in Sensation

27. *Underline the word(s) in parentheses that will make each statement correct. (Both options may be correct!)*

   A. A (feature detector/percept) is not just what we sense, but is the associated meaning also.

   B. One of the biggest mysteries of perceptual psychology is (feature detectors/the binding problem).

   C. The way in which various features of a stimulus are combined into a single unit is known as (bottom-up processing/the binding problem).

   D. The process of perception involves (bottom-up/top-down) processing.

   E. Top-down processing is also known as (stimulus-driven/conceptually driven) processing.

   F. Specialized brain cells dedicated to perceiving slant are called (feature detectors/percepts).

   G. The fact that we don't experience a door as changing shape when it is open versus when it is closed demonstrates the phenomenon of (change blindness/perceptual constancy).

   H. (Change blindness/Perceptual constancy) explains why we may not notice when a friend shaves his mustache.

I. (Top-down/Bottom-up) processing is involved when biases or stereotypes affect our perceptions.

J. The primary visual cortex receives information from the (what/where) pathway.

K. Blindsight involves damage to the (what/where) pathway.

L. Unlike (inattentional/change) blindness, (inattentional/change) blindness requires a person to access memory in order to compare a current scene to a past scene.

M. Perceptual constancy occurs with (color/size).

28. Why are perceptual constancies important for us to have?

29. This is a link to Dr. John Krantz's set of tutorials on sensation and perception. There are many topics to explore that can help you understand the concepts in this chapter.
http://psych.hanover.edu/Krantz/sen_tut.html

Perceptual Ambiguity and Distortion

30. What is the Hermann grid illusion, and why is it so difficult to overcome?

31. *Indicate whether each statement is True (T) or False (F) by circling the appropriate letter after the statement.*

    A. Stimulus patterns that can be interpreted in more than one way are referred to as ambiguous figures.   T F

    B. Ambiguous figures mainly involve bottom-up processing.   T F

    C. Research suggests that the alternating perceptions of the Necker cube may involve the shifting of perceptual control between the left and right eyes.   T F

    D. The vase/faces figure is an illusion that makes use of brightness constancy.   T F

32. What is the Müller-Lyer illusion and what has cross-cultural research revealed concerning a likely explanation for this illusion?

33. This is a wonderful collection of illusions by Dr. David Landrigan of the University of Massachusetts at Lowell. Some will be familiar to you, but there are many others as well.
http://dragon.uml.edu/psych/illusion.html

Theoretical Explanations for Perception

34. *Fill in the blanks of the following concept map with the correct information.*

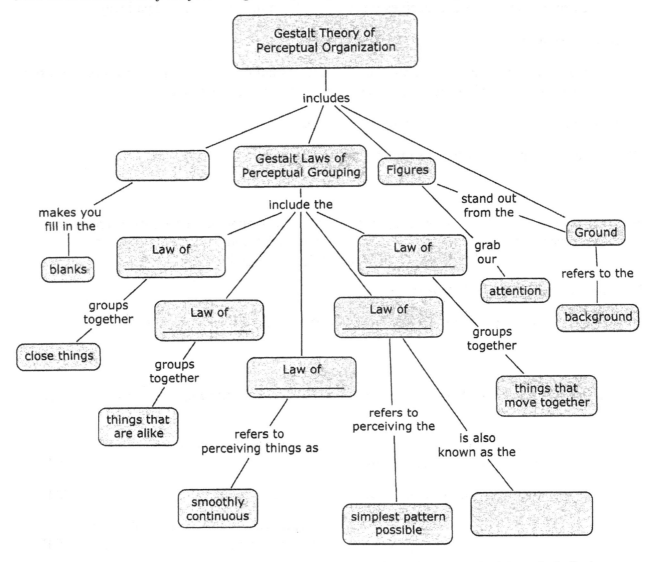

35. The following web site has an excellent discussion of the Gestalt principles of similarity, continuity, closure, proximity, and figure and ground.
http://graphicdesign.spokanefalls.edu/tutorials/process/gestaltprinciples/gestaltprinc.htm

36. Explain Helmholtz's theory of learning-based inferences.

37. What are three of the most important factors for successfully forming an accurate percept?

A. _____ B. _____ C. _____

38. *Fill in the blanks with the correct information.*

A. A readiness to notice and respond to certain stimulus cues is called _____.

B. The surrounding environment can affect our perceptions. In other words, what we perceive is often influenced by the _____.

C. Researchers have assessed babies' depth perception using an apparatus called the _____, and have shown that babies show reluctance to crawl over the "deep side" after they are _____ months of age.

D. Using virtual reality images, research shows that _____-old infants see depth.

39. Using the examples of individuals from Guam, the U.S., and China, explain how culture can play a role in perception.

40. *Fill in the blanks in the following table with the correct information about monocular cues.*

Name of Monocular Cue	Description
A. _____	If two objects are assumed to be the same size, the one that casts the _____ retinal image is assumed to be farther away.
B. _____	Two parallel lines seem to come together in the distance, so the apparent convergence of lines serves as a depth cue.
C. light and shadow	
D. _____	We assume that closer objects will cut off our view of more distant objects behind them.
E. relative motion	
F. _____	Haze or fog makes distant objects appear fuzzy, less distinct, or invisible.

41. This is the homepage for the work of artist M. C. Escher. His work is a good demonstration of how artists use the Gestalt principles and monocular depth perception cues. Click on Gallery to see his work. Visit:

http://www.mcescher.com

42. Explain the similarities and differences between "binocular convergence" and "retinal disparity."

Psychology Matters: Using Psychology to Learn Psychology

43. How does Gestalt psychology relate to studying?

Thinking Critically about Subliminal Perception and Subliminal Persuasion

44. What are "subliminal perception" and "subliminal persuasion" and what evidence is there to support the existence of each of these?

PRACTICE TEST #1

1. Negative afterimages are explained by which theory of color vision?
   A. Frequency   B. Trichromatic   C. Place   D. Opponent-process

2. The _____ convert incoming stimulus information into electrochemical signals.
   A. brain receptors   C. sensory receptors
   B. perceptory receptors   D. neural receptors

3. Sensation is to _____ as perception is to _____.
   A. interpretation; memory   C. transduction; interpretation
   B. processing; construction   D. interpretation; processing

4. If you close your eyes and press gently with your finger on the insider corner of one eye, you will see a pattern caused by the pressure of your finger—not the light on the opposite side of your visual field. These light sensations are called _____.
   A. phosphenes   B. phospheres   C. posphenes   D. protosphenes

5. The diminishing responsiveness of sensory systems to prolonged stimulation is called _____.
   A. sensory relocation   C. sensory differentiation
   B. sensory adoption   D. sensory adaptation

6. The idea that the size of the just noticeable difference is proportional to the intensity of the stimulus is known as _____.
   A. Muller's law   C. Weber's law
   B perceptual threshold   D. the difference threshold

7. You cannot stand the taste of Brussels sprouts. You would most likely be classified as a(n) _____.
   A. supertaster   B. nontaster   C. sensitive taster   D. extreme taster

8. When you are able to correctly identify that the noise you hear after going to bed is just your cat jumping on the dining room table, your ability to accurately identify that noise is due to
   A. your cochlea.   C. sensation principles.
   B. feature detectors.   D. signal detection theory.

9. The _____ is the part of the retina with the greatest visual acuity.
   A. rod   B. fovea   C. optic nerve   D. cornea

10. Place theory explains which characteristic of sound?
    A. Timbre   B. Pitch   C. Amplitude   D. Loudness

PRACTICE TEST #2

1. In vision, _____ of light are transduced by the photoreceptors into color sensations transmitted to the brain.
   A. wavelengths   B. intensities   C. amplitudes   D. electrical charges

2. You arrive at your friend's house and something is cooking that smells very delicious. However, after your study group has studied for fifteen minutes, you are not longer aware of the odor. You have experienced _____.
   A. psychophysics   C. sensory adaptation
   B. your difference threshold   D. Weber's law

3. The _____ cells are responsible for collecting impulses from photoreceptors and shuttling them to the ganglion cells.
   A. bipolar   B. retinal   C. foveal   D. rod and cone

4. When we hear the melody in a song as opposed to the individual notes in the song, we are using the Gestalt law of _____.
   A. continuity   B. similarity   C. Prägnanz   D. proximity

5. The two physical properties of simple sound waves are _____.
   A. frequency and amplitude   C. amplitude and timbre
   B. timbre and frequency   D. pitch and frequency

6. The correct sequence for the process of hearing is: _____.
   A. eardrum; pinna; bones; basilar membrane; cochlea; auditory nerve
   B. pinna; eardrum; bones; cochlea; basilar membrane; auditory nerve
   C. pinna; bones; basilar membrane; cochlea; auditory nerve; eardrum
   D. pinna; eardrum; cochlea; basilar membrane; bones; auditory nerve

7. The primary organ of hearing, a coiled tube in the inner ear where sound waves are transduced into nerve messages, is called the _____.
   A. pinna   B. cochlea   C. auditory nerve   D. semicircular canal

8. Some stores have reported that the subliminal messages played in stores to prevent shoplifting are successful. However, research does not support this finding. The most likely explanation for the success reported is that _____.
   A. the research was not really valid   C. the stores did not have accurate records
   B. purchasers were being more careful   D. employees in those stores were more vigilant

9. The cells that are responsible for daytime vision are called the _____.
   A. ganglions   B. cones   C. rods   D. bipolars

10. The sense that communicates most directly with brain areas associated with memory is _____.
    A. vision   B. sound   C. taste   D. smell

PRACTICE TEST #3

1. Susan developed an inner ear infection and her doctor told her to refrain from driving until it is cured. The sense most affected by this infection would be the _____ sense.
   A. olfactory   B. vestibular   C. kinesthetic   D. gustation

2. Which of the following illusions is usually hardest to overcome?
   A. The Ponzo illusion   C. The Necker cube
   B. The Hermann grid   D. The vase versus faces

3. The _____ theory best explains how we hear high-pitched sounds, whereas the _____ theory best explains how we hear low-pitched sounds.
   A. place; frequency   C. amplitude; wavelength
   B. wavelength; amplitide   D. frequency; place

4. The theory of perception that states that the observer makes reasonable guesses about what sensations mean based on previous experience is known as _____.
   A. the Gestalt perspective   C. bottom-up processing
   B. learning-based inference D. trial-and-error learning

5. If you hold your finger about twelve inches from your face and look at it first with your right eye and then with your left eye, you will see it differently. This is due to the depth cue of _____.
   A. convergence   B. relative size   C. interposition   D. retinal disparity

6. The law of Prägnanz is also referred to as _____.
   A. the grouping principle   C. the minimum principle of perception
   B. law of common fate   D. the principle of least resistance

7. You run into your psychology professor at a baseball game after you have completed her course. You cannot remember why you know her. This best illustrates the concept of _____.
   A. context   B. perceptual set   C. percepts   D. ambiguous figures

8. Rena read a story about movie theaters briefly presenting messages about buying soda and popcorn. This story involves false claims about _____.
   A. light perception   C. sensory experience
   B. subliminal persuasion   D. absolute threshold

9. All of the following are monocular cues EXCEPT _____.
   A. interposition   B. relative size   C. retinal disparity   D. linear perspective

10. All of the following are involved in the process of hearing EXCEPT the _____.
    A. pinna   B. hair cells   C. anvil   D. semicircular canals

COMPREHENSIVE REVIEW TEST

1. Maher can detect the slight increased volume of the radio, but Ahn doesn't think the volume has changed at all. Maher's _____ threshold is _____ than Ahn's.
   A. absolute; lower
   B. difference; lower
   C. difference; higher
   D. absolute; higher

2. According to Weber's law, _____.
   A. the greater the strength of the stimulus, the greater in degree is the change that is needed for an organism to notice a change
   B. a weak stimulus is less likely to be noticed than a strong stimulus
   C. organisms are most likely to notice changes in the transduction of body sense information than visual information
   D. we eventually "get used to" most stimuli when we are exposed to them for a long time

3. The idea that competing stimuli can reduce pain comes from the _____ theory of pain.
   A. drug-control   B. gate-control   C. placebo effect   D. sensory pathway

4. A pilot looks down and sees an island surrounded only by blue ocean. In this case, the ocean is _____.
   A. the figure   B. the ground   C. an illusion   D. an ambiguous figure

5. The receptor cells for which of these senses can renew themselves?
   A. Vision   B. Hearing   C. Gustation   D. Vestibular

6. You read about a plane that crashed off the shore of the local beach. It was a hazy night and there were no lights. One reason for the crash could be the perceptual cue of _____.
   A. convergence
   B. atmospheric perspective
   C. retinal disparity
   D. relative size

7. The most general principle of all Gestalt laws is the law of_____, which states that the mind organizes the world in the way that requires the least amount of cognitive effort to interpret.
   A. closure   B. common fate   C. Prägnanz   D. proximity

8. Sharon had trouble hearing the teacher so the school gave her a hearing test. Some of the sounds presented were at such a low level of intensity that she couldn't hear them. These sounds were below her _____ threshold.
   A. absolute.   B. difference   C. discriminative   D. adaptive

9. All of the following are important factors in signal detection theory EXCEPT _____.
   A. the detector.   B. the stimulus.   C. psychophysics.   D. background stimulation.

10. A "carpentered" world appears to play a role in which illusion?
    A. Ponzo   B. Necker cube   C. Müller-Lyer   D. Hermann grid

11. Natasha experiences stabbing pain as bright orange and dull pain as blue. She likely has _____.

A. JND   B. synesthesia   C. phosphenes   D. the placebo effect

12. Brain cells specialized to respond to only one aspect of a stimulus are called _____.
    A. percepts   B. JNDs   C. perceptual sets   D. feature detectors

13. Josh read in the newspaper about numerous break-ins around town. When he hears a tapping on the window one windy night, he is sure someone is trying to break in, rather than it being the tree branches hitting the window. Josh is demonstrating _____.
    A. closure   B. figure/ground   C. perceptual set   D. the law of continuity

14. The _____ theory explains what happens in the bipolar cells and beyond.
    A. trichromatic   B. gate-control   C. opponent-process   D. learning-based inference

15. After _____ of age, babies are reluctant to cross over to the "deep" side of the visual cliff.
    A. six months   B. three months   C. one month   D. two weeks

CRITICAL THINKING ESSAYS

1. Based on what you've learned about sensation and perception, explain why it is not a good idea to listen to interesting or favorite music while studying for exams. Use correct terms.

2. Discuss what you have learned about pain and how top-down and bottom-up processing play a role.

CHAPTER 4
Learning and Human Nature

Make flashcards using the following terms or, even better, develop mnemonics (memory strategies) to help you remember the different concepts and terms. Use the definitions in the margins of this chapter for help. Numbers refer to page numbers in the textbook.

acquisition (138)
behavioral learning (135)
classical conditioning (136)
cognitive map (158)
conditioned reinforcer (147)
conditioned response (CR) (138)
conditioned stimulus (CS) (138)
continuous reinforcement (145)
extinction (in classical conditioning) (138)
extinction (in operant conditioning) (146)
fixed interval (FI) schedule (147)
fixed ratio (FR) schedule (146)
habituation (135)
insight learning (158)
instinctive drift (148)
intermittent reinforcement (146)
interval schedule (146)
law of effect (143)
learning (134)
long-term potentiation (161)
mere exposure effect (135)
negative punishment (149)
negative reinforcement (144)

neutral stimulus (137)
observational learning (160)
operant chamber (144)
operant conditioning (143)
positive punishment (149)
positive reinforcement (144)
Premack principle (148)
primary reinforcer (147)
punishment (149)
ratio schedule (146)
reinforcement contingencies (145)
reinforcer (144)
schedule of reinforcement (146)
secondary reinforcer (147)
shaping (145)
spontaneous recovery (138)
stimulus discrimination (139)
stimulus generalization (139)
token economy (148)
unconditioned response (UCR) (138)
unconditioned stimulus (UCS) (137)
variable interval (VI) schedule (147)
variable ratio (VR) schedule (14

Lecture Assistant *for Chapter 4*

Tear this outline out and bring it with you to class in order to facilitate your note taking. Spend more time listening to the lecture and less time writing!

Chapter Opening Problem: Assuming that Sabra's fear of flying was a response that she had learned, could it also be treated by learning? If so, how?

- *Learning =*

1) <u>Behavioral Learning versus Cognitive Learning</u> =

2) <u>Learning versus Instincts</u> =

3) <u>Simple and Complex Forms of Learning</u> =

- *Habituation =*

- *Mere exposure effect =*

- *Behavioral learning =*

4.1 WHAT SORT OF LEARNING DOES CLASSICAL CONDITIONING EXPLAIN?

Core Concept 4.1 =

A) The Essentials of Classical Conditioning

- *Neutral stimulus =*

1) <u>Acquisition</u> =

- *Unconditioned stimulus (UCS) =*

- *Unconditioned response (UCR) =*

- *Conditioned stimulus (CS) =*

- *Conditioned response (CR) =*

2) <u>Extinction and Spontaneous Recovery</u> =

- *Extinction =*

- *Spontaneous recovery =*

3) <u>Generalization</u> =

- *Stimulus generalization =*

4) <u>Discrimination Learning</u> =

- *Stimulus discrimination =*

B) Applications of Classical Conditioning

1) <u>The Notorious Case of Little Albert</u> =

- John Watson and Rosalie Rayner =

  o *Counterconditioning =*

2) <u>Conditioned Food Aversions</u> =

- John Garcia and Robert Koelling =

3) <u>Biological Predispositions: A Challenge to Pavlov</u> =

4) <u>Real-World Applications of Classical Conditioning</u> =

C) Psychology Matters: Taste Aversions and Chemotherapy =

4.2 HOW DO WE LEARN NEW BEHAVIORS BY OPERANT CONDITIONING?

Core Concept 4.2 =

A) Skinner's Radical Behaviorism=

- *Thorndike's law of effect =*

B) The Power of Reinforcement =

- *Reinforcer =*

- *Positive reinforcement =*

- *Negative reinforcement =*

1) <u>Reinforcing Technology: The "Skinner Box"</u> =

- *Operant chamber =*

2) <u>Contingencies of Reinforcement</u> =

- *Reinforcement contingencies =*

3) <u>Continuous versus Intermittent Reinforcement</u> =

- *Continuous reinforcement =*

- *Shaping =*

- *Intermittent reinforcement =*

- *Extinction =*

4) <u>Schedules of Reinforcement</u> =

- *Ratio schedule =*

- *Interval schedule =*

- *Fixed ratio (FR) Schedule =*

- *Variable ratio (VR) Schedule =*

- *Fixed interval (FI) Schedule =*

- *Variable interval (VI) Schedule =*

5) <u>Primary and Secondary Reinforcers</u> =

- *Primary reinforcers* =

- *Secondary reinforcers (conditioned reinforcers)* =

6) <u>Piggy Banks and Token Economies</u> =

- *Instinctive drift* =

- *Token economy* =

7) <u>Preferred Activities as Reinforcers: The Premack Principle</u> =

- *Premack principle* =

8) <u>Reinforcement across Cultures</u> =

C) The Problem of Punishment

- *Punishment* =

- *Positive punishment* =

- *Negative punishment* =

1) <u>Punishment versus Negative Reinforcement</u> =

2) <u>The Uses and Abuses of Punishment</u> =

3) <u>Does Punishment Ever Work?</u>

D) A Checklist for Modifying Operant Behavior =

E) Operant and Classical Conditioning Compared =

F) Psychology Matters: Using Psychology to Learn Psychology =

4.3 HOW DOES COGNITIVE PSYCHOLOGY EXPLAIN LEARNING?

Core Concept 4.3 =

A) Insight Learning: Köhler in the Canaries with the Chimps =

- *Insight learning* =

B) Cognitive Maps: Tolman Finds Out What's on a Rat's Mind =

1) Mental Images—Not Behaviors =

- *Cognitive map* =

2) Learning without Reinforcement =

- o *Latent learning* =

3) The Significance of Tolman's Work =

C) Observational Learning: Bandura's Challenge to Behaviorism =

- o *BoBo doll* =

1) Learning by Observation and Imitation =

- *Observational learning (social learning)* =

2) Effects of Media Violence =

- o *Psychic numbing* =

3) Observational Learning Applied to Social Problems Around the Globe =

D) Brain Mechanisms and Learning =

- *Long-term potentiation =*

1) <u>The Brain on Extinction</u> =

2) <u>Linking Behavioral Learning with Cognitive Learning</u> =

3) <u>Observational Learning and Mirror Neurons</u> =

E) "Higher" Cognitive Learning =

F) Psychology Matters: Fear of Flying Revisited =

ADDITIONAL NOTES

What Sort of Learning Does Classical Conditioning Explain?

1. *Fill in the blanks with the correct terms.*

"A process through which experience produces a lasting change in behavior or mental

processes" is the definition of _____ . In contrast, _____

refer to motivated behaviors that have a strong innate basis.

2. *Match each term with its best description by placing the letter corresponding to the term in the space next to its description. (Terms may be used more than once.)*

TERMS
A. Mere exposure effect
B. Cognitive learning
C. Habituation
D. Behavioral learning
E. Walden Two
F. Species-typical behavior

DESCRIPTIONS
_____ Includes insight and imitation
_____ Leonard no longer notices or responds to the smell of the room deodorizer.
_____ Classical and operant conditioning are two kinds
_____ Babies know how to nurse immediately after birth.
_____ Jessica cries when she sees doctors because of all the shots she's been given by doctors in the past.
_____ A preference for stimuli we've experienced before
_____ Instincts
_____ Emphasizes that nurture is more important than nature

The Essentials of Classical Conditioning

3. *Fill in the blanks with the correct terms.*

A. Pavlov's research on learning focused on manipulating simple, automatic responses

known as _____ by associating such responses with

_____ stimuli that had previously produced no response.

B. The initial stage of learning in classical conditioning is referred to as

_____.

C. In classical conditioning, the stimulus that automatically brings on a reflexive response is called the _____ stimulus, and the reflexive response is called the _____ response.

D. Through classical conditioning, the neutral stimulus becomes the _____ stimulus, which then elicits a behavior called the _____ response.

4. *Indicate whether each statement is True (T) or False (F) by circling the appropriate letter after the statement.*

A. During the initial stages of acquisition, the conditioned stimulus usually elicits strong responses.   T F

B. For classical conditioning to take place, the UCS and CS need to occur only a few seconds apart.   T F

C. During classical conditioning, a conditioned stimulus becomes an unconditioned stimulus.   T F

D. According to the text, the building blocks of classical conditioning are the CS, CR, UCS, UCR, and the timing that connects them.   T F

E. Extinction of the CR occurs when the UCS is no longer presented with the CS.   T F

5. Complete the following chart with the elements of Pavlov's famous experiment that match the terminology.

Terminology	Element from the Experiment
Unconditioned Stimulus (UCS)	
Unconditioned Response (UCR)	
Neutral Stimulus (NS)	
Conditioned Stimulus (CS)	
Conditioned Response (CR)	

6. *Apply classical conditioning terminology to the following example.*

Ann is a twelve-year-old girl who has been diagnosed with diabetes and must now get daily insulin injections from her parents. The shots are painful and anxiety-producing for her, so her heart races during the injections. After several weeks of painful shots, Ann's heart now races when she merely smells the rubbing alcohol used to sterilize the injection site. In fact, any sort of alcohol smell—including the wine her parents drink with dinner—makes her heart race.

Her parents notice this newfound behavior and buy lemon-scented alcohol wipes. After a few weeks of using the lemon-scented alcohol wipes, Ann no longer experiences a racing heart when she smells rubbing alcohol, wine, or other alcohol smells. However, two months later when she helps her mother use rubbing alcohol to remove some glue, Ann's heart begins racing again.

_____

_____

_____

_____

_____

_____

_____

7. *Underline the word(s) in parentheses that will make each statement correct. (Both options may be correct!)*

   A. Extinction (weakens/completely eliminates) the conditioned response.

   B. When spontaneous recovery occurs, the CR nearly always reappears at a (higher/lower) intensity.

   C. When an organism learns to respond to one stimulus but not to other similar stimuli, this is called stimulus (generalization/discrimination).

   D. (Extinction/Spontaneous recovery) demonstrates that (extinction/spontaneous recovery) involves the weakening of—rather than the elimination of—a behavior.

Applications of Classical Conditioning

8. Watson and Rayner classically conditioned an eleven-month-old named Albert to fear a white rat. When Albert first saw the rat, he showed no fear and tried to reach for it. Then whenever Albert reached for the rat, Watson and Rayner made a loud noise behind Albert, which scared Albert and made him cry. After Watson and Rayner did this many times, just seeing the rat was enough to make Albert scared and cry.

   Match the classical conditioning terms with the stimuli and responses from Albert's case.

   A. unconditioned stimulus   D. conditioned response
   B. conditioned stimulus   E. neutral stimulus
   C. unconditioned response

   _____ The white rat when Albert was first introduced to it
   _____ Fear of the white rat
   _____ Fear due to the loud noise
   _____ The white rat after it was paired numerous times with the loud noise
   _____ The loud noise

9. *Fill in the blanks with the correct information.*

   In _____ therapy for phobias, the strategy is to combine

   _____ of the conditioned fear response with learning a

   _____ response to the conditioned stimulus.

10. This site contains a very helpful explanation of the process of classical conditioning.
    http://www.edpsycinteractive.org/topics/behsys/classcnd.html

11. Garcia and Koelling (1966) found that they could condition rats to avoid water when that water became associated with the nausea caused by radiation. However, they could not condition the rats to associate water with pain from electric shocks.

    A) Use an evolutionary perspective to explain these findings.

    B) Then, explain how these findings challenge Pavlov's theory.

12. *Fill in the blanks in the following concept map about classical conditioning.*

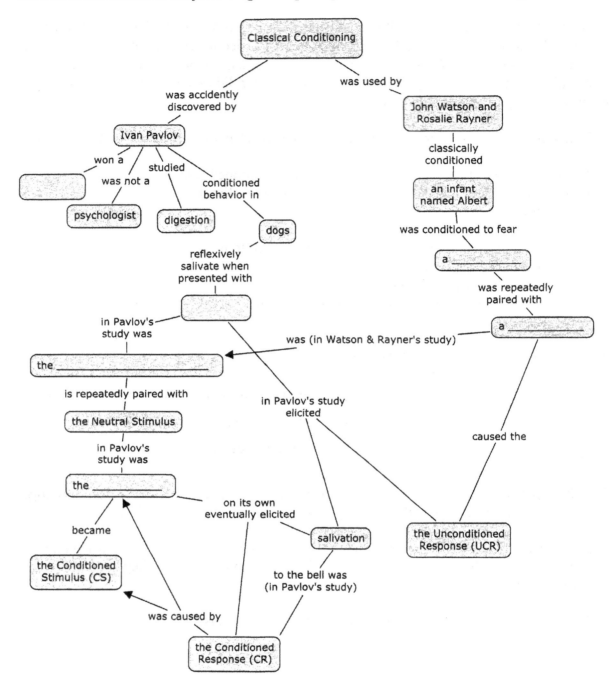

13. Explain how researchers classically conditioned coyotes to dislike eating sheep.

Psychology Matters: Taste Aversion and Chemotherapy

14. Briefly explain how knowledge about conditioned taste aversions has been used to help chemotherapy patients.

How Do We Learn New Behaviors By Operant Conditioning?

15. *Fill in the blanks with the correct information.*

   A. A(n) _____ is an observable behavior that an organism uses to have an effect on the environment.

   B. In operant conditioning, the _____ of behavior, such as _____ and _____, influence the probability that the behavior will occur again.

   C. _____ conditioning accounts for a much wider spectrum of behaviors than does _____ conditioning.

   D. Operant conditioning explains _____ behaviors, not just _____ behaviors.

Skinner's Radical Behaviorism

16. *Underline the word(s) in parentheses that will make each statement correct. (Both options may be correct!)*

   A. (Skinner/Thorndike) believed that what happens immediately (after/before) a behavior is what influences the behavior the most.

   B. Thorndike's idea that responses that produce desirable consequences would be learned is called (radical behaviorism/the law of effect).

   C. According to (Skinner's/Thorndike's) (law of effect/radical behaviorism), the subjective and unscientific speculations about an organism's thoughts, feelings, and intentions are not considered.

103

The Power of Reinforcement

17. *Indicate whether each statement is True (T) or False (F) by circling the appropriate letter after the statement.*

   A. Negative reinforcement makes a behavior less likely to occur.   T F

   B. Continuing to fasten one's seatbelt in order to get rid of the awful
   buzzing sound is an example of positive reinforcement.   T F

   C. A "Skinner box" is also known as an operant chamber.   T F

   D. The word "negative" in negative reinforcement refers to the removal
   of an unpleasant or aversive behavior.   T F

   E. The Skinner box is used to study classical conditioning in animals.   T F

   F. Both the timing and frequency of reinforcement can be controlled in
   an operant chamber.   T F

   G. Skinner preferred the term "Skinner box" to "operant chamber."   T F

   H. According to Skinner, a "reward" and a "reinforcer" are the same thing.   T F

18. *For each example, identify whether positive reinforcement, negative reinforcement, <u>or neither</u> is affecting YOUR behavior.*

   A. You take your cousin to the store and he whines until you buy him a candy bar. You
   tend to buy him a lot of candy to keep him from whining. _____

   B. Your parents praise you when you show them the good grade on your psychology final
   exam, so you continue to get good grades. _____

   C. The judge takes away your driver's license because you have received ten speeding
   tickets. You no longer speed. _____

   D. You miss curfew once again, and your parents make you clean the garage. You hate
   cleaning the garage, so you don't miss curfew as often in the future.

   _____

   E. You get tired of hearing your mother nag about how dirty your room is, so you start
   cleaning it more often to keep her from nagging you. _____

19. *For each example, identify whether positive reinforcement, negative reinforcement, <u>or</u> <u>neither</u> is affecting the OTHER PERSON'S behavior (rather than your own).*

    A. You take your cousin to the store and he whines until you buy him a candy bar. He tends to whine whenever he goes to the store with you. _____

    B. Your parents praise you when you show them the good grade on your psychology final exam. They continue to praise you, because the praise seems to get rid of your bad exam scores. _____

    C. The judge takes away your driver's license because you have received ten speeding tickets. You no longer speed. The judge is likely to continue taking away speeders' driver's licenses. _____

    D. You miss curfew once again, and your parents make you clean the garage. You hate cleaning the garage, so you don't miss curfew as often in the future. Your parents are now more likely to make you clean the garage because it keeps you from misbehaving and missing curfew. _____

    E. You get tired of hearing your mother nag about how dirty your room is, so you start cleaning it more often to keep her from nagging you. Her nagging is likely to continue in the future. _____

20. Explain the difference between continuous reinforcement and intermittent (partial) reinforcement. Then, explain which is better to use early in the learning process—and which is better for maintaining behaviors already learned. Be sure to explain why!

21. What is "shaping," and why is it used?

22. This great tutorial from Athabasca University in Canada explains what positive reinforcement is—and what it isn't. The site also gives you some practice exercises with instant feedback. http://psych.athabascau.ca/html/prtut/reinpair.htm

23. *Match each term with its correct description by placing the letter corresponding to the term in the space next to its description. (Terms may be used more than once.)*

TERMS

A. Ratio schedule   F. Fixed-ratio schedule
B. Interval schedule   G. Primary reinforcers
C. Variable ratio schedule   H. Secondary reinforcers
D. Variable interval schedule   I. Instinctive drift
E. Fixed interval schedule   J. Extinction

DESCRIPTIONS

_____ They fulfill basic biological needs.

_____ You buy lottery tickets every week because you win money now and then.

_____ Occurs more quickly with continuous reinforcement than partial reinforcement

_____ Dogs trained to pick things up gently often revert back to chewing the items instead.

_____ Schedule that usually results in a low response rate

_____ Reinforcement occurs after a number of responses.

_____ The local coffee shop gives you a "buy nine, get the tenth free" card for buying drinks, so you buy a lot of drinks there.

_____ Also known as conditioned reinforcers

_____ You keep staring at the night sky because sometimes you get to see a shooting star, which is exciting for you.

_____ Produces a "scalloped" pattern of behavior

_____ Reinforcement occurs after an amount of time goes by.

_____ You find yourself clicking on the oven light more and more as it gets closer to the time that your favorite cookies are done.

_____ Your job is to pick strawberries, and you receive twenty-five cents for every six quarts you pick.

_____ Usually produces more responding than any other partial reinforcement schedule

_____ Schedule most widely adopted by businesses

24. *Fill in the blanks with the correct terms.*

A. A preferred activity can reinforce a less preferred one. This fact is referred to as the

_____.

B. An organization that uses small, plastic "coins" as reinforcers (that people in the organization can exchange for privileges or other rewards) is referred to as a

_____.

C. Cynthia loves playing basketball with her father, so he uses that as a reinforcer to get her to clean he room. Psychologists would say that Cynthia's father is using the

_____.

The Problem of Punishment

25. *For each of the examples below, indicate whether it is an example of reinforcement (R) or of punishment (P).*

    A. Rima's swearing declines after her parents take away her car privileges.   _____
    B. Terrance shares a lot because his parents praise him when he does.   _____
    C. Jordan argues with his parents. His parents keep sending him to his room, which
        gets him away from their nagging. The arguing now happens more frequently.   _____
    D. Mei-Chin stops going to birthday parties because she hates loud noise.   _____
    E. Hilda gets the teacher's attention when she yells, so she continues to yell.   _____
    F. Attiq doesn't crawl near steps anymore after falling down the stairs.   _____

26. *Underline the word(s) in parentheses that will make each statement correct. (Both options may be correct!)*

    A. To decrease the likelihood of a behavior occurring again, one can use (positive punishment/negative reinforcement).

    B. Negative punishment differs from positive punishment in that negative punishment involves the (removal/presentation) of (a pleasant/an unpleasant) stimulus to weaken a behavior.

    C. Darnell takes away his daughter's cell phone privileges after she swears at him, so her swearing declines drastically. Darnell has successfully utilized (positive punishment/negative punishment).

    D. Freddy is acting up in class, so his teacher yells at him. Freddy loves the attention, so he continues to act up in class. His teacher's yelling was a (positive reinforcer/positive punisher) for Freddy.

    E. Rachael sprays her cat with water every time it jumps on the counter, so the cat is not jumping on the counter as often. Rachael has used (positive punishment/negative punishment) on her cat.

    F. In order to weaken a behavior, you can use (positive/negative) punishment.

    G. The most effective punishment is usually (negative/positive) punishment.

    H. Not touching a hot stove after being burned is (negative/positive) punishment.

27. The following site has a compendium of strategies for pet owners and others who work with animals. They are explicitly based on operant conditioning, particularly positive reinforcement and negative punishment. Try them with your own pets!
http://www.wagntrain.com/OC/

28. Explain five main reasons that punishment is difficult to use effectively.

A. _____

B. _____

C. _____

D. _____

E. _____

29. Your friend Robert's five-year-old daughter keeps hitting her three-year-old brother. Needless to say, your friend wants to make that behavior go away. Knowing what you now know about punishment, what would you tell Robert concerning punishment and the ways to make it most effective?

A Checklist for Modifying Operant Behavior

30. In the table below, explain the effects of each operant conditioning technique, including the potential problems with it.

Operant Conditioning Technique	Effects
A. Positive Reinforcement	
B. Negative Reinforcement	
C. Punishment	
D. Extinction	

31. *Fill in the blanks in the following concept map about operant conditioning.*

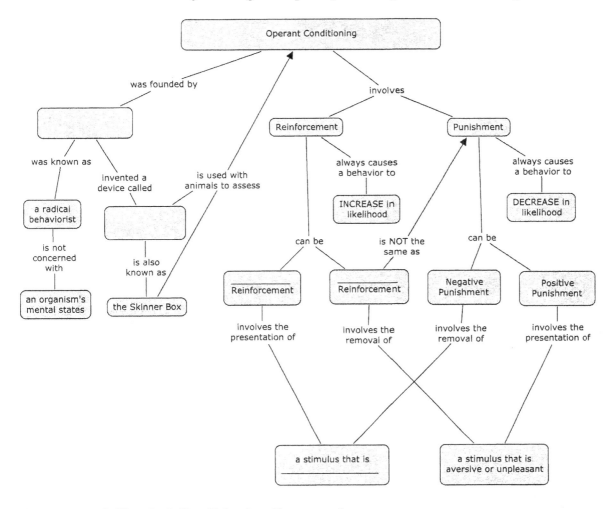

Operant and Classical Conditioning Compared

32. Fill in the following chart comparing operant and classical conditioning.

Question	Operant Conditioning	Classical Conditioning
A. When does the stimulus occur?		
B. What type of stimuli is used?	both pleasant and unpleasant	
C. What type of behavior is produced?		"old," reflexive behaviors
D. How does extinction occur?	reinforcement is withheld	
E. Is the learner passive or active?		

33. NEED A BREAK?
   To get a better understanding of classical conditioning, operant conditioning, and other learning theories, visit MyPsychLab.

How Does Cognitive Psychology Explain Learning?

34. In your own words, describe Core Concept 3.3, which deals with cognitive learning.

Insight Learning: Köhler in the Canaries with the Chimps

35. Define "insight learning" and then explain how Köhler was able to demonstrate its existence in chimps.

Cognitive Maps: Tolman Finds Out What's on a Rat's Mind

36. What is a "cognitive map"? Describe Tolman's studies with rats that provided evidence of the existence of cognitive maps.

Observational Learning: Bandura's Challenge to Behaviorism

37. Describe how Bandura was able to demonstrate the occurrence of observational learning in young children through the use of a BoBo doll.

38. What is meant by "psychic numbing"?

39. Dr. Boeree's site from Shippensburg University tells you all about Albert Bandura and his social learning theory.
       http://www.ship.edu/~cgboeree/bandura.html

40. *Match each researcher's name with concepts related to his theory and research by placing the letter corresponding to his name in the space next to the concept.*

NAMES
   A. Tolman   B. Bandura   C. Köhler

CONCEPTS
___ showed the importance of social learning   ___ showed the existence of insight learning
___ showed the existence of cognitive maps   ___ worked with young children
___ worked with chimps   ___ showed the importance of observation
___ showed the existence of latent learning   ___ worked with rats

Brain Mechanisms and Learning

41. *Fill in the blanks with the correct terms.*

   A. The term _____ refers to physical changes that strengthen the synapses in a group of neurons.

   B. In operant conditioning, the brain's reward circuitry gets activated, especially the _____ and parts of the _____ cortex.

   C. Neuroscientists have found that extinction occurs when certain _____, such as _____ and _____, are blocked.

   D. _____ neurons are specifically involved in observational learning.

111

PRACTICE TEST #1

1. Tolman's work with rats demonstrated the existence of _____ learning.
   A. latent   B. observational   C. insight   D. social

2. The type of learning in which associations between stimuli play a major role is _____.
   A. classical conditioning   C. social learning
   B. operant conditioning   D. insight learning

3. Pavlov discovered _____ while studying _____.
   A. cognition; mazes   C. operant conditioning; rabbits
   B. classical conditioning; cats   D. classical conditioning; dogs

4. When you learn to ignore the sounds of traffic on the busy street where you live, you are exhibiting _____.
   A. unlearning   B. habituation   C. conditioning   D. prompting

5. Acquisition is most likely to occur when the conditioned stimulus is presented _____.
   A. after the UCS   C. along with the UCS
   B. before the UCS   D. only once

6. In Pavlov's studies, when salivation was elicited by food, the food was _____.
   A. a reflex   C. a conditioned stimulus
   B. an unconditioned stimulus   D. a conditioned response

7. In Pavlov's studies, when the bell elicited salivation, the salivation was _____.
   A. a reflex   C. a conditioned stimulus
   B. an unconditioned response   D. a conditioned response

8. In classical conditioning, sometimes an extinguished behavior suddenly reappears. This is known as _____.
   A. extinction   C. spontaneous recovery
   B. reconditioning   D. generalization

9. You were frightened by a yellow cat when you were a child. Now you get scared whenever you see any cat. In classical conditioning, this response would be known as _____.
   A. spontaneous recovery   C. generalization
   B. discrimination   D. insight

10. The behavior elicited by the unconditioned stimulus is _____ in nature.
    A. involuntary   B. voluntary   C. complex   D. prosocial

112

PRACTICE TEST #2

1. Janelle is trying to get her daughter, Leena, to play quietly by herself for twenty minutes. First Janelle gives Leena a favorite sticker after she plays alone quietly for just five minutes. Then Leena has to play quietly for ten minutes before she gets a sticker—and, after that, for fifteen minutes. Eventually, Leena only gets a sticker after twenty minutes of quiet play. This is _____.
   - A. extinction
   - B. habituation
   - C. classical conditioning
   - D. shaping

2. Portia has a client who is exhibiting an undesirable conditioned fear. Portia decides to try a therapeutic strategy called _____ to extinguish the response.
   - A. appetitive conditioning
   - B. aversive conditioning
   - C. reflex conditioning
   - D. counterconditioning

3. Thorndike trained animals to connect a stimulus with a response. His theory is called _____.
   - A. reflexive responses
   - B. Thorndike's principle
   - C. the law of effect
   - D. insight learning

4. Mark is babysitting Sue; Sue throws tantrums in order to get candy. In the future, when Mark continues to give Sue candy to make her tantrums stop, Mark's behavior is being
   - A. negatively punished
   - B. positively punished
   - C. negatively reinforced
   - D. positively reinforced

5. Mark is babysitting Sue, who throws tantrums in order to get candy. When Mark continues to give Sue candy to make her tantrums stop, Sarah's tantrums are likely to increase. Sue is being _____.
   - A. positively reinforced
   - B. negatively reinforced
   - C. positively punished
   - D. negatively punished

6. Pigs taught to pick up coins in their mouth and drop them in a slot often revert back to pushing the coins around with their snouts instead. This is known as _____.
   - A. shaping
   - B. instinctive drift
   - C. law of effect
   - D. spontaneous recovery

7. Gambling by using a slot machine is reinforced on a _____ schedule.
   - A. fixed ratio
   - B. variable ratio
   - C. continuous
   - D. variable interval

8. Which schedule of reinforcement is most likely to produce a "scalloped" pattern of behavior?
   - A. fixed ratio
   - B. variable ratio
   - C. fixed interval
   - D. variable interval

9. Which usually produces more responding than any other partial reinforcement schedule?
   - A. fixed ratio
   - B. variable ratio
   - C. fixed interval
   - D. variable interval

10. We tend to have a preference for stimuli we've experienced before. This is known as _____.
   A. the mere exposure effect
   B. shaping
   C. habituation
   D. classical conditioning

PRACTICE TEST #3

1. You throw a wild party while your parents are out of town. They find out, and you are grounded for two weeks. You never again throw a party when they are out of town. This is _____.
   A. negative reinforcement
   B. negative punishment
   C. positive reinforcement
   D. positive punishment

2. The law of effect is most similar to which of the following?
   A. the Premack principle
   B. classical conditioning
   C. operant conditioning
   D. habituation

3. Stimuli that fulfill basic needs and act as a reinforcer are called _____ reinforcers.
   A. secondary
   B. primary
   C. conditioned
   D. neutral

4. You show up at your little cousin's home wearing earplugs every time you babysit for an entire month. You watch him serenely as he throws a tantrum until he becomes exhausted and falls asleep. After two weeks, he no longer throws tantrums. This is an example of _____.
   A. negative reinforcement
   B. prompting
   C. shaping
   D. extinction

5. You promise your brother that when he finishes his history term paper you will buy him the new CD from his favorite group. This is an example of _____.
   A. the Premack principle
   B. a token economy
   C. classical conditioning
   D. shaping

6. Punishment _____ a behavior, and negative reinforcement _____ a behavior.
   A. increases; decreases
   B. decreases; increases
   C. increases; increases
   D. decreases; decreases

7. In Pavlov's research, when salivation was elicited by the presentation of food, salivation was _____.
   A. an unconditioned stimulus
   B. a conditioned stimulus
   C. a conditioned response
   D. an unconditioned response

8. When a characteristic in the environment decreases the probability that a behavior will be repeated, this is known as _____.
   A. punishment
   B. reinforcement
   C. an unconditioned response
   D. a conditioned response

9. Köhler developed his theory of cognitive learning by studying _____.
   A. rats
   B. dogs
   C. chimps
   D. monkeys

10. Lisa is goofing around in class, so her teacher yells at her. Lisa likes annoying the teacher, so she goofs around in class even more. The teacher has _____ Lisa's annoying behavior.

A. negatively reinforced

C. positively reinforced

B. negatively punished

D. positively punished

COMPREHENSIVE REVIEW TEST

1. When you push the buttons on the vending machine and get your favorite drink, you are likely in the future to use the vending machine again. This is an example of _____.
   A. classical conditioning
   B. operant conditioning
   C. habituation
   D. shaping

2. All of the following statements about classical conditioning are true EXCEPT _____.
   A. timing is relatively unimportant as long as the UCS is presented before the CS
   B. presenting the neutral stimulus before the UCS is important for conditioning to take place
   C. the organism must see a connection between the UCS and CS
   D. conditioning will occur only if the CS is a unique source of information about the UCS

3. Elmer rings a bell and blows a puff of air through a straw into Susie's right eye, causing her to blink. After seven trials, he rings a bell and there is no air puff. Susie blinks anyway. The bell was a _____ and is now a _____.
   A. CS; neutral stimulus
   B. neutral stimulus; UCS
   C. neutral stimulus; CS
   D. negative stimulus; positive stimulus

4. Maggie, the dog, hides under the bed when she hears her human saying he is going to take her to the V-E-T for her S-H-O-T-S. Through an unintentional process of _____, the spelled-out words have become a _____.
   A. classical conditioning; CS
   B. negative reinforcement; CS
   C. operant conditioning; CS
   D. conditioned reinforcement; CR

5. Which of the following pairings is correct?
   A. Skinner and operant conditioning
   B. Pavlov and operant conditioning
   C. Bandura and classical conditioning
   D. Skinner and classical conditioning

6. You are in the grocery store, waiting to check out. Your son cries because he wants candy, so you give in to his demands to make the tantrum stop. In the future, when he has tantrums, you are likely to give him candy. Your behavior of giving him candy has been _____.
   A. positively reinforced
   B. negatively reinforced
   C. positively punished
   D. classically conditioned

7. You are in the grocery store, waiting to check out. Your son cries because he wants candy, so you give in to his demands to make the tantrum stop. His tantrums now occur every time you take him to the grocery store. Your son's tantrums have been _____.
   A. positively reinforced
   B. negatively reinforced
   C. positively punished
   D. classically conditioned

8. The research of _____ suggests that watching violent television programs causes some children to become more aggressive.
   A. Bandura   B. Skinner   C. Premack   D. Watson

9. A garment worker earns $5.00 for every 30 sweaters she finishes. She is being reinforced on a
   _____ schedule.
   A. continuous   B. fixed interval   C. fixed ratio   D. variable ratio

10. I received a $150 ticket for speeding about a year ago. According to Skinner, the fact that I now
    no longer speed is an example of the effectiveness of _____.
    A. punishment   C. classical conditioning
    B. reinforcement   D. observational learning

11. A(n) _____ is an internal representation of an organism's environment that is acquired through
    experience.
    A. insight   B. concept map   C. cognitive map   D. latent structure

12. Köhler's study of chimpanzees suggests that they reorganize their perceptions, a mental
    process he called _____ learning.
    A. operant   B. latent   C. insight   D. perceptual

13. Jack learned how to shoot a basketball free throw by watching his older brother. Bandura
    called this _____ learning.
    A. insight   B. observational   C. latent   D. representational

14. A preferred activity can reinforce a less preferred one. This fact is referred to as _____.
    A. latent learning   C. the mere exposure effect
    B. insight learning   D. the Premack principle

15. The removal of a pleasant stimulus to weaken a behavior is referred to as _____.
    A. negative reinforcement   C. positive reinforcement
    B. negative punishment   D. positive punishment

CRITICAL THINKING ESSAYS

1. Using theory and terminology you learned in this chapter, explain how someone might now always get anxious and sweaty when approaching a revolving door after getting painfully pinched and caught in one two years earlier. Why do you think this anxiety about revolving doors has persisted for two years instead of going away?

2. Your friend's dog is chewing up his shoes and your friend is convinced that the best way to stop this behavior is to hit his dog with a rolled-up newspaper if he arrives home after work and finds his shoes chewed up. He asks you if you've learned anything in psychology that can help him stop the dog from destroying his shoes.

   Knowing what you know about operant conditioning, what suggestions would you make?

3. Your cousin tells you that there's no evidence that watching violent media causes people to behave aggressively. She points out that it's all a bunch of correlational research.
   Based on what you've learned in this chapter, what do you tell her?

CHAPTER 5
Memory

Before You Read . . . Term Identification

Make flashcards using the following terms or, even better, develop mnemonics (memory strategies) to help you remember the different concepts and terms. Use the definitions in the margins of this chapter for help. Numbers refer to page numbers in the textbook.

absent-mindedness (198)
acoustic encoding (182)
anterograde amnesia (187)
blocking (198)
childhood amnesia (186)
chunking (181)
consolidation (188)
declarative memory (184)
distributed learning (204)
eidetic imagery (175)
elaborative rehearsal (181)
encoding (174)
encoding specificity principle (193)
engram (187)
episodic memory (185)
explicit memory (191)
flashbulb memory (189)
forgetting curve (196)
gist (192)
implicit memory (191)
information-processing model (174)
levels-of-processing theory (183)
long-term memory (LTM) (177)
maintenance rehearsal (181)
memory (172)
method of loci (203)
misattribution (199)

misinformation effect (200)
mnemonic strategy (203)
mood-congruent memory (193)
natural language mediators (203)
persistence (202)
priming (192)
proactive interference (197)
procedural memory (184)
prospective memory (194)
recall (192)
recognition (193)
retrieval (175)
retrieval cue (191)
retroactive interference (197)
retrograde amnesia (188)
schema (185)
self-consistency bias (202)
semantic memory (185)
sensory memory (177)
serial position effect (197)
storage (175)
suggestibility (200)
TOT phenomenon (194)
transience (196)
whole method (204)
working memory (177)

Lecture Assistant *for Chapter 5*

Tear this outline out and bring it with you to class in order to facilitate your note taking.
Spend more time listening to the lecture and less time writing!

Chapter Opening Problem: How can our knowledge about memory help us evaluate claims of recovered memories?

5.1 WHAT IS MEMORY?

Core Concept 5.1 =

A) Metaphors for Memory:

- "Video recorder" =

- "Interpretive system" =

    o The most complete and accurate memories are made when:

- *Information-processing model* =

B) Memory's Three Basic Tasks:

- *Encoding* =

    o *Elaboration* =

- *Storage* =

- *Retrieval* =

C) Psychology Matters: Would You Want a "Photographic" Memory?

- *Eidetic memory* =

o   *Eidetikers* =

5.2 HOW DO WE FORM MEMORIES?

- *Sensory memory* =

- *Working memory* =

  o   *Short-term memory (STM)* =

- *Long-term memory (LTM)* =

Core Concept 5.2 =

A) The First Stage: Sensory Memory

1) The Capacity and Duration of Sensory Memory =

  o   George Sperling =

2) The Structure and Function of Sensory Memory =

  o   *Sensory register* =

  o   *Iconic memory* =

  o   *Echoic memory* =

3) The Biological Basis of Sensory Memory =

B) The Second Stage: Working Memory

1) The Capacity and Duration of Working Memory =

- *"Magic number"* 7±2 =

a) <u>Chunks and Chunking</u> =

- *Chunking* =

1) <u>The Capacity and Duration of Working Memory (Continued)</u> =

    b) <u>The Role of Rehearsal</u> =

        • *Maintenance rehearsal* =

        • *Elaborative rehearsal* =

2) <u>The Structure and Function of Working Memory</u> =

    a) <u>The Central Executive</u> =

    b) <u>Acoustic Encoding: The Phonological Loop</u> =

    c) <u>Visual and Spatial Encoding: The Sketchpad</u> =

    d) <u>Binding Information Together: The Episodic Buffer</u> =

3) <u>Levels of Processing in Working Memory</u> =

        • *Levels-of-processing theory* =

4) <u>The Biological Basis of Working Memory</u> =

C) The Third Stage: Long-Term Memory (LTM)

    1) <u>The Capacity and Duration of Long-Term Memory</u> =

    2) <u>The Structure and Function of Long-Term Memory</u> =

    • *Procedural memory* =

    • *Declarative memory* =

        • *Episodic memory* =

2) <u>The Structure and Function of Long-Term Memory (Continued)</u> =

- *Semantic memory* =

  o *Schemas* =

  o *Childhood amnesia* =

3) <u>The Biological Basis of Long-Term Memory</u> =

  o *Engram* =

a) <u>Clues from the Case of H. M.</u> =

- *Anterograde amnesia* =

b) <u>Parts of the Brain Associated with Long-Term Memory</u> =

- *Consolidation* =

c) <u>Memories, Neurons, and Synapses</u> =

- *Retrograde amnesia* =

D) Psychology Matters: "Flashbulb" Memories: Where Were You When . . . ?

- *Flashbulb memory* =

5.3 HOW DO WE RETRIEVE MEMORIES?

Core Concept 5.3 =

A) Implicit and Explicit Memory

- *Implicit memory* =

- *Explicit memory* =

B) Retrieval Cues

- *Retrieval cues =*

1) <u>Retrieving Implicit Memories by Priming</u> =

- *Priming =*

2) <u>Retrieving Explicit Memories</u> =

    a) <u>Meaningful Organization</u> =

- *Gist =*

    b) <u>Recall and Recognition</u> =

- *Recall =*

- *Recognition =*

C) Other Factors Affecting Retrieval =

1) <u>Encoding Specificity</u> =

- *Encoding specificity principle =*

2) <u>Mood and Memory</u> =

- *Mood-congruent memory =*

3) <u>Prospective Memory</u> =

- *Prospective memory =*

    o *Continuous monitoring =*

D) Psychology Matters: On the Tip of Your Tongue =

- *TOT phenomenon =*

5.4 WHY DOES MEMORY SOMETIMES FAIL US?

- *Schacter's "Seven Sins" of Memory:*

1)	*2)*	*3)*	*4)*
5)	*6)*	*7)*	

| Core Concept 5.4 | =

A) Transience: Fading Memories Cause Forgetting

1) Ebbinghaus and the Forgetting Curve =

- *Forgetting curve =*

2) Interference =

a) Three main causes:

_____

_____

_____

- *Proactive interference =*

- *Retroactive interference =*

- *Serial position effect =*

  o *Primacy effect =*

  o *Recency effect =*

B) Absentmindedness: Lapses of Attention Cause Forgetting =

- *Absentmindedness =*

  o *Change blindness =*

C) Blocking: Access Problems =

- *Blocking =*

D) Misattribution: Memories in the Wrong Context =

- *Misattribution =*

E) Suggestibility: External Cues Distort or Create Memories =

- *Suggestibility =*

1) <u>Memory Distortion</u> =

- *Misinformation effect =*

2) <u>Fabricated Memories</u> =

3) <u>Factors Affecting the Accuracy of Eyewitnesses</u> =

_____

_____

_____

_____

_____

4) <u>Bias: Beliefs, Attitudes, and Opinions Distort Memories</u> =

- o *Expectancy bias =*

- *Self-consistency bias =*

F) Persistence: When We Can't Forget =

- *Persistence =*

G) The Advantages of the "Seven Sins" of Memory =

H) Improving Your Memory with Mnemonics =

- *Mnemonic strategies =*

1) The Method of Loci =

- *The method of loci =*

2) Natural Language Mediators =

- *Natural language mediators =*

3) Remembering Names =

I) Psychology Matters: Using Psychology to Learn Psychology =

1) Studying to Avoid Transience =

- *Whole method =*

- *Distributed learning =*

2) Studying to Avoid Blocking on the Test =

- *Elaborative rehearsal =*

- *Encoding specificity =*

J) Critical Thinking Applied: The Recovered Memory Controversy =

- *Repression =*

- *Post hoc fallacy =*

What Is Memory?

1. *Fill in the blanks with the correct information.*

Memory is a system that _____, _____, and
_____ information.

Metaphors for Memory

2. In what ways is human memory like an artist?

3. What are the types of information that we remember most completely and accurately?

A. _____   D. _____

B. _____   E. _____

C. _____

4. The _____ model emphasizes that memory is functional.

Memory's Three Basic Tasks

5. *Fill in the blanks to complete this paragraph about memory.*

The first process in memory is to _____ the incoming sensory information. This
requires that you _____ some stimulus event from the array of input. Next you
must _____ the stimulus and finally you must mentally "tag," or _____, the
stimulus. Much of this process is _____. Sometimes, however, you need to use
_____ in which you connect new information to old information. The retention of
encoded information over time is called _____. Finally, your ability to access the
retained material in your memory is called _____.

Psychology Matters: Would You Want a "Photographic" Memory?

6. What is "eidetic memory" and how is it similar to and different from camera images? How
does it differ from normal memory?

7. Discuss the relationship between eidetic memory and language development.

How Do We Form Memories?

8. What are the three sequential stages of memory?

A. _____ B. _____ C. _____

The First Stage: Sensory Memory

9. *Fill in the table below with essential information about the stage of memory.*

Stage of Memory	Capacity	Duration	Structure/Function	Biological Basis
Sensory Memory				

10. Describe Sperling's famous experiment on sensory memory and explain what it demonstrated. (Refer to the boxed letters in your description.)

```
D J B W
X H G N
C L Y K
```

11. What is a "sensory register?" What do we call the sensory registers for vision and hearing?

The Second Stage: Working Memory

12. *Fill in the table below with essential information about the stage of memory.*

Stage of Memory	Capacity	Duration	Structure/Function	Biological Basis
Working Memory (used to be known as _____ memory)				

13. *Match each term with its best description by placing the letter corresponding to the term in the space next to its description. (Terms may be used more than once.)*

TERMS
- A. Episodic buffer
- B. Maintenance rehearsal
- C. Elaborative rehearsal
- D. Central executive
- E. Acoustic encoding
- F. Semantic buffer
- G. Sketchpad
- H. Chunking

DESCRIPTIONS

_____ Only repeat the material   _____ Connects to previously learned material

_____ Convert words into sounds   _____ Create meaningful units of material

_____ Helps us remember events   _____ Encodes visual representations

_____ Attaches meaning to words   _____ The "information clearinghouse"

_____ Directs our attention   _____ Involves a phonological loop

14. *Write the name of the working memory enhancement strategy (i.e., maintenance rehearsal, elaborative rehearsal, chunking) next to its example(s) in the table below.*

DESCRIPTION	STRATEGY
Your credit card number is 4 digits, a space, 4 more digits, a space, 4 more digits, a space, and the 4 final digits.	A.
Your repeat the word "semantic buffer" to yourself as you also remember the term "semantics" from English class. Because you learned in English that "semantics" has to do with the meaning of words, you relate that to your understanding of the memory term "semantic buffer."	B.
On the side of a bus you see the address of a store you want to find. Because you can't write it down, you keep repeating the address.	C.
You get a personalized license plate for your car with the letters and numbers you want so it's easy to remember.	D.

15. *Complete the following paragraph about memory by filling in the blanks.*

The _____ theory was proposed by Craik and Lockhart. It is an interaction between _____ memory and _____ memory. They believed that _____ processing makes memories more _____. Such processing requires establishing _____ with long-term memories.

16. Visit this terrific website that features a comprehensive collection of mnemonic (memory) strategies. The site was developed by Prof. Jaap Murre of the University of Amsterdam. http://memory.uva.nl/memimprovement/eng/

The Third Stage: Long-Term Memory

17. *Fill in the table below with essential information about the stage of memory.*

Stage of Memory	Capacity	Duration	Structure/Function	Biological Basis
Long-Term Memory				

18. *Underline the word(s) in parentheses that will make each statement correct. (Both options may be correct!)*

   A. Long-term memory can be divided into two main components: (semantic/declarative) memory and (procedural/episodic) memory.

   B. Much of (episodic/procedural) memory operates outside of awareness.

   C. We use (declarative/procedural) memory to store facts, impressions, and events.

   D. The fact that we can instantly ride a bicycle after not having ridden one for 10 years is an example of (episodic/procedural) memory.

   E. Part of our (semantic/episodic) memory is autobiographical memory.

   F. (Semantic/Episodic) memory is a division of declarative memory.

   G. The basic meanings of words are stored in (procedural/semantic) memory.

   H. Episodic memory is the division that stores (temporal/context) coding of events.

19. *Name the type of long-term memory best described by the examples in the table below.*

Event	Type of Memory
You move your fingers to type an email to your parents.	A.
You share your thoughts with your friend using words and grammar to express them.	B.
You tell your friends about things that happened in your childhood.	C.
You tell your father something interesting that you learned about memory.	D.
You tell your best friend about how depressed you were two weeks ago when you had a fight with your sister while the two of you were on vacation with your parents.	E.

20. *Fill in the blanks in the following concept map about memory.*

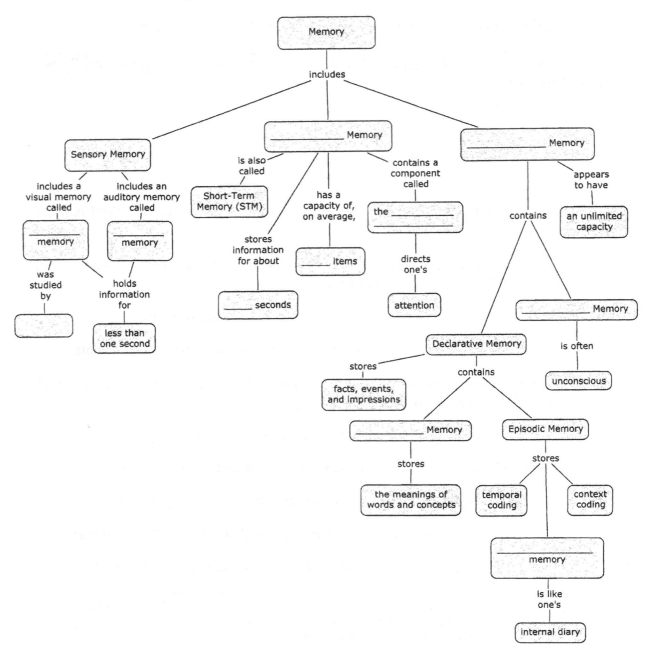

21. What are "schemas" and in what part of long-term memory are they located?

22. Explain what "childhood amnesia" is. Then, discuss why it likely occurs.

23. *Fill in the blanks to make each sentence correct.*

   A. Another term for the biological memory trace within neurons is the _____.

   B. The inability to form new memories is called _____ amnesia, whereas the inability to remember prior information is called _____ amnesia.

   C. The biological process by which new memories gradually form permanent memories is called _____.

24. *Indicate whether each statement is True (T) or False (F) by circling the appropriate letter after the statement.*

   A. The man named H. M. developed retrograde amnesia after brain surgery.   T F

   B. H. M.'s amnesia was caused by the removal of his hippocampus and amygdala.   T F

   C. The removal of his hippocampus may be why H. M. is upbeat and positive.   T F

   D. The amygdala and hippocampus are crucial for creating new episodic memories.   T F

   E. Negative emotions tend to make memories broader rather than restricted in focus. T F

   F. Epinephrine tends to enhance memory for emotional experiences.   T F

   G. H. M. can't form new memories of events, but he recognizes people he meets.   T F

25. The San Francisco Exploratorium (the Museum of Science, Art, and Human Perception) has an excellent site devoted to memory, including some wonderful interactive exhibits. Visit:
   http://www.exploratorium.edu/memory/

Psychology Matters: "Flashbulb" Memories: Where Were You When…?

26. What is a "flashbulb" memory?

27. Although flashbulb memories can be highly accurate, they often are not. The following site briefly describes recent research at Washington University about flashbulb memories: http://mednews.wustl.edu/tips/page/normal/516.html

How Do We Retrieve Memories?

Implicit and Explicit Memories

28. According to Core Concept 4.3, successful retrieval of memories depends on what two factors?

    A. _____   B. _____

29. What are "explicit" memory and "implicit" memory? Which of these two types of memory has been damaged in H. M. and how can researchers tell?

Retrieval Cues

30. What is a "retrieval cue?" Give an example of one.

31. Whether a retrieval cue is a good one depends on what two factors?

    A. _____   B. _____

32. *Fill in the blanks with the correct terms.*

    A. Researchers can activate unconscious memories in _____ memory. They do so by providing cues that stimulate people's memories without the people having any awareness of the connection between the cue and the retrieved memory. This technique is referred to as _____.

    B. Instead of remembering exact details, we tend to remember the meaning, in other words, the _____, of things.

    C. We can cue explicit memories in two main ways: _____ and _____.

33. Differentiate between *recall* and *recognition*. Which tends to be easier?

Other Factors Affecting Retrieval

34. *Underline the word(s) in parentheses that will make each statement correct. (Both options may be correct!)*

   A. The fact that successful recall depends on how well the retrieval cues match the cues present at the time of encoding and storage illustrates the importance of (mood-congruent memory/encoding specificity).

   B. Jonah is angry and he starts remembering many other occurrences that have infuriated him. This illustrates (prospective/mood-congruent) memory.

   C. Remembering to remember is referred to as (encoding specificity/prospective memory).

   D. (Mood-congruent memory/continuous monitoring) can easily be derailed by distraction.

35. NEED A BREAK?
   To get a better understanding of memory, visit MyPsychLab.

Psychology Matters: On the Tip of Your Tongue

36. What is the TOT phenomenon and what are the most common TOT experiences?

37. What are the two possible causes of the TOT phenomenon?

   A. _____   B. _____

Why Does Memory Sometimes Fail Us?

38. *Match each of Schacter's Seven "Sins" with its best description by placing the letter corresponding to the term in the space next to its description*

MEMORY "SIN"
A. Transience	C. Misattribution	E. Persistence	G. Bias
B. Absent-mindedness	D. Suggestibility	F. Blocking	

DEFINITIONS
_____ occurs due to retrieval failure
_____ attitude that distorts memory
_____ unwanted memories cannot be put out of mind
_____ impermanence of a long-term memory
_____ association with incorrect time/place
_____ caused by lapse in attention
_____ distortion due to deliberate or inadvertent suggestion

Transience: Fading Memories Cause Forgetting

39. Describe the work of Ebbinghaus and the "forgetting curve."

40. What are the three main factors that cause interference?

     A. _____

     B. _____

     C. _____

41. *Identify the following examples as either proactive or retroactive interference.*

A. _____ Lee remembers her former boyfriend's phone number but forgets her new boyfriend's phone number.

B. _____ You learned the combination for a new gym locker and now you can't remember the combination to the bicycle lock you've had for years.

C. _____ Mario learned several new dance steps and he now can't remember the steps to a previously learned dance to the same music.

42. *Indicate whether each statement is True (T) or False (F) by circling the appropriate letter after the statement.*

A. The impermanence of long-term memory is referred to as "transience."   T F

B. The serial position effect shows a steep initial memory decline, followed by a leveling off.   T F

C. The forgetting curves for meaningless and meaningful material are identical.   T F

D. The "savings method" involves how quickly people relearn material.   T F

E. The ease of remembering the last items in a series is the "recency effect."   T F

F. The ease of remembering the middle items in a list is the "primacy effect."   T F

G. Retroactive interference is when old memories get in the way of your remembering new material.   T F

Absent-Mindedness: Lapses of Attention Cause Forgetting

43. Explain why absent-mindedness happens.

Blocking: Access Problems

44. *Underline the word(s) in parentheses that will make each statement correct. (Both options may be correct!)*

   A. "Blocking" occurs when we cannot (access/get rid of) long-term memories.

   B. The most thoroughly studied form of blocking is (the TOT phenomenon/interference).

   C. (Stress/Age) plays a role in blocking.

Misattribution: Memories in the Wrong Context

45. *Fill in the blanks with the correct information about memory and retrieval.*

   _____ occurs when we retrieve memories but then associate
   them with the wrong time, place, or person. This stems from the _____
   nature of long-term memory. It also can cause people to believe mistakenly that other
   people's ideas are _____, such as in the case of unintentional
   plagiarism.

Suggestibility: External Cues Distort or Create Memories

46. Discuss what has been learned about "suggestibility" from the research of Loftus. What is the "misinformation effect"?

47. In eyewitness reports, what five factors should we be wary of?

   A. _____   D. _____
   B. _____   E. _____
   C. _____

Bias: Beliefs, Attitudes, and Opinions Distort Memories

48. Compare and contrast "expectancy bias" and "self-consistency bias."

Persistence: When We Can't Forget

49. *Match each of Schacter's memory sins to the event that best illustrates it by placing the letter corresponding to the term in the blank next to the event.*

MEMORY "SIN"

A. Transience   D. Misattribution   G. Persistence
B. Absent-mindedness   E. Suggestibility
C. Blocking   F. Bias

EVENT
_____ All during January 2011 you write 2010 on your checks.
_____ Anika just can't forget the description of the horrible crime that she read about in the paper this morning.
_____ Kevin keeps confusing the appearance of the person he saw rob the corner store with the features that the police detective asked him about in the interview.
_____ Rima is taking a test and can't remember a key term, but she knows it starts with a "C."
_____ Sebastian was sure the party would be great, and even though he was very bored during it, he later remembers it as being a lot of fun.
_____ Jen's dad told her about a family event that never occurred. Jen claims to remember it.
_____ Dave is studying while the TV and radio are on and can't remember what she read.

The Advantages of the "Seven Sins" of Memory

50. In what way is each of the "seven sins" of memory actually helpful (or adaptive)?

A. Transience _____

B. Absent-mindedness _____

C. Blocking _____

D. Misattribution _____

E. Suggestibility _____

F. Bias _____

G. Persistence _____

Improving Your Memory with Mnemonics

51. *Fill in the blanks in the following paragraph with the correct information.*

Mnemonic strategies help you encode new information by associating it with information in your _____ memory. One technique, called the _____, is to associate information with mental images of objects in familiar places (such as your house or room). This technique tends to work well because it involves both _____ and _____ memories. In fact, _____ is one of the most effective ways of encoding information. Memory techniques called _____ associate meaningful word patterns with new information to be remembered. An example is when you form an _____ by creating a word made up of initials. Overall, when trying to remember any information, it is best to create _____ associations.

Psychology Matters: Using Psychology to Learn Psychology

Studying to Avoid Transience

52. *Identify three studying strategies you can use that can help you avoid transience.*

     A. _____

     B. _____

     C. _____

53. *Fill in the blanks with the correct terms.*

    A. When using the _____ technique, a person first gets an overview of the material and then fills in the details afterwards.

    B. The technical term for studying repeatedly at frequent intervals (rather than cramming it all into one session) is _____.

Studying to Avoid Blocking on the Test

54. To avoid blocking on tests, the text authors suggest study techniques that apply two ideas you've learned about in this chapter. What are those ideas and how can they help you study?

    A._____

    B. _____

PRACTICE TEST #1

1. _____ is broadly defined as any system that encodes, stores and retrieves information.
   A. Perception   B. Cognition   C. Memory   D. Learning

2. Scientists have found that we remember most easily all of the following types of material EXCEPT information
   A. in which we are interested.   C. that connects with previous experience.
   B. that affects us emotionally.   D. that is very important for success.

3. The current model of memory most often cited is called the
   A. computer analogy model.   C. video-recorder model.
   B. information-processing model.   D. cognitive learning model.

4. All of the following are one of memory's essential functions EXCEPT
   A. encoding.   B. storage.   C. decoding.   D. retrieval.

5. Your friend can look at a complex figure and remember most every detail. The memory involved in this type of task is _____ memory.
   A. picture   B. pattern   C. eidetic   D. echoic

6. The best reason why a video recorder is NOT a good metaphor for human memory is
   A. memory is a more vivid record of what happened than is videotape.
   B. memory is a constructive process that interprets and organizes information according to perceived meaning.
   C. memory is a destructive process that erases segments that are upsetting to the individual.
   D. memory may not last forever.

7. All of the following are stages of memory EXCEPT _____ memory.
   A. working   B. long-term   C. initial   D. sensory

8. All of the following are involved in the process of encoding EXCEPT
   A. storage   B. identification   C. selection   D. labeling

9. The sensory memory for hearing is known as _____ memory.
   A. icoic   B. autonic   C. iconic   D. echoic

10. You have studied the terms you need to pass this test. When you read the terms, you hold them in _____ memory in order to process them.
    A. sensory   B. long-term   C. working   D. retrieval

PRACTICE TEST #2

1. _____ is a special kind of encoding that adds meaning to information.
   A. Access   B. Elaboration   C. Priming   D. Structuring

2. Your sensory memory holds images in _____ memory, whereas it holds memory for sounds in _____ memory.
   A. iconic; echoic   C. eidetic; echoic
   B. echoic; iconic   D. iconic; eidetic

3. You have a list of 15 words you need to learn for your Spanish test. You have trouble remembering them all. That is because working memory only holds, on average, about _____ items.
   A. 10   B. 8   C. 4   D. 7

4. You have been studying all night for your psychology test. You are having trouble remembering how to spell Erik Erikson's name, so you keep repeating it over and over as you go to take the test. This is an example of _____ rehearsal.
   A. visual   B. maintenance   C. elaborative   D. working

5. Tony remembers the names of the U.S.'s five great lakes (i.e., Huron, Ontario, Michigan, Erie, Superior) by using the acronym HOMES. Tony is making use of
   A. visual imagery.   C. natural language mediators.
   B. elaborative rehearsal.   D. the method of loci.

6. Craik and Tulving's experiment with words and meaning examined the concept of
   A. visual memory.   C. levels of processing.
   B. meaningful organization.   D. visual encoding.

7. _____ memory takes information from sensory memory and connects it to information that has been stored in long-term memory.
   A. Encoding   B. Working   C. Explicit   D. Declarative

8. Your father asks you what you did three weeks ago. In order to answer the question, you must access _____ memory.
   A. sensory   B. implicit   C. procedural   D. declarative

9. The job of sensory memory is to
   A. briefly store images.   C. sort images for storage.
   B. add meaning to images.   D. categorize images.

10. You had to learn a list of 30 terms for your French exam. You rely mostly on your _____ memory for this task.
    A. working   B. declarative   C. procedural   D. episodic

PRACTICE TEST #3

1. Two useful methods for dealing with the limitations of short-term memory storage are
   A. chunking and rehearsal.
   B. sensing and elaborating.
   C. decoding and retrieving.
   D. encoding and relating.

2. You have not ridden a bicycle for many years. While on vacation, your friend talks you into riding one again. You have no trouble climbing on and going off down the road. Your _____ memory was at work here.
   A. episodic   B. declarative   C. explicit   D. procedural

3. The type of memory that is helping you complete this practice test is
   A. implicit.   B. declarative.   C. episodic.   D. procedural.

4. Your "encyclopedia of knowledge" is a reasonably good metaphor for your _____ memory.
   A. semantic   B. episodic   C. procedural   D. working

5. In your English class, you are asked to write an essay about what you did on summer vacation. To write this essay, you rely most strongly on _____ memory.
   A. implicit   B. eidetic   C. procedural   D. episodic

6. Taneesha has a mental list of 12 grocery items to buy. She is most likely to forget
   A. the first few items in the list.
   B) the last few items in the list.
   C) the middle items in the list.
   D) the first few and the last few items in the list.

7. _____ refers to our looking back at events that occurred closely in succession and believing that the first event caused the second event.
   A. Retrograde amnesia
   B) The post hoc fallacy
   C) Absent-mindedness
   D) The TOT phenomenon

8. H. M. was unable to transfer new memories from short-term to long-term memory. His condition is known as
   A. retrograde amnesia.
   B. anterograde amnesia.
   C. absent-mindedness.
   D. epileptic amnesia.

9. The part of the brain that is involved in new episodic memories is the
   A. thalamus.   B. hypothalamus.   C. hippocampus.   D. limbic system.

10. When you know that you know the answer but you just can't seem to tell other people what it is, you are experiencing
   A. anterograde amnesia disorder.
   B. a transience problem.
   C. an absent-mindedness dilemma.
   D. the TOT phenomenon.

COMPREHENSIVE REVIEW TEST

1. Encoding is
    A. the retention of learned material.
    B. the selection, identification and labeling of information.
    C. the recovery and expression of stored material.
    D. necessary to prevent learned material from decaying over time.

2. The human memory is proficient at processing information that is all of these EXCEPT
    A. very emotional.
    B. very interesting to us.
    C. given attention by us.
    D. new and unfamiliar.

3. The type of retrieval that you use to answer essay questions is
    A. recall.   B. priming.   C. remembrance.   D. recognition.

4. What is the best way to remember, in order, the list ABCCBSABCCNBCESPNTNTHGTV?
    A. Chunk it into seven letter segments
    B. Make it into a rhyme
    C. Repeat it over and over again to yourself
    D. Chunk it into bits that have some meaning

5. _____ memory is the part of long-term memory that stores mental directions for how to do things, whereas _____ memory is the part that stores information that we can describe.
    A. Working; implicit
    B. Episodic; sensory
    C. Declarative; explicit
    D. Procedural; declarative

6. According to Schacter, _____ memory affects our behavior even though we have no conscious awareness of the information held in it.
    A. implicit   B. explicit   C. declarative   D. sensory

7. You are at the airport waiting to check in for your flight home. You see a man who looks very familiar. You cannot remember his name. Later when you get airborne, you remember that he is on one of your favorite television shows. Your inability to remember his name highlights
    A. a hippocampal failure.
    B. anterograde amnesia.
    C. the encoding-specificity principle.
    D. blocking.

8. _____ is a technique for cuing the recall of implicit memories.
    A. Encoding   B. Priming   C. Decoding   D. TOT

9. You are at lunch with some friends. Someone tells a joke and everyone begins to giggle. Whenever you feel happy, you remember these lunches. This best illustrates the concept of
    A. encoding specificity.
    B. mood-congruent memory.
    C. explicit memory.
    D. episodic memory.

10. All of the following are one of Schacter's "seven sins of memory" EXCEPT
    A. bias.   B. transience.   C. serial position.   D. absent-mindedness.

11. All of the following are components of working memory EXCEPT a(n)
    A. sketchpad.　　B. episodic buffer.　　C. sensory register.　　D. phonological loop.

12. You are dating a girl named Susan. Your old girlfriend was named Sharon. When you meet some friends, you introduce Susan but you call her Sharon. This is likely due to
    A. proactive interference.
    B. retroactive interference.
    C. misattribution.
    D. suggestibility.

13. Your favorite radio station is having a contest in which you could win a new iPod. To win, you must name all of Snow White's Seven Dwarfs. You cannot think of the name of the seventh one although you know you know it. This is due to
    A. a transience problem.
    B. the TOT phenomenon.
    C. proactive interference.
    D. anterograde amnesia.

14. Dr. Smyth is studying soldiers who have just returned from the war and are suffering from post-traumatic stress disorder. She is most likely looking at what part of the brain?
    A. Hippocampus
    B. Reticular formation
    C. Amygdala
    D. Limbic system

15. Much of our _____ memory operates outside of awareness.
    A. episodic　　B. procedural　　C. semantic　　D. declarative

CRITICAL THINKING ESSAYS

1. Discuss the issue of recovered memories of child abuse. Present both sides of the debate and identify principles related to memory that would impact on this issue.

2. Based on what you've learned in this chapter, what suggestions about studying would you give your undergraduate friends who are having trouble remembering material for their tests?

CHAPTER 6
Thinking and Intelligence

Before You Read ... Term Identification

Make flashcards using the following terms or, even better, develop mnemonics (memory strategies) to help you remember the different concepts and terms. Use the definitions in the margins of this chapter for help. Numbers refer to page numbers in the textbook.

algorithms (225)
analytical intelligence (244)
anchoring bias (229)
aptitudes (231)
artificial concepts (217)
availability bias (230)
base rate information (230)
chronological age (CA) (236)
computer metaphor (216)
concept hierarchies (217)
concepts (217)
creative intelligence (245)
creativity (231)
crystallized intelligence (244)
experts (231)
fluid intelligence (244)
functional fixedness (227)
g factor (244)
giftedness (240)
hereditability (254)
heuristics (225)
hindsight bias (228)

intelligence (235)
intuition (221)
intelligence quotient (IQ) (237)
mental age (MA) (236)
mental retardation (240)
mental set (226)
multiple intelligences (245)
natural concepts (217)
normal distribution (normal curve) (238)
normal range (239)
practical intelligence (244)
prototype (217)
representativeness bias (229)
savant syndrome (243)
script (222)
self-fulfilling prophecy (250)
stereotype threat (258)
theory of mind (248)
triarchic theory (245)
tyranny of choice (230)
wisdom (245)

Lecture Assistant *for Chapter 6*

Tear this outline out and bring it with you to class in order to facilitate your note taking.
Spend more time listening to the lecture and less time writing!

Chapter Opening Problem: What produces "genius," and to what extent are the people we call "geniuses" different from others?

- *Computer metaphor =*

6.1 WHAT ARE THE COMPONENTS OF THOUGHT?

Core Concept 6.1 =

A) Concepts

- *Concepts =*

  o *Déjà vu =*

1) Two Kinds of Concepts =

- *Natural concepts =*

- *Prototype =*

- *Artificial concepts =*

2) Concept Hierarchies =

- *Concept hierarchies =*

3) Culture, Concepts and Thought =

B) Imagery and Cognitive Maps

  o *Cognitive map =*

C) Thought and the Brain

D) Intuition

- *Intuition* =

E) Psychology Matters: Schemas and Scripts Help You Know What to Expect

- o *Schema* =

1) <u>Expectations</u> =

2) <u>Making Inferences</u> =

3) <u>Schemas and Humor</u> =

4) <u>Scripts As Event Schemas</u> =

- *Script* =

5) <u>Cultural Influences on Scripts</u> =

6.2 WHAT ABILITIES DO GOOD THINKERS POSSESS?

$\boxed{Core\ Concept\ 6.2}$ =

A) Problem Solving

1) <u>Identifying the Problem</u> =

2) <u>Selecting a Strategy</u> =

- *Algorithms* =

- *Heuristics* =

3) <u>Some Useful Heuristic Strategies</u> =

   a) <u>Working Backward</u> =

   b) <u>Searching for Analogies</u> =

      o *Analogy* =

   c) <u>Breaking a Big Problem into Smaller Problems</u> =

      o *Subgoals* =

4) <u>Obstacles to Problem Solving</u> =

   a) <u>Mental Set</u> =

      • *Mental set* =

   b) <u>Functional Fixedness</u> =

      • *Functional fixedness* =

   c) <u>Self-Imposed Limitations</u> =

   d) <u>Other Obstacles</u> =

B) Judging and Making Decisions

1) <u>Confirmation Bias</u> =

      o *Confirmation bias* =

2) <u>Hindsight Bias</u> =

   • *Hindsight bias* =

3) <u>Anchoring Bias</u> =

•   *Anchoring bias*

4) <u>Representativeness Bias</u> =

- *Representativeness bias* =

5) <u>Availability Bias</u> =

- *Availability bias* =

6) <u>Tyranny of Choice</u> =

- *Tyranny of choice* =

7) <u>Decision Making and Critical Thinking</u> =

C) Becoming a Creative Genius

- *Creativity* =

1) <u>Creative Genius as Not So Superhuman</u> =

2) <u>Knowledge and Understanding</u> =

- *Experts* =

3) <u>Aptitudes, Personality Characteristics, and Creativity</u> =

- *Aptitudes* =
-
- Five Main Personality Traits Possessed by Creative People:

    1)
    2)
    3)
    4)
    5)

4) <u>The Role of Intelligence in Creativity</u> =

D) Psychology Matters: Using Psychology to Learn Psychology

1) <u>A Study of Chess Experts</u> =

2) <u>Expertise as Organized Knowledge</u> =

3) <u>Practice versus Talent</u> =

3) <u>So, How Do You Become an Expert?</u>

6.3 HOW IS INTELLIGENCE MEASURED?

- *Intelligence =*

    - *Hypothetical construct =*

Core Concept 6.3 =

A) Binet and Simon Invent a School Abilities Test

- Alfred Binet =

- Theophile Simon =

- Four Important Features of the Binet-Simon Approach:
    - a)
    - b)
    - c)
    - d)

- *Mental age (MA) =*

- *Chronological age (CA) =*

B) American Psychologists Borrow Binet and Simon's Idea

1) <u>The Appeal of Intelligence Testing in America</u> =

2) <u>The Stanford-Binet Intelligence Scale</u> =

- Lewis Terman =

- *Intelligence Quotient (IQ)* =

3) Problems with the IQ Formula =

4) Calculating IQs "on the Curve" =

- *Normal distribution (normal curve)* =

- *Normal range* =

    o *Flynn effect* =

5) IQ Testing Today =

- David Wechsler =

B) Psychology Matters: What Can You Do for an Exceptional Child?

- *Mental retardation* =

- *Giftedness* =

1) Mental Retardation =

   a) Causes of Mental Retardation =

      o *Down syndrome* =

      o *Fetal alcohol syndrome* =

   b) Dealing with Mental Retardation =

      o *PKU* =

2) Giftedness =

   a) Terman's Study of Giftedness =

   a) Dealing with Giftedness =

6.4 IS INTELLIGENCE ONE OR MANY ABILITIES?

- *Savant syndrome* =

$\boxed{\textit{Core Concept 6.4}} =$

A) Psychometric Theories of Intelligence =

- o *Psychometrics* =

1) Spearman's g Factor =

- *g factor* =

2) Cattell's Fluid and Crystallized Intelligence =

- *Crystallized intelligence* =

- *Fluid intelligence* =

B) Cognitive Theories of Intelligence =

1) Sternberg's Triarchic Theory =

- *Practical intelligence* =

- *Analytical intelligence* =

- *Creative intelligence* =

- *Triarchic theory* =

- *Wisdom* =

2) Gardner's Multiple Intelligences =

- *Multiple intelligences* =

- The List and Descriptions of the Multiple Intelligences:

C) **Assessing Cognitive Theories of Intelligence =**

D) **Cultural Definitions of Intelligence =**

1) African Concepts of Intelligence =

2) A Native American Concept of Intelligence =

E) **The Question of Animal Intelligence**

1) What Abilities Make Humans Unique?

- *Theory of mind =*

2) Language of the Apes =

3) What Are the Lessons of Research on Animal Language and Intelligence?

F) **Psychology Matters: Test Scores and the Self-Fulfilling Prophecy =**

1) Expectations Influence Student Performance =

- *Self-fulfilling prophecy =*

2) The Self-Fulfilling Prophecy: Beyond the Classroom =

6.5 HOW DO PSYCHOLOGISTS EXPLAIN IQ DIFFERENCES AMONG GROUPS?

Core Concept 6.5 =

A) **Intelligence and the Politics of Immigration =**

B) **What Evidence Shows That Intelligence Is Influenced By Heredity?**

C) What Evidence Shows That Intelligence Is Influenced By Environment?

D) Heritability (not Heredity) and Group Differences =

- *Heritability =*

1) The Jensen Controversy =

2) The Scarr and Weinberg Adoption Study =

3) Social Class and IQ =

4) Head Start: A Successful Intervention Program =

5) Test Biases and Culture-Fair Tests =

6) *The Bell Curve*: Another Hereditarian Offensive =

E) Psychology Matters: Stereotype Threat =

- *Stereotype threat =*

F) Critical Thinking Applied: The Question of Gender Differences =

- *Gender similarities hypothesis =*

What Are the Components of Thought?

Concepts

1. *Complete the following paragraph about the components of thought.*

    Mental groupings of similar objects, ideas, or experiences are called _____.

They often let us organize our declarative memory into _____,

arranged from general to specific. Imprecise mental representations of everyday experiences

are called _____. They are sometimes called

_____ because of their imprecision. Sometimes we develop

a_____—the most representative example in a category—to organize

mental information. _____ are defined by a set of rules or

characteristics, and are precisely defined abstractions or ideas.

Imagery and Cognitive Maps

2. Explain what "imagery" is. How is imagery involved in cognitive maps?

Thought and the Brain

3. *Underline the word(s) in parentheses that will make each statement correct. (Both options may be correct!)*

    A. Brain research shows that thinking is an activity involving (narrowly/widely) distributed areas of the brain.

    B. The brain generates many of the images used in thought with (different circuitry than/the same circuitry) it uses for sensation.

    C. Neuroscientists see the brain as a community of highly specialized (modules/nerves), each of which deals with different components of thought.

    D. Neuroscientists have found that most jokes activate the areas of the brain that process (language/visual imagery).

E. The (temporal/frontal) lobes of the brain play an important role in coordinating mental activity when we solve problems and make decisions.

F. The prefrontal cortex of the brain is responsible for (keeping track of the situation/understanding the context).

Intuition

4. *Indicate whether each statement is True (T) or False (F) by circling the appropriate letter after the statement.*

A. The emotional component of thinking involved in intuition activates regions of the temporal lobes just above the ears.   T F

B. Intuition tends to be most reliable in complex situations when time is short.   T F

C. Research shows that employers make better judgments about people's abilities when they use intuition rather than test scores or educational background.   T F

D. Research has shown that people make very accurate judgments about a person's personality even after only seeing a six-second video clip of that person.   T F

E. One area of very reliable intuitions concerns statistical judgments.   T F

Psychology Matters: Schemas and Scripts Help You Know What to Expect

5. *Fill in the blanks with the correct terms.*

A. A _____ is a cluster of related concepts that provides a framework for thinking about objects, events, or ideas.

B. Five-year-old Pasha knows exactly what her bedtime routine is. It starts with a bedtime snack, then a bedtime story, and finishes with being tucked into bed and given a kiss. Pasha's knowledge of this event is called a _____.

C. Another term for script is _____ schema.

D. Humor often involves two or more incongruous _____ at once.

E. People from different cultures can feel uncomfortable around each other when they don't follow the same _____.

F. Akiko has never been to the local all-you-can-eat buffet, but she knows that she will select and dish out her own food. She also knows she can go back and get more food. Akiko's knowledge of this even is a _____.

What Abilities Do Good Thinkers Possess?

Problem Solving

6. What are the two basic steps involved in problem solving?

    A. _____ B. _____

7. Compare and contrast "algorithms" and "heuristics." Give an example of each.

8. List and explain the three useful heuristic strategies that are discussed in the text. What common element do the three strategies share?

    A. _____

    B. _____

    C. _____

    Common Element = _____

9. *Fill in the name of the obstacle to problem solving next to the example in the table below.*

EXAMPLE	OBSTACLE TO PROBLEM SOLVING
Joe can't figure out how to solve an arithmetic problem. He keeps using the strategies that have always worked in the past.	A.
Sam and Jack were hiking when Sam fell and cut his leg. He can't see that his shirtsleeve can be used as a makeshift bandage for his injury.	B.
Sharonda won't consider applying for a job as a park ranger because she believes it is work suitable only for males.	C.

10. *Complete the following table with information about obstacles to problem solving.*

Obstacle	Description
A. Mental set	
B. Functional fixedness	
C. Self-imposed limitations	

Judging and Making Decisions

11. *Match each term with its best example(s) by placing the letter corresponding to the term in the space next to its example. (Terms may be used more than once.)*

TERMS
A. Confirmation bias   C. Hindsight bias   E. Representativeness bias
B. Anchoring bias   D. Availability bias

EXAMPLES

_____ Betsy believes that there are more words in the English language that start with the letter K than words with K as the third letter.

_____ Jason is certain that people in red cars are the most irresponsible drivers and he notices how many red cars go zipping by him on the road, while ignoring the other cars.

_____ You and your friend go to a murder mystery movie. At the end of the film when it's revealed who the murderer is, your friend says that it was obvious at the very beginning.

_____ Although she didn't buy a lottery ticket this time, Leslie's number is finally the winner in the state "quick pick" lottery. She says that she should have played it because she "knew all along that it would win."

_____ You're shown a very expensive apartment in your new city and then five more places after that. You believe that the fifth apartment you visit is a huge bargain, because it's so much cheaper than the first one.

_____ Gordon believes that the full moon makes people behave weirdly because he only notices weird behavior on nights when the moon is full.

_____ Sara visits a college where only 10 percent of students major in computer science and the majority major in English. When she meets a guy there with thick glasses and mismatched clothes, she believes it's more likely he's a computer science major than an English major.

12. Define "tyranny of choice" and explain how it can affect people.

13. What is "base rate information," and with which bias is it most associated?

14. Have fun testing your problem-solving and decision-making skills at the following web site:
http://www.greylabyrinth.com/puzzles

15. *Fill in the blanks in the following concept map about good thinkers.*

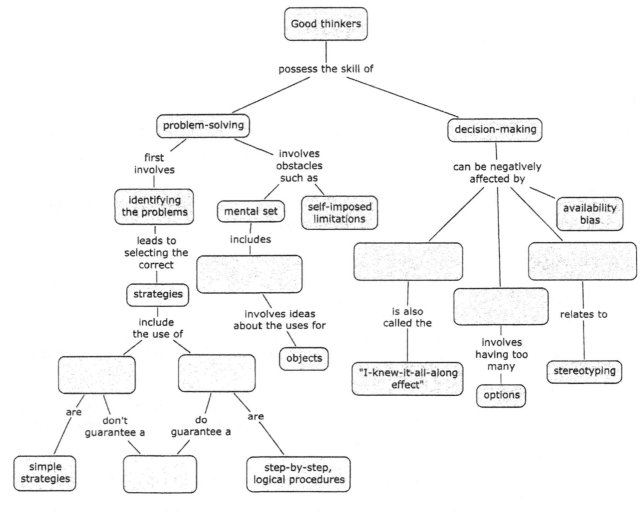

Becoming a Creative Genius

16. According to Weisberg, what are three characteristics that produce extraordinary creativity?

A. _____ B. _____ C. _____

17. Explain Gardner's idea that extraordinary creativity involves "aptitudes."

18. What are five personality traits commonly possessed by creative people?

A. _____   D. _____

B. _____   E. _____

C. _____

19. What has research found about the relation between intelligence and creativity? And what is Sternberg's view?

Psychology Matters: Using Psychology to Learn Psychology

20. To become an expert, what cognitive and behavioral strategies appear to be particularly important? List at least three.

A. _____

B. _____

C. _____

How is Intelligence Measured?

Binet and Simon Develop a School Abilities Test

21. *Fill in the blanks in the following paragraph with the correct information.*

Binet and Simon developed a _____ abilities test in the country of _____. Their goal was to identify students who needed _____. Four features distinguished this approach: (a) They interpreted scores as a measure of _____ and not of _____ intelligence; (b) They did not want to _____ children; (c) They emphasized that _____ and _____ could affect intelligence; and (d) The test was not tied to a certain theory, but instead was constructed _____. On the test, children were given a number corresponding to their years since birth, their _____ age, and a number corresponding to their score on the test as it compared to the average age at which children achieve this particular score. This latter number is referred to as children's _____ age.

American Psychologists Borrow Binet and Simon's Idea

21. What three forces in American society during the early twentieth century increased the popularity of intelligence testing?

    A. _____

    B. _____

    C. _____

22. What have been some of the consequences of the large-scale intelligence testing in the United States?

23. *In the table below, provide the answers to the questions.*

QUESTIONS	ANSWERS
A. Who developed the Stanford-Binet Intelligence Scale?	
B. What do the initials "IQ" stand for?	
C. Who originally coined the term "IQ"?	
D. In terms of intelligence tests, what do the initials "MA" and "CA" stand for?	
E. Who believed that the Stanford-Binet test precisely measured innate intelligence?	
F. What is the formula used to calculate the intelligence quotient?	
G) Is the Stanford-Binet test administered in groups, or individually?	

24. What was one of the biggest criticisms of the Stanford-Binet test, and what did test makers do in response to this criticism?

Problems with the IQ Formula

25. What is the problem with using the IQ formula for adults?

Calculating IQs "on the Curve"

26. Define the "Flynn Effect." Then, give some of the possible explanations for it.

27. *Underline the word(s) in parentheses that will make each statement correct. (Both options may be correct!)*

A. The bell-shaped pattern is also called the normal (distribution/curve).

B. IQ scores are (normally/not normally) distributed.

C. To calculate adults' IQ scores, their scores are compared with other adults' scores (who are the same age/regardless of their age).

D. IQ scores are statistically adjusted so that the average for each group is set at (100/110).

E. IQ scores near the middle of the distribution are considered to be in the (normal/bell-shaped) range.

F. Scores above 130 on IQ tests are sometimes said to indicate (genius/giftedness).

G. IQ scores below (80/70) are often said to be in the mentally retarded range.

IQ Testing Today

28. Explain what the WAIS and WISC are.

Psychology Matters: What Can You Do for an Exceptional Child?

29. *Indicate whether each statement is True (T) or False (F) by circling the appropriate letter after the statement.*

A. About 2 percent of the population have IQ test scores in the mental retardation range.   T F

B. The American Association of Mental Retardation has a cutoff IQ score of 65 in its definition of mental retardation.   T F

C. Fetal alcohol syndrome is a cause of mental retardation.   T F

D. PKU, a genetic disorder, produces mental retardation that can't be prevented.   T F

E. Terman's giftedness study showed that those who were most successful had extraordinary motivation and someone at home or school who was very encouraging. T F

30. NEED A BREAK?
To get a better understanding of thinking and intelligence, visit MyPsychLab.

Is Intelligence One Ability or Many?

31. Explain "savant syndrome."

Psychometric Theories of Intelligence

32. Define "psychometrics."

33. Explain what Spearman's "g factor" is. Describe neuroscience support for this theory.

34. *Fill in the blanks in the following paragraph with the correct information.*

     Cattell developed his theory of intelligence using _____ techniques.
He broke intelligence into two factors he called _____ intelligence and
_____ intelligence. He believed that these factors are relatively
_____. _____ intelligence is the knowledge a person
has acquired and the ability to _____ and _____ information
from _____ memory. This intelligence is measured by tests of
_____ (for example). By contrast, _____ intelligence
is the ability to see _____ and solve _____. It
is measured, for example, by tests of _____.

35. To see a timeline of important people in the history of intelligence testing, visit this site:
http://www.wilderdom.com/personality/L1-5KeyPlayers.html

Cognitive Theories of Intelligence

36. Name and explain the three components of Sternberg's triarchic theory of intelligence.

    A. _____

    B. _____

    C. _____

37. *Identify each of the following examples as practical, analytical, or creative intelligence.*

A. _____ You get all As this semester in college.
B. _____ You have been promoted to head manager at work because you deal with employees so well.
C. _____ You won an award for writing the best new screenplay.
D. _____ You can easily find your way around new cities.

38. *Match each of Gardner's intelligences with its best example by placing the letter corresponding to the term in the space next to its example.*

TERMS

A. Linguistic   D. Musical   G. Intrapersonal
B. Logical-mathematical   E. Bodily-kinesthetic   H. Naturalistic
C. Spatial   F. Interpersonal

EXAMPLES

_____ Celia is a soloist in the choir.
_____ Jenny spends a lot of time thinking about who she is and what she wants from life.
_____ Spencer is a top surgeon at the hospital.
_____ Sasha scores well on her vocabulary tests.
_____ Aaron gets excellent reviews of his architectural drawings.
_____ Jocelyn gets good evaluations from her supervisor on her counseling internship.
_____ Megan is majoring in physics and has an A average.
_____ Shawn spends a lot of time in the local park, exploring the woods and flowers.

39. In Gardner's theory, which two intelligences are similar to "emotional intelligence"?

A. _____   B. _____

40) Explain the major contribution and the main challenge for cognitive theories of intelligence.

Major Contribution: _____

Main Challenge: _____

41. Visit Howard Gardner's homepage. It contains links to his projects and articles.
http://www.howardgardner.com

42. Give three different examples of what is viewed as "intelligence" in other cultures.

A. _____
B. _____
C. _____

The Question of Animal Intelligence

43. *Indicate whether each statement is True (T) or False (F) by circling the appropriate letter after the statement.*

    A. Humans are the only animals that use and understand language.   T F

    B. Jane Goodall discovered that chimpanzees make and use tools.   T F

    C. Jane Goodall taught a young gorilla named Washoe to use sign language.   T F

    D. Unlike humans, animals do not show evidence of theory of mind.   T F

    E. Nonhuman primates are the only animals that have been taught human language.   T F

    F. Theory of mind refers to knowing that one's own thoughts may differ from someone else's thoughts.   T F

Psychology Matters: Test Scores and the Self-Fulfilling Prophecy

44. What is the "self-fulfilling prophecy," and how did Rosenthal and Jacobson demonstrate it in humans?

How do Psychologists Explain IQ Differences among Groups?

45. How is the nature-nurture controversy related to both (a) the ideas about the causes of an individual's intelligence and (b) the debate over group differences in IQ scores? What evidence supports these different views?

Intelligence and the Politics of Immigration

46. Who was Henry Goddard and what role did he play in the 1924 Immigration Restriction Act?

What Evidence Shows That Intelligence Is Influenced by Heredity?

47. *Underline the word(s) in parentheses that will make each statement correct. (Both options may be correct!)*

   A. The correlation between the IQs of children and their (biological/adoptive) parents is greater than that with their (biological/adoptive) parents.

   B. Twin and adoption studies have revealed genetic influences on (personality traits/hypnotizability).

   C. Identical twins reared apart have more similar IQ scores than do (identical/fraternal) twins reared together.

What Evidence Shows That Intelligence Is Influenced by Environment?

48. *Underline the word(s) in parentheses that will make each statement correct. (Both options may be correct!)*

   A. Evidence about environmental influences on intelligence has come from a (longitudinal/cross-sectional) study of 110 children from impoverished homes.

   B. The study revealed a strong correlation between a stimulating environment and children's (language/memory) abilities.

   C. The study revealed a strong correlation between parents' nurturance and children's (language/memory) abilities.

   D. Young monkeys who are trained to solve problems show more active curiosity and higher intelligence when they are given (food rewards/companionship with other monkeys).

   E. Research shows that the IQ gap between African Americans and Euro-Americans is (stabilized/narrowing).

Heritability (not Heredity) and Group Differences

49. *Fill in the blanks with the correct information.*

   _____ refers to the amount of trait variation _____ that can be attributed to genetic differences. It refers only to individuals who have shared the same _____. It does not explain _____ between groups.

50. *Indicate whether each statement is True (T) or False (F) by circling the appropriate letter after the statement.*

A. There are only a few biological boundaries defining different races.   T F

B. Jensen believes that IQ differences between racial groups are mostly due to genetic differences between races.   T F

C. Culture-fair intelligence tests do a better job of predicting academic success than do traditional IQ tests.   T F

D. Scarr and Weinberg did a study of black and white children who were adopted into similar home environments.   T F

E. In Scarr & Weinberg's adoption study, they found that adoptees in late adolescence had IQ scores higher than both their biological and adoptive parents.   T F

F. Head Start provides disadvantaged children with education, nutrition, and medical support, but parents are not involved in the program.   T F

G. Compared to a control group, children enrolled in Head Start score higher on IQ tests and have higher school achievement, even into adolescence.   T F

H. Asians are more likely than Americans to believe that a child's academic success is due to innate ability.   T F

I. "Culture-fair" tests are free of cultural biases.   T F

51. List at least six different environmental effects that limit the intellectual potential of individuals who live in poverty.

A. _____   D. _____

B. _____   E. _____

C. _____   F. _____

Psychology Matters: Stereotype Threat

52. Define "stereotype threat" and explain how it relates to the self-fulfilling prophecy and expectancy bias.

PRACTICE TEST #1

1. _____ is broadly defined as the process by which the brain uses information to create and manipulate mental representations.
   A. Perception   B. Thinking   C. Memory   D. Learning

2. Mental groupings of similar objects, ideas, or experiences are called _____.
   A. concepts   B. prototypes   C. heuristics   D. algorithms

3. When you hear the term flower, you think of a rose. Rose is your _____ of a flower.
   A. concept   B. heuristic   C. prototype   D. script

4. A trapezoid is an example of a(n) _____ concept.
   A. prototype   B. artificial   C. natural   D. fuzzy

5. A mental representation of a physical space is called a _____.
   A. mental concept   C. cognitive map
   B. sensory map   D. cognitive concept

6. When we are asked to think of a tree, few of us picture a giant cactus. This suggests that _____.
   A. we use the artificial concept approach to forming concepts
   B. we frequently use prototypes for our natural concepts
   C. we live according to implicit memories
   D. a cactus cannot be a tree

7. Kim is an American participant in an experiment in which she is shown photos of fruits and vegetables. She is asked to classify as quickly as possible the kind of item shown in each photo. Kim would most likely classify the _____ most quickly.
   A. avocado   B. persimmon   C. carrot   D. mango

8. _____ refers to the probability of a characteristic occurring in the general population.
   A. Heritability   C. Normal distribution
   B. Theory of mind   D. Base rate information

9. An awareness that our own thoughts may differ from other people's thoughts is called _____.
   A. intuition   C. wisdom
   B. interpersonal intelligence   D. theory of mind

10. "Feed a cold, starve a fever" is an example of a(n) _____.
    A. heuristic   B. algorithm   C. script   D. analogy

PRACTICE TEST #2

1. All of the following are part of the problem-solving process EXCEPT_____.
   A. identifying the problem
   B. selecting a strategy
   C. avoiding obstacles, such as biases
   D. using hindsight to evaluate the solution

2. _____ is possibly time-consuming, but if followed correctly, it guarantees a solution; _____ is a quicker, more common-sense approach that works in most situations.
   A. A heuristic; an algorithm
   B. An algorithm; a heuristic
   C. A mental set; an artificial concept
   D. An artificial concept; a natural concept

3. Harriet is planning the courses she needs for completion of her major. She identifies the courses taught only once a year, then those that are taught by interesting professors, and then she looks at the times when the courses are available. What heuristic is she using?
   A. working backward
   B. searching for analogies
   C. breaking a large problem into smaller ones
   D. availability

4. It is registration day at the college. You know that you need to collect the proper forms, fill them out with your chosen classes, get the forms signed by your advisor, pay your fees, and obtain your ID card. This is your _____ for college registration.
   A. script   B. heuristic   C. pattern   D. prototype

5. A good way to solve a maze puzzle is by _____.
   A. working backwards
   B. using an analogy
   C. using an algorithm
   D. trial and error

6. Because it is a characteristic that is not directly observable but must be inferred from behavior, psychologists would say that intelligence is a _____ concept.
   A. fuzzy   B. useless   C. hypothetical   D. vague

7. When Carla uses nail polish to keep the run in her stocking from getting longer, she is demonstrating her ability to overcome _____.
   A. a script
   B. anchoring bias
   C. functional fixedness
   D. availability bias

8. Mary completed Algebra I last year. Now, in Algebra II, she tries to solve the problems in the same way as she did last year. She cannot seem to use the new strategies she has been taught. Mary is demonstrating _____.
   A. functional fixedness
   B. anchoring bias
   C. the availability bias
   D. a mental set

9. According to Sternberg, _____ involves using one's intelligence toward a common good, rather than toward a selfish pursuit.
   A. creativity   B. wisdom   C. a mental set   D. practical intelligence

172

10. Ken saw several news reports about a plane crash last month. Now he is much more frightened to fly to Daytona Beach for spring break than to drive there. He is operating under the influence of _____ bias.
    A. availability   B. anchoring   C. hindsight   D. representativeness

PRACTICE TEST #3

1. During the presidential election, most people watched the debates but did not change their minds. The debates most likely reinforced their previous beliefs because of the _____ bias.
   A. availability   B. confirmation   C. hindsight   D. representativeness

2. The day after her team lost, Addie was analyzing the baseball game. She maintained that the manager obviously should have changed pitchers in the third inning (although she made no such comment during the game). This is likely an example of the _____ bias.
   A. availability   B. confirmation   C. hindsight   D. representativeness

3. Austin played quarterback on his college football team. He overheard some people talking about how dumb football players are. Because Austin was just awarded a Rhodes scholarship, he knows that those people are guilty of using the _____ bias.
   A. availability   B. confirmation   C. hindsight   D. representativeness

4. All of the following are personality characteristics of creative people EXCEPT _____.
   A. independent thinking   C. willingness to restructure problems
   B. need for stimulating interaction D. preference for keeping things simple

5. Arnold does well on tests that measure the ability to see relationships and solve problems. Cattell would say he is strong in _____ intelligence.
   A. fluid   B. analytical   C. crystallized   D. general

6. Your psychology professor has assigned a term paper; she requires you to turn in several preliminary steps. She is teaching you to use a problem-solving strategy called _____.
   A. searching for analogies   C. creating subgoals
   B. working backward   D. preliminary work

7. The first intelligence test was developed by Binet and Simon in _____.
   A. France   B. Germany   C. Britain   D. the United States

8. The purpose of Binet and Simon's first test was to _____.
   A. identify students who were gifted   C. decide who went on to high school
   B. measure the IQ of French students   D. identify students who needed special help

9. When all intelligence test scores fall under a bell-shaped curve, we call that a(n) _____.
   A. intelligence curve   C. normal distribution
   B. random distribution   D. intelligence distribution

10. The amount of variation within a group that is due to genetic factors is _____.
    A. the normal distribution   C. heredity
    B. the normal range   D. heritability

COMPREHENSIVE REVIEW TEST

1. All of the following are generally true about highly creative people EXCEPT _____.
   A. they are independent thinkers
   B. they prefer simplicity
   C. they have an intense interest in their subject
   D. they are willing to restructure a problem

2. The person most associated with the study of giftedness is _____.
   A. Binet   B. Simon   C. Terman   D. Gardner

3. Your friend claims that intelligence is a single, general construct. She is referring to _____ theory.
   A. Spearman's   B. Terman's   C. Binet's   D. Gardner's

4. You do really well on tests that tap into your semantic memory, such as tests of vocabulary and arithmetic. According to Cattell, you are strong in _____ intelligence.
   A. general   B. analytical   C. crystallized   D. fluid

5. Gardner's theory of multiple intelligences includes all of the following EXCEPT _____ intelligence.
   A. spatial   B. emotional   C. musical   D. naturalistic

6. In a concept hierarchy, the most _____ concepts are "at the top."
   A. specific   B. well-defined.   C. concrete   D. general

7. Jennifer hears the following words: cheerleader, tackle, pass, wide receiver, fourth down, goal line, halfback, and coach. When asked to list the words that she just heard, she includes the word "football." This most likely occurred because of her _____.
   A. schema   B. script   C. prototypes   D. motivated forgetting

8. Fritz is 8 years old. He has a mental age of 10. According to the traditional formula, his IQ is _____.
   A. 119   B. 80   C. 100   D. 125

9. Your favorite basketball team wins the championship. You proclaim, "I knew they would do it all along!" This is an example of _____ bias.
   A. availability   B. hindsight   C. anchoring   D. representativeness

10. All of the following are types of intelligence from Sternberg's theory EXCEPT _____.
   A. analytical   B. triarchical   C. practical   D. creative

11. According to research on creativity, one cannot become extraordinarily creative without first _____.

   A. becoming an expert.   C. using cognitive maps.
   B. developing wisdom.   D. recognizing one's intuition.

12. Research has found that teachers' expectations can influence how well their students perform. This is known as the _____.
   A. expectation bias   C. self-fulfilling prophecy
   B. confirmation bias   D. expectancy prophecy

13. Melissa has been studying intelligence in her psychology class. One term she finds interesting is "heritability." She explains to her mother that the term means _____.
   A. that almost all of intelligence is inherited
   B. the amount of trait similarity between groups attributed to genetics
   C. the amount of trait variation within a group attributed to genetics
   D. that some intelligence may be inherited but some may not be inherited

14. In experiments, when African-American students are asked to take a test of academic ability and are told that white students get higher scores, the African-American students perform worse than they do when they are told that African-American students get higher scores. This is an example of _____.
   A. mental set   B. the Flynn effect   C. anchoring bias   D. stereotype threat

15. The "Flynn effect" refers to the fact that the average score on IQ tests has _____.
   A. steadily increased over the last 100 years   C. drastically increased in the past 20 years
   B. not changed in the past 100 years   D. steadily declined over the last 100 years

CRITICAL THINKING ESSAYS

1. In what ways do prejudice and stereotyping tie in with some of the obstacles to good decision making, problem solving, and judgments? Give examples.

2. Discuss the evidence for each side of the nature/nurture debate in intelligence. Give the research support for the heritability of intelligence and for the role of environment.

CHAPTER 7
Development over the Lifespan

Make flashcards using the following terms or, even better, develop mnemonics (memory strategies) to help you remember the different concepts and terms. Use the definitions in the margins of this chapter for help. Numbers refer to page numbers in the textbook.

accommodation (283)
adolescence (296)
adoption study (267)
Alzheimer's disease (312)
animistic thinking (285)
anxious-ambivalent attachment (274)
assimilation (282)
attachment (274)
attention-deficit hyperactivity disorder (294)
authoritarian parent (289)
authoritative parent (289)
autonomy (293)
avoidant attachment (274)
babbling (280)
body image (297)
centration (285)
cognitive development (282)
concrete operational stage (285)
conservation (285)
contact comfort (273)
developmental psychology (266)
embryo (268)
egocentrism (284)
ego-integrity (310)
emerging adulthood (307)
executive function (278)
fetus (268)
fetal alcohol syndrome (FAS) (269)
formal operational stage (300)
generativity (309)
genetic leash (273)
goal-directed behavior (284)
grammar (281)
identity (303)

imprinting (274)
industry (293)
infancy (271)
initiative (293)
innate ability (268)
innate reflex (270)
intimacy (306)
irreversibility (285)
Language Acquisition Device (LAD) (280)
maturation (271)
menarche (297)
mental operation (286)
mental representation (284)
mimicry (270)
morpheme (281)
nature-nurture issue (267)
neonatal period (269)
object permanence (283)
peer marriage (308)
permissive parent (289)
placenta (269)
prenatal period (268)
preoperational stage (284)
psychosocial stage (276)
puberty (297)
revolution in aging (306)
rite of passage (297)
scaffolding (288)
schema (282)
secure attachment (274)
selective social interaction (312)
self-control (277)
sensitive period (271)

Make flashcards using the following terms or, even better, develop mnemonics (memory strategies) to help you remember the different concepts and terms. Use the definitions in the margins of this chapter for help. Numbers refer to page numbers in the textbook.

sensorimotor intelligence (283)
sensorimotor stage (283)
separation anxiety (274)
sexual orientation (298)
socialization (289)
stage of moral reasoning (302)
stage theory (282)
synaptic pruning (271)
synchronicity (270)
telegraphic speech (281)

temperament (288)
teratogen (269)
theory of mind (287)
transition (309)
trust (276)
twin study (267)
uninvolved parent (290)
wave metaphor (288)
zygote (268)

Lecture Assistant *for Chapter 7*

Tear this outline out and bring it with you to class in order to facilitate your note taking.
Spend more time listening to the lecture and less time writing!

Chapter Opening Problem: Do the amazing accounts of similarities in twins reared apart indicate that we are primarily a product of our genes? Or do genetics and environment work together to influence growth and development over the lifespan?

- *Developmental psychology =*

- *Nature-nurture issue =*

    o   *Nature-nurture interaction =*

- *Twin study =*

- *Adoption study =*

7.1 WHAT INNATE ABILITIES DOES THE INFANT POSSESS?

- *Innate ability =*

Core Concept 7.1 =

A) Prenatal Development

- *Prenatal period =*

1) Three Phases of Prenatal Development =

- *Zygote =*

    o   *Germinal phase =*

- *Embryo =*

    o   *Embryonic phase =*

- *Fetus =*

2) Teratogens: Prenatal Toxins

- *Placenta =*

- *Teratogen =*

- *Fetal alcohol syndrome (FAS) =*

B) The Neonatal Period: Abilities of the Newborn Child

- *Neonatal period =*

1) Sensory Abilities in Newborns =

2) Social Abilities =

- *Mimicry =*

- *Synchronicity =*

3) Innate Reflexes =

- *Innate reflex =*

  o *Postural reflex =*

  o *Grasping reflex =*

  o *Rooting reflex =*

  o *Stepping reflex =*

C) Infancy: Building on the Neonatal Blueprint

- *Infancy =*

1) Neural Development =

- *Sensitive period =*

- *Synaptic pruning =*

2) <u>Maturation and Development</u> =

- *Maturation* =

- *Genetic leash* =

3) <u>Contact Comfort</u> =

  - o Harry and Margaret Harlow =

- *Contact comfort* =

4) <u>Attachment</u> =

- *Attachment=*

- *Imprinting* =

  a) <u>Attachment Styles</u> =

  - o *Mary Ainsworth's "Strange Situation"* =

    - *Secure attachment* =

    - *Separation anxiety* =

    - *Anxious-ambivalent attachment* =

    - *Avoidant attachment* =

  b) <u>Culture and Attachment</u> =

  c) <u>Long-Term Effects of Attachment</u> =

5) <u>Psychosocial Development: Trust versus Mistrust</u> =

- *Psychosocial stage* =

- *Trust*

D) Psychology Matters: Not Just Fun and Games—The Role of Child's Play in Life Success

- *Executive function* =

7.2 WHAT ARE THE DEVELOPMENTAL TASKS OF CHILDHOOD?

Core Concept 7.2 =

A) How Children Acquire Language

1) Language Structures in the Brain =

- *Language Acquisition Device (LAD)* =

2) Acquiring Vocabulary and Grammar =

- *Babbling* =

a) Practice Makes Perfect =

b) Grammar Turns Vocabulary into Language =

- *Grammar* =

c) First Sentences =

- *Telegraphic speech* =

- *Morphemes* =

o *Overregularization* =

d) Other Language Skills =

o *Social rules of conversation* =

B) Cognitive Development: Piaget's Theory

- *Cognitive development* =

- *Stage theory of development* =

- *Schema* =

1) <u>Assimilation and Accommodation</u> =

- *Assimilation* =

- *Accommodation* =

2) <u>Piaget's Stages of Cognitive Development</u> =

    a) <u>The Sensorimotor Stage (Birth to about Age Two)</u> =

- *Sensorimotor stage* =

- *Sensorimotor intelligence* =

- *Object permanence* =

- *Goal-directed behavior* =

- *Mental representations* =

    b) <u>The Preoperational Stage (from about Two to Seven Years of Age)</u> =

- *Preoperational stage* =

- *Egocentrism* =

- *Animistic thinking* =

- *Centration* =

- *Irreversability* =

    b) <u>The Concrete Operational Stage (from about Seven to about Eleven Years of Age)</u> =

- *Concrete operational stage* =

- *Conservation* =

- *Mental operation =*

3) Beyond Piaget: Contemporary Perspectives on Cognitive Development =

    a) Hints of Abilities Appear Earlier Than Piaget Thought =

    b) A Theory of Mind =

- *Theory of mind =*

    c) Stages or Waves? =

- *Wave metaphor =*

    d) The Importance of Culture in Learning =

- *Scaffolding =*

C) Social and Emotional Development

1) Temperament =

- *Temperament =*

2) Socialization =

- *Socialization =*

    a) Four Parenting Styles and Their Effects =

- *Authoritarian parent =*

- *Authoritative parent =*

- *Permissive parent =*

- *Uninvolved parent =*

    b) Effects of Daycare =

    c) Leisure Influences =

d) Gender Differences in Socialization =

3) Psychosocial Development in Childhood: Erikson's Stages =

a) Autonomy versus Shame and Doubt =

- *Autonomy =*

b) Initiative versus Guilt =

- *Initiative =*

C) Industry versus Inferiority =

- *Industry =*

D) Psychology Matters: The Puzzle of ADHD

- *Attention-deficit hyperactivity disorder (ADHD) =*

7.3 WHAT CHANGES MARK THE TRANSITION OF ADOLESCENCE?

Core Concept 7.3 =

- *Adolescence =*

A) Adolescence and Culture

- *Rite of passage =*

B) Physical Maturation in Adolescence

- *Puberty =*

- *Menarche =*

- *Body image =*

C) Adolescent Sexuality

- *Sexual orientation =*

D) Neural and Cognitive Development in Adolescence

1) <u>Teens: Guided by Reason or Emotion?</u> =

2) <u>The Brain Undergoes Major Pruning</u> =

3) <u>Piaget's Final Stage: Formal Operational Thought</u> =

- *Formal operational stage =*

E) Moral Development: Kohlberg's Theory

- o *Moral dilemmas =*

- *Stages of moral reasoning =*

1) <u>Critiques of Kohlberg's Theory</u> =

- o Carol Gilligan =

F) Social and Emotional Issues in Adolescence

1) <u>Do Parents Still Matter?</u> =

2) <u>Erikson's Psychosocial Development in Adolescence</u> =

- *Identity =*

3) <u>Is Adolescence a Period of Turmoil?</u> =

G) Using Psychology to Learn Psychology: Cognitive Development in College Students =

7.4 WHAT DEVELOPMENTAL CHALLENGES DO ADULTS FACE?

Core Concept 7.4 =

- *Revolution in aging* =

A) Early Adulthood: Explorations, Autonomy, and Intimacy

1) Intimacy versus Isolation =

- *Intimacy* =

2) Emerging Adulthood: The In-Between Stage =

- *Emerging adulthood* =

3) Modern Approaches to Intimacy =

- *Peer marriage* =

B) The Challenges of Midlife: Complexity and Generativity

1) Generativity versus Stagnation =

- *Generativity* =

2) Transitions =

- *Transition* =

C) Late Adulthood: The Age of Integrity =

1) Ego-Integrity versus Despair =

- *Ego-integrity* =

2) <u>Physical Changes</u> =

3) <u>Cognitive Changes</u> =

- *Alzheimer's disease* =

4) <u>Social and Emotional Changes</u> =

- *Selective social interaction* =

5) <u>Keys to Successful Aging</u> =

D) Psychology Matters: A Look Back at the Jim Twins and Your Own Development =

E) Critical Thinking Applied: The Mozart Effect =

ADDITIONAL NOTES

As You Read . . . Practice Activities

1. *Fill in the blanks with the correct terms.*

    A. _____ psychology is the psychology of growth, change, and
consistency through the lifespan.

    B. In terms of nature and nurture, _____ establishes your potential, but
_____ determines how your potential will be realized.

    C. Heredity effects should show up more strongly in _____ twins than in
_____ twins.

    D. In adoption studies, adopted children's similarities with their _____
family point to the effects of nature, whereas similarities with their
_____ family point to the effects of nurture.

What Innate Abilities Does the Infant Possess?

2. According to Core Concept 6.1, what three main innate abilities do newborns have?

    A. _____   B. _____

                C. _____

Prenatal Development

3. *In the table below, fill in the empty boxes with the correct information.*

Prenatal Stage	Name of Organism	Major Developments during the Stage
A) Germinal	Zygote	Rapid cell _____ occurs. Zygote _____ itself in lining of _____. Other cells become the _____.
B) _____	_____	Cells specialize in process of _____. First _____ occurs in the fifth week. Especially sensitive time to effects of _____.
C) Fetal	Fetus	Basic _____ appear. By the sixteenth week, the _____ is fully formed. By the twenty-seventh week, the fetus can _____.

4. Visit this site to view amazing three-dimensional MRI images of the human embryo.
http://embryo.soad.umich.edu/

5. Define "teratogens" and then list four examples.

6. *Underline the word(s) in parentheses that will make each statement correct. (Both options may be correct!)*

   A. Women who smoke while pregnant are more likely to have children with (ADHD/low birth weight).

   B. Fetal alcohol syndrome is a leading cause of (SIDS/mental retardation).

   C. The herb (gingko/ginseng) has been shown to have harmful effects on the fetus.

   D. The (placenta/uterus) separates the bloodstreams of the mother and her fetus.

The Neonatal Period: Abilities of the Newborn Child

7. *Complete the following paragraph about the sensory abilities of the newborn.*

   The _____ period refers to the first month after birth. Research tells us a lot about the sensory abilities of a newborn. Infants prefer _____ tastes. As early as _____ hours after birth, they show pleasure at the taste of sugar water or vanilla. They smile when they smell _____. Newborns prefer to look at _____ more than most other visual patterns, and they prefer looking at patterns with a high degree of _____. Their optimal focus is a distance of about _____ inches. They prefer _____ voices over _____ voices.

8. Why did researchers have expectant mothers read *The Cat in the Hat* aloud twice a day for the last six weeks of their pregnancy? What did the researchers discover?

9. *Fill in the blanks with the correct terms.*

   A. Mirror neurons explain why babies engage in the _____ of many behaviors.

   B. The close coordination between the gazing, touching, vocalizing, and smiling of caregivers and infants is referred to as _____.

10. Name and describe four of the innate reflexes infants possess.

A. _____   C. _____

B. _____   D. _____

Infancy: Building on the Neonatal Blueprint

11. *Indicate whether each statement is True (T) or False (F) by circling the appropriate letter after the statement.*

A. When infants are exposed to new stimuli, the dendrites and axons in the brain grow and branch out.   T F

B. "Windows of opportunity" for the development of certain abilities are called "genetic leashes."   T F

C. "Synaptic pruning" refers to the destruction of unused neurons.   T F

D. "Maturation" refers to the occurrence of genetically programmed processes of growth and development.   T F

E. Sensitive periods have been found for hearing and vision.   T F

F. Research has found that infants who receive more physical contact experience faster intellectual development.   T F

G. German families tend to prefer avoidant attachment over secure attachment.   T F

H. Japanese parenting encourages avoidant attachment in children.   T F

I. Attachment problems in infancy predict later problems with social relationships.   T F

J. Between the ages of four and six months, most babies start to crawl.   T F

12. *Fill in the blanks with the correct terms.*

A. Edward Wilson refers to the constraints placed on development by heredity as the

_____.

B. Harry and Margaret Harlow tested their theory using baby _____.

C. The Harlows discovered that infants prefer a caregiver that provides _____ over a caregiver that only provides food.

D. Rather than the term "bonding," most psychologists use the term _____ to refer to the caregiver-child emotional relationship.

E. The powerful attraction of some infant animals to the first moving object or individual they see is referred to as _____.

F. Psychologist John Bowlby believed that _____ is innate.

G. To measure attachment, Mary Ainsworth developed a laboratory procedure called the _____.

H. Erik Erikson's theory includes eight _____ stages, and he believed that babies go through a developmental crisis that he called the _____ stage.

I. Erik Erikson's theory of human development was the first theory to encompass the entire _____.

13. *Match each term with its best description(s) by placing the letter corresponding to the term in the space next to its description. (Terms may be used more than once.)*

TERMS
    A. Separation anxiety   C. Avoidant attachment
    B. Secure attachment   D. Anxious-ambivalent attachment

DESCRIPTIONS
    _____ Fourteen-month-old Ahmed is angry and fearful when his mother leaves the room, and then cannot be consoled by his mother once she returns
    _____ Russell is two years old, and cries whenever his parents leave for work.
    _____ Lea is fifteen months old and becomes upset when her father leaves the room. When he returns, she calms down immediately and goes back to playing.
    _____ Nimita is a thirteen-month-old who doesn't show distress when her mother leaves, and doesn't show interest or happiness when her mother returns.
    _____ Eleven-month-old Michael is interested in new experiences, is tolerant of strangers, and uses his parents as a "secure base" when he explores.

14. An outstanding explanation and animated demonstration of Ainsworth's Strange Situation procedure can be found at the following web site:
    http://bpc.digitalbrain.com/bpc/web/LearningObjects/Ainsworth/home/?backto&verb

Psychology Matters: Not Just Fun and Games—The Role of Child's Play in Life Success

15. *Fill in the blanks with the correct information about children's play.*

A. Low _____ is a strong predictor of delinquency and criminal behavior.

B. _____ play requires more thinking, self-management, planning, and creativity than does _____ play.

C. Even when the effects of social class and intelligence are taken into account, _____ is one of the most important predictors of life success.

D. _____ refers to the frontal lobe areas related to self-regulation and goal attainment.

What Are the Developmental Tasks of Childhood?

How Children Acquire Language

16. *Fill in the blanks with the correct information about theories of language development.*

The psycholinguist named _____ has proposed that children are born with mental structures built into the brain that help them learn language. He calls these language structures the _____. Research based on the _____ provides evidence of a genetic contribution to language.

17. *Fill in the following table with information about (a) the typical age at which the language ability is seen, (b) an example of the sounds and/or vocabulary that are associated with the ability.*

STAGE	AGE	SOUNDS/VOCABULARY
A. Babbling		
B. One-Word		
C. Two-Word		

18. *Underline the word(s) in parentheses that will make each statement correct. (Both options may be correct!)*

A. Parents in low-SES households read to their children an average of (25/250) hours between the ages of 1 and 5 years, compared to (100/1000) hours for middle-SES parents.

B. Mothers talk significantly more with young (daughters/sons) than with (daughters/sons).

C. The meaningful units that make up words are called (grammars/morphemes).

D. Simple sequences of nouns and verbs without plurals or function words are called (one-word/telegraphic) speech.

E. A child who thinks that all plurals are formed by adding an "s" and therefore says "mouses" rather than "mice" is showing (overextension/overregularization).

F. (Grammar/Morpheme) refers to the rules of a language.

G. Infants are born with the ability to make (all/about half) the sounds in the approximately (40,000/4,000) languages spoken in the world.

19. What are some of the social rules of conversation that children must master in order to be effective users of language?

Cognitive Development: Piaget's Theory

20. *Fill in the blanks with the correct terms.*

A. Piaget referred to mental structures used to interpret stimuli as _____.

B. _____ is the process of incorporating new information into an existing schema.

C. The process of reorganizing or changing one's schema to adapt to new information is called _____.

D. According to Piaget, cognitive development results from a continual interplay between the dynamic processes of _____ and _____.

E. According to Piaget's terminology, if a child can manipulate concepts entirely in his or her mind, he or she is able to perform _____.

21. *Write the name of the cognitive process each child is exhibiting, according to Piaget.*

EXAMPLE	COGNITIVE PROCESS
A. Four-year-old Johnny knows that he has a brother, but doesn't know that his brother has a brother.	
B. Julia understands that pouring milk from a small, wide glass into a tall, slender glass does not change the amount of milk.	
C. Billy says "Mean sidewalk!" after he falls down and scrapes his knee.	
D. Nine-month-old Sara tries to move the cloth away to find the toy that is hidden under it.	
E. Three-year-old Lamees thinks that other people see things the same way she does.	
F. Brandon watches milk being poured from a small, wide glass into a tall, slender glass and sees that the level of milk in the tall glass is higher up than it was before, so he believes there is more milk.	

22. *Match each Piagetian term with its best description(s) or example(s) by placing the letter corresponding to the term in the space next to its description or example. (Terms may be used more than once.)*

TERMS
    A. Centration   C. Egocentrism   E. Assimilation
    B. Animistic thinking   D. Irreversibility   F. Accommodation

DESCRIPTIONS
_____ Joelle has a schema that all psychologists are therapists, but then completely changed her schema once she found out that lots of psychologists are NOT therapists.
_____ Five-year-old André is certain that all the other children know exactly what he knows.
_____ Four-year-old Frank believes that his shadow is following him because it likes him.
_____ It is the inability to pay attention to more than one aspect of a situation at a time.
_____ Three-year-old Deanna has a schema that cars have feelings.
_____ Teisha understands that 1 + 2 = 3, but doesn't understand that 3 − 2 = 1.
_____ Pete found out at school that some cats do not have tails, so he incorporated that information into his existing schema about cats.
_____ Four-year-old Jimmy says, "He put it under there," and expects everyone to know exactly who "he" is, what "it" is, and where "there" is.
_____ Piaget believes that it is one of the dynamic processes underlying all cognitive growth.

23. *Fill in the blanks of this concept map about Piaget's theory.*

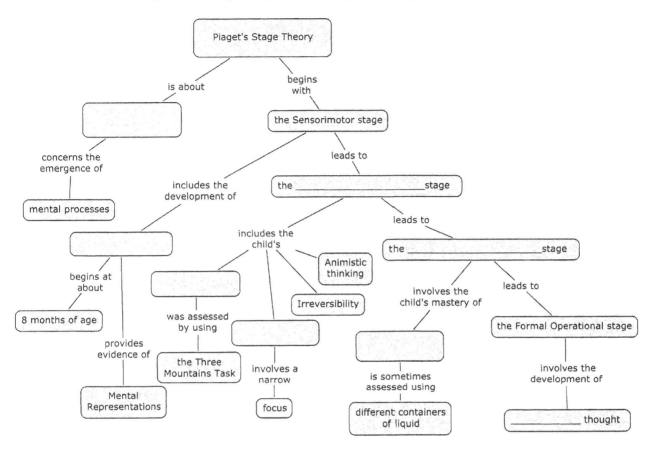

24. What five pieces of evidence demonstrate that Piaget was not correct in terms of the ages at which he believed certain cognitive changes occur in children?

    A. _____

    B. _____

    C. _____

    D. _____

    E. _____

25. To see a demonstration of children attempting a Piagetian conservation task, view the following site:

        http://youtube.com/watch?v=MpREJIrpgv8&feature=related

26. What is the "wave metaphor," and how does it relate to Piaget's theory?

Social and Emotional Development

27. Define "temperament." How does temperament relate to socialization?

28. *Indicate whether each statement is True (T) or False (F) by circling the appropriate letter after the statement.*

    A. According to Jerome Kagan's research, about 5 percent of babies are born with a tendency toward shyness.   T F

    B. Brain-imaging studies show that bold babies have more active amygdalas than do shy babies.   T F

    C. Temperament is quite stable over time.   T F

    D. Socialization is the lifelong process of shaping a person's behaviors, attitudes, values, motives, skills, and standards to those that are considered desirable in a given society.   T F

29. *Identify the most likely parenting style in each of the following vignettes.*

_____A. Sharon likes to stay out past curfew just because she does not want to miss any of the fun. Her mom doesn't want Sharon's adolescence to be full of rules, so she looks the other way when her daughter comes in late.

_____B. Casey's parents have set curfews and other rules for her and her brothers. While they expect their children to obey the rules, they also have explained that the rules are there to help their children stay safe and learn to manage their social lives.

_____C. Bill's parents both work outside of the home, and they often must travel for days at a time. Bill cannot remember the last time either of them attended his soccer games, ate a meal with him, or even asked him how things are going.

_____D. Jerald's father has set curfews for his son. He expects his son to abide by the curfews without questioning them, and when Jerald breaks a curfew, he is disciplined severely.

30. *Underline the word(s) in parentheses that will make each statement correct. (Both options may be correct!)*

    A. Research shows that children of (authoritarian/authoritative) parents tend to be confident, happy, and self-reliant.

B. Studies show that children of (permissive/uninvolved) parents tend to be more immature, impulsive, and demanding.

C. Chinese, Hispanic, and Asian Pacific Island parents tend to be (less strict/stricter) with their children than Western parents are with their children.

D. In the U.S., over (60 percent/80 percent) of women with children under 6 years of age work outside the home.

E. Intellectually and socially, most children in daycare do (worse than/as well as) children raised at home by a full-time parent.

F. In terms of daycare, more children in the U.S. are cared for by (paid providers/relatives) than by (paid providers/relatives).

G. Poor-quality daycare can influence children to be (aggressive/depressed).

31. *Indicate whether each statement is True (T) or False (F) by circling the appropriate letter after the statement.*

A. American children spend between 40 and 50 percent of their waking hours involved in leisure activities. T F

B. On average, American children spend about three hours per day with media. T F

C. Reading for pleasure increases as children approach adolescence. T F

D. Children and teens spend twice as much time with friends and family as they do with media. T F

E. Watching entertainment television before the age of three is linked with attention problems in later childhood. T F

F. Boys watch more television than girls do. T F

G. Viewing violent TV and playing violent video games increase aggression. T F

H. As children get older, they typically spend more time in physical activities. T F

32. What gender differences have been observed consistently in social interactions between children?

33. NEED A BREAK?
To get a better understanding of developmental psychology, visit MyPsychLab.

34. *In the table below, fill in the empty spaces or boxes with the correct information about Erikson's psychosocial stages.*

Name of the Stage	Age of Child	Description of Stage
A. _____ versus Inferiority		
B. _____ versus Shame or Self-Doubt		
C. Initiative versus _____		

Psychology Matters: The Puzzle of ADHD

35. *Indicate whether each statement is True (T) or False (F) by circling the appropriate letter after the statement.*

A. Attention-deficit hyperactivity disorder is found in about 10-15 percent of school-aged children in America.   T F

B. Cross-culturally, about 5 percent of school-age children have ADHD.   T F

C. Of children who are diagnosed with ADHD, about 10 percent are girls.   T F

D. A key criterion for diagnosing ADHD is that it must affect multiple domains.   T F

E. In girls rather than boys, ADHD more often looks like disorganization and a tendency to lose things.   T F

F. In about 30 percent of cases, ADHD fades away as the child enters adolescence.   T F

G. Research shows that a diet high in sugar causes ADHD.   T F

H. Viewing non-educational TV before the age of three predicts childhood ADHD.   T F

I. Prenatal exposure to alcohol and to nicotine increases the likelihood of ADHD.   T F

J. The prefrontal cortex in ADHD brains develops up to five years later than it does in non-ADHD brains.   T F

K. People with ADHD receive fewer bursts of the neurotransmitter serotonin.   T F

L. The brains of people with ADHD do not reach normal size.   T F

What Changes Mark the Transition of Adolescence?

36. What marks the beginning of adolescence? _____

Adolescence and Culture

37. What is meant by the term "rite of passage"? List some rites of passage that are found in different world cultures.

Physical Maturation in Adolescence

38. *Fill in the blanks with the correct information.*

    A. The name for the onset of menstruation is _____.

    B. The onset of menstruation is usually between the ages of _____ and _____.

    C. One's personal and subjective view of one's own appearance is referred to as one's

    _____.

    D. The onset of sexual maturity is referred to as _____.

39. How are gender, age of maturation, and culture related to adolescents' body image?

Adolescent Sexuality

40. *Underline the word(s) in parentheses that will make each statement correct. (Both options may be correct!)*

A. By age (13/17), about 40 percent of teens in the U.S. and Canada have had their first sexual experience.

    B. By age 20, about (75 percent/90 percent) of individuals in the U.S. and Canada have had their first sexual experience.

    C. By age 16, about (75 percent/90 percent) of boys and (40 percent/60 percent) of girls in the U.S. report that they have masturbated.

    D. For the vast majority of (females/males), emotional involvement is an important part of sexual attraction.

    E. Studies show that (1 to 6 percent/8 to 12 percent) of teens report having had sexual contact with a same-sex partner.

    F. Most gay and lesbian individuals become aware of their sexual orientation in (early/late) adolescence.

Cognitive Development in Adolescence

41. What brain structure development likely contributes to adolescent thinking being generally more emotional and less rational than adult thinking?

42. In terms of synaptic pruning, what happens in the brain during adolescence?

43. According to Piaget, what cognitive development stage are adolescents in, and what abilities go along with this level of thinking? Does research support Piaget's ideas?

Moral Development: Kohlberg's Theory

44. *Complete the following paragraph about Lawrence Kohlberg's theory of moral development.*

Lawrence Kohlberg used _____ to study moral development. His most famous one involved a character named _____. Kohlberg proposed _____ stages of moral development. In Stage 1, people reason on the basis of _____ and _____. In Stage 2, there is awareness of other people's _____. In Stage 3, decisions are based on _____. _____ is most important in Stage 4. Stage 5 is called the _____ stage, whereas the individual bases decisions in Stage 6 on _____.

45. In what ways does Carol Gilligan believe males and females differ in their moral reasoning? Does most research support her ideas?

46. *Match each Kohlberg stage of moral development with its best description(s) by placing the letter corresponding to the stage in the space next to its description. (Stages may be used more than once.)*

STAGE
A. Stage 1   B. Stage 2   C. Stage 3   D. Stage 4   E. Stage 5   F. Stage 6

DESCRIPTIONS
_____ Marcia believes that it's important not to shoplift because it's against the law.
_____ Derek won't drive over the speed limit because he doesn't want to get a ticket.
_____ Katelyn tells the teacher about her classmates who cheated so that the teacher will be proud of her.
_____ Zack decides to tell the police about the crime he witnessed because the police are now offering witnesses $200.
_____ Javon believes in assisted suicide because he believes all people deserve to die with dignity and should not have to suffer.
_____ Hussein believes that drivers should be allowed to speed if they are trying to get an expectant mother to the hospital so she can give birth safely.
_____ Ricardo doesn't cheat because he wants to get into heaven.

_____ Diana takes her sick friend to the doctor, thinking that in the future she may then get her friend to drive her places she needs to go.

47. Besides issues related to gender, give three other criticisms of Kohlberg's theory of moral reasoning.

A. _____

B. _____

C. _____

Social and Emotional Development in Adolescence

48. *Fill in the blanks with the correct information.*

A. According to Erikson's theory, adolescents are in the _____ stage.

B. Adolescents report spending four times as much time talking with _____ as with _____.

C. Studies of adolescent suicide show that the triggering experience is often a _____ event.

D. For most teens, the adolescent years _____ a time of anxiety and despair.

E. Adolescents who have the least trouble tend to be those whose parents have a(n) _____ parenting style.

49. This is a comprehensive collection of links covering biological, social, and emotional development from infancy to adolescence. The website is refereed by students in the Human Development program at Tufts University.
http://www.cfw.tufts.edu/

Using Psychology to Learn Psychology: Cognitive Development in College Students

50. Psychologist William Perry discovered five distinct stages that college students go through during their time in college. Explain the general progression over time, as well as how students' views of both their professors and the different subject areas change with this progression.

What Developmental Challenges Do Adults Face?

51. What is meant by the "revolution in aging"?

52. *Fill in the table below with the correct information regarding theories of adult development.*

THEORISTS	NEEDS OF ADULTHOOD
A. Freud	_____ and _____
B. Maslow	_____ and _____ which, when satisfied, allow for the emergence of the needs for _____ and _____
C. McClelland	_____ and _____ and _____
D. Erikson	_____ and _____

Early Adulthood: Explorations, Autonomy, and Intimacy

53. *Indicate whether each statement is True (T) or False (F) by circling the appropriate letter after the statement.*

   A. According to Erikson, a person must resolve the crisis of intimacy before he or she can work on obtaining a sense of identity.　　　T F

   B. Arnett's term for the transitional time between adolescence and adulthood is "emerging adulthood."　　　T F

   C. Adolescence is the period of time during which individuals take the most risks.　　　T F

   D. About one-fourth of emerging adults move out of their parents' homes and then move back in with them again.　　　T F

   E. Research on early adulthood shows that people name financial success as the key to a happy life.　　　T F

   F. For couples, the optimal ratio of positive interactions to negative interactions has been found to be about 5:1.　　　T F

   G. Partners in peer marriages view each other as having a specific, traditional role.　　　T F

The Challenges of Midlife: Complexity and Generativity

54. *Underline the word(s) in parentheses that will make each statement correct. (Both options may be correct!)*

   A. According to Erikson, the task of middle adulthood is (integrity/generativity).

   B. Research shows that most people (do/do not) go through a midlife crisis, and that midlife is a time of (upheaval/transition).

   C. Studies of cognitive development in midlife show that middle-aged adults have developed good skills in (mental operations/dialectical thinking), which is the ability to compare and evaluate contradictory viewpoints.

   D. Middle-aged adults tend to be good at integrating cognitions and emotions, which results in more (deliberate/reflective) coping responses to stressful events.

   E. Not resolving earlier crises of identity or intimacy may lead a person to develop (guilt/a midlife crisis).

Late Adulthood: The Age of Integrity

55. *Fill in the blanks with the correct information.*

A. _____ seems to be the key to healthy aging.

B. Erikson believed elderly adults face a crisis, called _____,

the healthy end of which involves looking back at life without regrets and enjoying a sense

of _____.

C. Problems with memory can be an early symptom of the degenerative brain disorder called

_____.

D. Brain-imaging research shows that older adults' brains compensate for cognitive decline by

processing information _____.

E. Middle-aged and older adult men and women define "well-being" in terms of

_____.

F. _____ refers to older adults only maintaining their most rewarding contacts.

56. The United States Administration on Aging has a comprehensive site with many links. Visit:
http://www.aoa.gov/

Psychology Matters: A Look Back at the Jim Twins and Your Own Development

57. Discuss three of the main criticisms leveled at Bouchard's twin studies.

Critical Thinking Applied: The Mozart Effect

58. Describe the "Mozart effect" and explain what research has found concerning this topic.

PRACTICE TEST #1

1. Kyrsten is twenty-nine years old. According to Erikson, what developmental task is Kyrsten working on?
   A. Intimacy B. Identity C. Integrity D. Emerging adulthood

2. Children's exposure to non-educational television before three years of age has been linked to the development of _____.
   A. autonomy B. ADHD C. centration D. superior memory

3. The meaningful units that make up speech are called _____.
   A. phonemes B. morphemes C. grammar D. language

4. During the embryonic phase, cells begin to specialize in a process known as _____.
   A. division B. separation C. discrimination D. differentiation

5. The time in life when individuals take the most risks is _____.
   A. early adolescence C. emerging adulthood
   B. late adolescence D. childhood

6. According to Erikson, individuals in adolescence experience what crisis?
   A. Initiative vs. guilt C. Identity vs. role confusion
   B. Integrity vs. despair D. Industry vs. inferiority

7. Samantha says she doesn't hit her younger brother, Justin, because if she did hit him her mother would punish her. According to Kohlberg's theory, this demonstrates which level of moral development?
   A. Stage 1 B. Stage 2 C. Stage 3 D. Stage 4

8. _____ is a leading cause of mental retardation.
   A. SIDS B. LAD C. FAS D. CBT

9. Gilligan's criticized Kohlberg's theory of moral reasoning because _____.
   A. Kohlberg never revised his theory or redefined his stages
   B. she believes women use justice reasoning more than care reasoning
   C. there was bias against females in Kohlberg's work
   D. there are no differences in moral reasoning between men and women

10. Attachment was studied, using the Strange Situation, by _____.
    A. Mary Ainsworth C. Noam Chomsky
    B. Harry Harlow D. Jerome Kagan

PRACTICE TEST #2

1. JoEllen is at a point in her life when she wants to do things that are meaningfully productive, so she is volunteering at a children's hospital. Erikson would say JoEllen is experiencing _____.

   A. autonomy   B. generativity   C. integrity   D. industry

2. According to Harlow, contact comfort is important because _____.
   A. it forms the basis for attachment
   B. it helps us understand primate behaviors
   C. it provides an empirical basis for Freudian personality theory
   D. it explains the development of the various temperaments

3. Noam Chomsky believes that we are born with speech-enabling structures he calls a(n)_____ device.
   A. innate language   C. language acquisition
   B. language learning   D. language controller

4. "Daddy car!" is an example of _____ speech.
   A. morpheme   B. grammatical   C. modified   D. telegraphic

5. Newborn infants have a visual acuity of _____.
   A. 20/500   B. 20/20   C. 20/50   D. 200/500

6. When Omar says "I eated all my carrots," he is demonstrating _____.
   A. overextension   C. telegraphic speech
   B. egocentrism   D. overregularization

7. _____ refers to the process in which unused neural connections in the newborn's brain are destroyed.
   A. Imprinting   B. Genetic leashing   C. Synaptic pruning   D. Neural detachment

8 During Piaget's sensorimotor stage, the one of the most critical skills developed is _____.
   A. conservation   C. object permanence
   B. irreversibility   D. centration

9. Robin's mother encourages her to try her best and to work toward her own goals. While she sets rules, she explains the reasons for those rules to Robin. This is an example of the _____ parenting style.
   A. permissive   B. authoritative   C. authoritarian   D. uninvolved

10. Our innate disposition is also called our _____.
    A. attachment style   C. character
    B. personality   D. temperament

1. Whenever it rains, three-year-old Sophia says, "The clouds are sad!" Piaget would say Sophia is exhibiting _____.
   A. conservation   C. centration
   B. egocentrism   D. animistic thinking

2. Some developmental psychologists have criticized Piaget's theory because _____.
   A. children learn in a diverse series of stages
   B. the transition between the cognitive stages is less abrupt than he believed
   C. current research methods have shown that children are less sophisticated than he predicted
   D. children cannot express concepts, and therefore probably cannot understand them

3. Gayle is a thirteen-month-old who doesn't show distress when her mother leaves and doesn't show interest or happiness when her mother returns. Gayle likely has what attachment style?
   A. Secure   B. Avoidant   C. Mistrusting   D. Anxious-ambivalent

4. Which parenting style is associated with the most self-reliant, happy children?
   A. Permissive   B. Authoritative   C. Authoritarian   D. Uninvolved

5. Between conception and the time at which the fertilized egg implants itself in the uterine wall, the egg is referred to as a(n) _____.
   A. zygote   B. embryo   C. fetus   D. teratogen

6. The primary task of young adulthood, according Erikson, is focused on _____.
   A. identity versus confusion   C. generativity versus stagnation
   B. intimacy versus isolation   D. competence versus inferiority

7. The understanding that the physical properties of an object or substance do not change when appearances change but nothing is added or taken away is called _____.
   A. object permanence   B. centration   C. animistic thought   D. conservation

8. All of the following are teratogens EXCEPT _____.
   A. alcohol   B. ginseng   C. SIDS   D. HIV

9. In terms of marriage, one recent trend for young adults has been _____ marriages.
   A. early   B. serial   C. traditional   D. peer

10. Muhammad does not shoplift because it is against the law. Max does not shoplift because he does not want to be arrested. According to Kohlberg, Muhammad is in the _____ stage and Max is in the _____ stage.
    B. third; fifth   D. sixth; fourth   C) fourth; first   D) fifth; second

COMPREHENSIVE REVIEW TEST

1. According to Piaget's theory, children in the sensorimotor stage develop ____.
   A. centration   B. conservation   C. egocentrism   D. object permanence

2. According to developmental theorists, which of the following individuals would most likely face a midlife crisis?
   A. Joe, who never resolved his own identity crisis as a young adult
   B. Jerry, who tends to be overly cautious
   C. Sue, who married young and focuses her life concerns mainly upon her family
   D. Sally, who lived with her boyfriend for a few years before marrying him

3. The percentage of people over age 85 who have Alzheimer's disease is estimated to be about ____.
   A. 10 percent   B. 30 percent   C. 50 percent   D. 70 percent

4. The powerful attraction of some infant animals to the first moving object or individual they see is referred to as ____.
   A. mimicry   B. imprinting   C. attachment   D. the genetic leash

5. The wave metaphor is an alternative to the idea that ____.
   A. adolescence is a time of turmoil   C. development occurs in distinct stages
   B. sensitive periods wax and wane   D. children only mimic facial expressions

6. Research has shown that midlife is best viewed as being a time of ____.
   A. crisis   B. integrity   C. transitions   D. separations

7. Erikson views _____ as the primary challenge facing elderly adults.
   A. identity versus confusion   C. generativity versus stagnation
   B. intimacy versus isolation   D. ego-integrity versus despair

8. According to Piagetian theory, adolescents in the formal operational stage would be better suited for which of the following tasks than someone in the concrete operational stage would be?
   A. Designing an experiment   C. Learning to speak a second language
   B. Memorizing all fifty state capitals   D. Solving a series of multiplication problems

9. Even though Carrie knows that she could be arrested, she helps illegal immigrants because of her belief that everyone is entitled to live free from dictatorships. Carrie is operating at which of Kohlberg's stages of moral reasoning?
   A. Stage 1   B. Stage 4   C. Stage 5   D. Stage 6

10. Marjorie is seventy-nine and only phones or writes family and her one close friend. This demonstrates ___.
    A. ego-integrity versus isolation   C. selective social interaction
    B. depression that comes with aging   D. the revolution in aging

11. You ask four-year-old Leslie if she has a sister. She says yes. You ask her if her sister has a sister. She looks puzzled and says no. This is an example of ___.
    A. object permanence   C. egocentric thinking
    B. lack of conservation   D. hypothetical reasoning

12. Dimitri is eighteen months old and cries whenever his parents leave the house. He is experiencing ___.
    A. avoidant attachment   C. anxious-ambivalent attachment
    B. separation anxiety   D. theory of mind

13. Matthew thought that fraternal twins always have to be the same gender because they have the exact same genes, but now he knows this idea is wrong. According to Piaget's theory, Matthew has changed his _____ by using _____.
    A. mental operation; a schema   C. schema; accommodation
    B. schema; assimilation   D. theory of mind; a mental operation

14. The _____ lobes of the brain are the last to develop in adolescents.
    A. frontal   B. temporal   C. parietal   D. occipital

15. Heredity puts constraints on development. Edward Wilson calls this ___.
    A. maturation   C. the nature-nurture issue
    B. the sensitive period   D. the genetic leash

CRITICAL THINKING ESSAYS

1. How do Piaget's stages of cognitive development relate to Kohlberg's stages of moral development?

2. Discuss a stereotype regarding midlife and a stereotype regarding late adulthood. Then, discuss whether research supports or undermines each of these stereotypes.

CHAPTER 8
States of Consciousness

Before You Read . . . Term Identification

Make flashcards using the following terms or, even better, develop mnemonics (memory strategies) to help you remember the different concepts and terms. Use the definitions in the margins of this chapter for help. Numbers refer to page numbers in the textbook.

activation-synthesis theory (340)
addiction (355)
attention (326)
cognitive neuroscience (325)
coma (330)
consciousness (325)
circadian rhythm (333)
daydreaming (332)
depressant (352)
general anesthetic (354)
hallucinogen (348)
hypnosis (345)
insomnia (342)
latent content (339)
manifest content (339)
meditation (347)
narcolepsy (343)

night terrors (343)
nonconscious process (325)
non-REM (NREM) sleep (335)
opiate (351)
physical dependence (355)
preconscious (327)
psychoactive drug (348)
psychological dependence (355)
REM rebound (336)
REM sleep (335)
sleep apnea (342)
sleep debt (337)
sleep paralysis (335)
stimulant (353)
unconscious (328)
tolerance (355)
withdrawal (355)

Lecture Assistant *for Chapter 8*
Tear this outline out and bring it with you to class in order to facilitate your note taking.
Spend more time listening to the lecture and less time writing!

Chapter Opening Problem: How can psychologists objectively examine the worlds of dreaming and other subjective mental states?

8.1 HOW IS CONSCIOUSNESS RELATED TO OTHER MENTAL PROCESSES?

- *Cognitive neuroscience =*

- *Nonconscious process =*

Core Concept 8.1 =

- *Consciousness =*

- *Attention =*

    o *Selective attention (the cocktail party phenomenon) =*

A) Tools for Studying Consciousness

1) Mental Rotation =

2) Zooming in with the Mind =

B) Models of the Conscious and Nonconscious Minds

1) Freud's Levels of Consciousness =

- *Preconscious =*

- *Unconscious =*

2) James's Stream of Consciousness =

3) The Modern Cognitive Perspective =

C) What Does Consciousness Do for Us?

Three especially important functions:

D) Coma and Related States

- *Coma =*

  - o *Minimally conscious state =*

  - o *Persistent vegetative state =*

E) Psychology Matters: Using Psychology to Learn Psychology

8.2 WHAT CYCLES OCCUR IN EVERYDAY CONSCIOUSNESS?

Core Concept 8.2 =

A) Daydreaming

- *Daydreaming =*

1) Why Do We Daydream? =

2) Is Daydreaming Helpful or Harmful? =

B) Sleep: The Mysterious Third of Our Lives

1) <u>Circadian Rhythms</u> =

- *Circadian rhythm* =

    o *Jet lag* =

2) <u>The Main Events of Sleep</u> =

- *REM sleep* =

    o *Sleep paralysis* =

- *Non-REM (NREM) sleep* =

3) <u>The Sleep Cycle</u> =

    Stage 1 =

    Stage 2 =

    Stage 3 =

    Stage 4 =

- *REM rebound* =

4) <u>Why Do We Sleep?</u>

5) <u>The Need for Sleep</u> =

6) <u>Sleep Debt Wreaks Havoc</u> =

- *Sleep debt* =

C) Dreaming: The Pageants of the Night

1) <u>Dreams as Meaningful Events</u> =

- *Manifest content* =

- *Latent content* =

2) <u>Dreams as Random Activity of the Brain</u> =

- *Activation-synthesis theory* =

3) <u>Dreams as a Source of Creative Insights</u> =

D) Psychology Matters: Sleep Disorders =

- *Insomnia* =

- *Sleep apnea* =

  - *Sudden Infant Death Syndrome (SIDS)* =

- *Night terrors* =

- *Narcolepsy* =

8.3 WHAT OTHER FORMS CAN CONSCIOUSNESS TAKE?

Core Concept 8.3 =

A) Hypnosis

- *Hypnosis* =

1) <u>Hypnotizability</u> =

2) <u>Is Hypnosis a Distinct State of Consciousness?</u> =

      o   *"Hidden observer"* =

3) <u>Practical Uses of Hypnosis</u> =

      o   *Posthypnotic amnesia* =

B) Meditation

- *Meditation* =

C) Psychoactive Drug States =

- *Psychoactive drug* =

1) <u>Trends in Drug Use</u> =

2) <u>Hallucinogens</u> =

- *Hallucinogen* =

      o   *Mescaline* =

      o   *Psilocybin* =

      o   *LSD (acid)* =

      o   *PCP* =

      o   *Cannabis and THC* =

      o   *Endocannabinoids* =

2) <u>Opiates</u> =

- *Opiate* =

  - *Morphine* =

  - *Heroin* =

  - *Codeine* =

    - *Endorphins* =

  - *Methadone* =

3) <u>Depressants and Antianxiety Drugs</u> =

- *Depressant* =

  - *Barbiturates* =

  - *Benzodiazepines* =

  - *Alcohol* =

4) <u>Stimulants</u> =

- *Stimulant* =

  - *Cocaine and crack* =

  - *Methamphetamine* =

  - *MDMA (Ecstasy)* =

  - *Caffeine* =

  - *Nicotine* =

5) The Altered States of Anesthesia =

- *General anesthetic* =

D) Psychology Matters: Dependence and Addiction =

- *Tolerance* =

- *Physical dependence* =

- *Addiction* =

- *Withdrawal* =

- *Psychological dependence* =

E) Critical Thinking Applied: The Unconscious—Reconsidered =

- ○ *Repress* =

How is Consciousness Related to Other Mental Processes?

1. *Underline the word(s) in parentheses that will make each statement correct. (Both options may be correct!)*

    A. (Structuralists/Behaviorists) used introspection to understand consciousness.

    B. (William Wundt/John Watson) believed that mental processes are little more than by-products of our actions.

    C. (Behavioral/Cognitive) neuroscience is the interdisciplinary field that makes connections between mental processes and the brain.

    D. Conscious processing occurs (serially/in parallel).

    E. (Conscious/Nonconscious) processes can work on many tasks simultaneously.

2. *Fill in the blanks with the correct terms.*

    _____ is the brain process that creates our mental representation of the world and our current thoughts. One process linked with consciousness is _____, which makes one item stand out from the others. For instance, when you are able to follow one conversation while there are many other conversations going on at the same time, you are experiencing _____, also called _____. Everything entering consciousness passes through _____. Some psychologists believe that _____ is the seat of consciousness.

Tools for Studying Consciousness

3. What did the mental rotation tasks and "zooming in" tasks demonstrate?

Models of the Conscious and Nonconscious Minds

4. William James, Sigmund Freud, and modern cognitive psychologists all use different metaphors for consciousness. What are these metaphors, and what do they mean?

5. *Indicate whether each statement is True (T) or False (F) by circling the appropriate letter after the statement.*

    A. Freud believed that unconscious processing can influence our conscious thoughts. T F

    B. The preconscious is essentially the same as working memory. T F

    C. Preconscious processing is parallel processing. T F

    D. The preconscious can engage in deliberate thinking. T F

    E. Freud used the terms "preconscious" and "unconscious" interchangeably because they essentially mean the same thing. T F

What Does Consciousness Do for Us?

6. Describe three important functions of consciousness.

    A. _____

    B. _____

    C. _____

7. *Indicate whether each statement is True (T) or False (F) by circling the appropriate letter after the statement.*

    A. Comas are generally stable, long-term states of unconsciousness. T F

    B. When people wake up from a coma, it is usually sudden and relatively quick. T F

    C. In a comatose state, individuals do not have normal sleep/wake cycles. T F

8. Explain the differences between a "minimally conscious state" and a "persistent vegetative state."

9. To find out more about comas, visit the following Merck Manual site:
    http://www.merckmanuals.com/home/print/sec06/ch079/ch079a.html

Psychology Matters: Using Psychology to Learn Psychology

10. What are the three main strategies suggested by your text authors for studying in such a way as to keep information readily accessible in your preconscious long-term memory?

What Cycles Occur in Everyday Consciousness?

Daydreaming

11. *Underline the word(s) in parentheses that will make each statement correct. (Both options may be correct!)*

   A. Most people daydream (every day/once a week).

   B. On average, about (15/30) percent of our waking hours is spent daydreaming.

   C. The incidence and intensity of daydreaming (increase/decline) as we age.

   D. Daydreaming can (enhance/interfere with) memories of recently learned material.

   E. Daydreaming can help us (be creative/solve problems)

12. In what ways does daydreaming differ from night dreaming?

Sleep: The Mysterious Third of Our Lives

13. *Match each term with its best description(s) by placing the letter corresponding to the term in the space next to its description. (Terms may be used more than once.)*

TERMS
A. Circadian rhythms	E. NREM sleep	I. REM rebound
B. REM sleep	F. Stage 2 sleep	J. Sleep debt
C. Stage 1 sleep	G. Stage 3 sleep	
D. Sleep paralysis	H. Stage 4 sleep	

DESCRIPTIONS
   _____ Characterized by the lack of rapid eye movement
   _____ When sleep talking and sleep walking most often occur
   _____ Indicates that there is a biological need for this kind of sleep
   _____ Bodily patterns that repeat approximately every twenty-four hours
   _____ Occurs during REM sleep
   _____ Associated with weight gain and a shortened life span
   _____ During the first sleep cycle, this usually only lasts ten minutes
   _____ The hypothalamus controls this bodily process
   _____ Sleep spindles show up on the EEG during this period
   _____ Most vivid dreaming occurs during this period
   _____ The stage that generally occurs after Stage 4 in the sleep cycle
   _____ EEGs show theta and beta waves during this period
   _____ The cause of jet lag and "Monday morning blues"

14. According to the text, what are the three most important features of normal sleep?

        A. _____

        B. _____

        C. _____

15. What is "REM rebound"? What does it indicate?

16. Give four different explanations for why we sleep.

        A. _____

        B. _____

        C. _____

        D. _____

17. *Underline the word(s) in parentheses that will make each statement correct. (Both options may be correct!)*

    A. Those who sleep (shorter/longer) than average tend to be more nervous, artistic, creative, and nonconforming.

    B. Strenuous activity during the day (decreases/increases) the amount of (REM/Stage 4) sleep.

    C. Newborns sleep about (13/16) hours per day, with half of that time devoted to (REM/Stage 4) sleep.

    D. Teens need more than (eight/nine) hours of sleep, but generally get about (five and a half /seven and a half).

    E. By old age, about (15/30) percent of sleep is REM sleep.

    F. A (gain/loss) of hours in your circadian rhythm creates greater jet lag than a (gain/loss) of hours.

    G. The normal response to boredom is (sleepiness/restlessness).

    H. Sleep debt is associated with (weight gain/shortened lifespan).

    I. After twenty-four hours of sleep loss, volunteers in an experiment performed (the same as/only slightly better than) volunteers who were legally intoxicated.

Dreaming: The Pageants of the Night

18. *Match each culture with its view of dreaming by placing the letter corresponding to the view of dreaming in the space next to its culture.*

_____ ancient Israelites	A. Extension of waking reality
_____ ancient Egyptians	B. Religious significance from Vedas
_____ people of ancient India	C. Messages from God
_____ ancient Chinese	D. Soul wanders outside the body
_____ Cherokee Indians	E. Temples were dedicated to god of dreaming
_____ some African cultures	

19. According to Freud, what are the two purposes of dreaming? What did Freud believe are the two components of dreams—and how are they related? What scientific evidence supports Freud's theory?

20. How does culture relate to the kinds of dreams a person has?

21. *Indicate whether each statement is True (T) or False (F) by circling the appropriate letter after the statement.*

A. Research shows that the brain replenishes neurotransmitters during REM sleep.　　T F

B. Women are more likely than men to dream about children.　　T F

C. When you try very hard not to dream about something, it is much less likely to appear in your dreams.　　T F

D. Typically, the first dream of the night connects with events that occurred during the previous day.　　T F

E. Memories for facts and locations appear to be consolidated in REM sleep.　　T F

22. According to nineteenth-century physiologist Herman von Helmholtz's belief, what three things are necessary for creative dreaming?

A. _____　　B. _____

C. _____

23. NEED A BREAK?
To better understand states of consciousness, visit MyPsychLab.

24. *Fill in the blanks with the correct information about dreaming.*

The _____ theory says dreams result when the _____ brain tries to makes sense of its own activity. In this theory, dreams originate from neural discharges coming from the _____. Energy sweeps over the _____, and the sleeper experiences many sensations. The activity is _____, and the images may not be logically connected. The dream, thus, can be the brain's way of _____ out of _____.

Psychology Matters: Sleep Disorders

25. *Match each term with its best description(s) by placing the letter corresponding to the term in the space next to its description. (Terms may be used more than once.)*

TERMS
   A. Insomnia   B. Sleep apnea   C. Narcolepsy   D. Night terrors

DESCRIPTIONS
_____ Involves the cessation of breathing many times during sleep
_____ Treatments can cut short REM sleep periods
_____ Very successfully treated by cognitive behavioral therapy
_____ REM sleep disorder
_____ Occurs in Stage 4 sleep; the sleeper is difficult to awaken
_____ Genetics and low hypocretin levels are possible causes
_____ A possible cause of Sudden Infant Death Syndrome (SIDS)
_____ Triggered by excitement
_____ The most common sleep disorder
_____ Can damage brain cells and put stress on blood vessels and heart
_____ Occasional episodes are likely to occur in premature babies
_____ May be preceded by cataplexy
_____ Usually disappears by adulthood
_____ Suddenly falling asleep without warning

26. Read all about sleep at The Sleep Foundation homepage. Explore the site at:
http://www.sleepfoundation.org

What Other Forms Can Consciousness Take?

Hypnosis

27. Most authorities would say that hypnosis involves three characteristics. What are the three?

   A. _____   B. _____   C. _____

28. *Indicate whether each statement is True (T) or False (F) by circling the appropriate letter after the statement.*

    A. Research has shown a unique EEG signature for hypnosis.   T F

    B. "Hypnotizability" refers to a person's ability to go into a trance.   T F

    C. Approximately 10 to 15 percent of adults are highly hypnotizable.   T F

29. Your textbook authors discuss five different theories concerning what hypnosis is. Briefly describe those five competing perspectives.

A. _____

B. _____

C. _____

D. _____

E. _____

30. Explain three main practical uses of hypnosis.

    A. _____

    B. _____

    C. _____

31. *Skeptic* magazine examines the topic of hypnosis using a scientific, skeptical perspective. Visit the following website for a comprehensive summary of the topic:
                 http://skepdic.com/hypnosis.html

Meditation

32. *Complete the following paragraph with the correct information.*

Meditation begins by _____ on a _____ behavior, assuming body positions, and minimizing _____. The Western view is that meditation is _____ state of consciousness. In the Buddhist view, meditation more accurately _____. Experienced meditators show changes in their brain-wave patterns, particularly in the _____ lobes. A first-of-its-kind MRI study showed _____ size of meditators' hippocampus and decreased density of their _____. However, some research does not show meditation to be superior to other _____ techniques.

Psychoactive Drug States

33. Describe some of the general, physical effects of psychoactive drugs.

34. *Fill in the blanks of the following concept map with the correct information.*

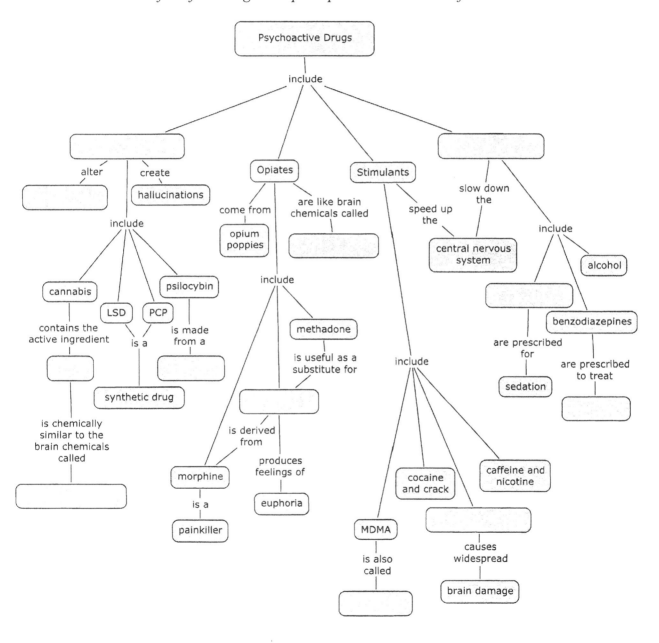

35. *Underline the word(s) in parentheses that will make each statement correct. (Both options may be correct!)*

   A. Cannabis impairs (memory/motor coordination) and its effects last (a shorter time/longer) than the effects of alcohol do.

   B. Cannabis has a medical use for the treatment of nausea associated with (glaucoma/chemotherapy).

   C. THC causes the release of (endorphins/dopamine) and there are THC receptors in (many/a select few) parts of the brain.

   D. Opiates are used medically as (pain relievers/cough suppressants) and in managing severe cases of (nausea/diarrhea).

   E. Barbiturates are commonly used in (sleeping pills/anti-anxiety drugs).

   F. In the absence of pain, (opiates/stimulants) give the user a strong rush of pleasurable sensations, and there (are/are not) major changes in cognitive abilities.

   G. An opiate-based drug that has recently appeared on the market is (OxyContin/Vicodin).

   H. (Barbiturates/Benzodiazepines) are safer than (barbiturates/benzodiazepines).

   I. Methadone (has/doesn't have) the same addictive effects as heroin, and its levels in the brain increase more (slowly/rapidly) than do the levels of heroin.

   J. Sleeping pills (increase/decrease) REM-sleep time.

   K. A leading cause of mental retardation in the U.S. is (opiate/alcohol) use by expectant mothers.

   L. The negative impact of (alcohol/smoking) on health is greater than that of all other psychoactive drugs combined.

   M. (MDMA/Methamphetamine) produces elevated temperature, increased blood pressure and heart rate, and dehydration.

   N. Use of (methamphetamine/cocaine) can lead to physical damage in the brain.

36. What four sleep-like components do general anesthetics produce in individuals?

   A. _____   C. _____
   B. _____   D. _____

Psychology Matters: Dependence and Addiction

37. *Fill in the blanks with the correct information.*

The reduced effectiveness of a drug with repeated use is called _____.
The body's adjustment to and need for the drug is called _____,
and when the drug is no longer present, the person will suffer unpleasant symptoms of
_____. When a person continues to use a drug, even in the face of
negative effects on his or her health or life, this is referred to as _____.
Craving a drug without having a physical dependence on it is called

_____.

38. *Indicate whether each statement is True (T) or False (F) by circling the appropriate letter.*

A. Addiction is a biological response, rather than a learned response.   T F

B. The general public tends to view addiction as a disease.   T F

C. Heroin addicts can tolerate larger doses when they shoot up in their typical
environment than when they shoot up in a new location.   T F

39. Explain the pros and cons of viewing drug addiction as a disease. Use the research
concerning treatment for heroin and alcohol addictions to illustrate some of your points.

PROS	CONS

40. The National Institute of Drug Abuse is a U.S. government-sponsored website with a lot of
excellent information on all psychoactive substances, legal and not legal. Visit:
http://www.nida.nih.gov/nidahome.html

Critical Thinking Applied: The Unconscious—Reconsidered

41. According to the textbook authors, how do the logical fallacies of (a) the confirmation bias,
(b) "begging the question," and (c) circular reasoning play a role in Freud's theory of the
unconscious?

PRACTICE TEST #1

1. The study of consciousness in modern psychology had its roots in _____.
   A. humanism   B. behaviorism   C. structuralism   D. functionalism

2. Benzodiazepines such as Valium and Xanax fall into this class of medications.
   A. Opiates   B. Stimulants   C. Depressants   D. Hallucinogens

3. Janelle is in the middle of REM sleep. Research shows that she _____.
   A. may engage in sleep walking   C. will show sleep spindles on her EEG
   B. will show delta waves on her EEG   D. will likely report a vivid dream if awakened

4. _____ would say that consciousness is a by-product of our actions.
   A. Freud   B. Watson   C. Rogers   D. Crick

5 Freud compared consciousness to a(n) _____.
   A. iceberg tip   C. carousel ride
   B. floating feeling   D. flowing stream

6. All of the following are functions of consciousness EXCEPT _____.
   A. it restricts our attention   C. it provides a mental meeting place
   B. it allows us to sleep easily   D. it allows creation of a mental model

7. All of the following are opiates EXCEPT _____.
   A. morphine   B. codeine   C. cocaine   D. heroin

8. We "lose" approximately _____ of our lives to sleep.
   A. one-fourth   B. one-fifth   C. one-third   D. one-half

9. The locus of circadian rhythms resides in the _____.
   A. thalamus   B. hippocampus   C. medulla   D. hypothalamus

10. All of the following are key features of the activation-synthesis model of dreaming EXCEPT
    _____.
    A. dreams are caused by random bursts of activity in brain-stem structures
    B. the cerebral cortex constructs coherent stories from spontaneous brain stem discharge
    C. dreams are biologically based
    D. dream images produced in the brain stem are laden with significance related to the
       dreamer's waking life

PRACTICE TEST #2

1. Sleeping pills reduce _____ sleep.
   A. Stage 2 B. Stage 3   C. Stage 4   D. REM

2. Sleep spindles are associated with what stage of sleep?
   A. Stage 1 B. Stage 2   C. Stage 3   D. Stage 4

3. Conscious processing occurs _____ and nonconscious processing occurs _____.
   A. serially; in parallel   C. in the cortex; in the medulla
   B. in parallel; serially   D. in the medulla; in the cortex

4. The reduced effectiveness with repeated use of a drug is called _____.
   A. withdrawal   C. addiction
   B. psychological dependence D. tolerance

5. Individuals describe mental activity during REM sleep as _____, while describing NREM
   sleep as _____.
   A. vivid; ordinary   C. dull; exciting
   B. ordinary; vivid   D. exciting; vivid

6. Evolutionary psychology suggests that the purpose of sleep is to _____.
   A. refresh brain cells   C. fill up the time
   B. stay out of harm's way   D. digest dinner

7. The deepest point in the sleep cycle occurs in _____.
   A. Stage 1 B. Stage 2   C. REM sleep   D. Stage 4

8. Sleep debt can make people behave _____.
   A. as though they are intoxicated C. very slowly because they are tired
   B. as normal if it is not a habit   D. a bit irrationally, but generally fine

9. The ancient Chinese were reluctant to awaken a sleeper hastily because they believed _____.
   A. the person might have a heart attack
   B. it would disturb a good dream
   C. the soul wanders outside of the body
   D. it would disrupt a sound sleep

10. All of the following are features that can be applied to states of consciousness EXCEPT
    _____.
    A. restriction   C. combination
    B. perception   D. manipulation

PRACTICE TEST #3

1. Which of the following is an opiate?
   A. Cocaine   B. Heroin   C. Valium   D. PCP

2. Recent research shows that daydreaming may interfere with _____.
   A. solving problems   C. memories of material learned long ago
   B. developing creative insight   D. being happy

3. The negative impact on health and life of _____ is greater than that of all other psychoactive drugs combined.
   A. alcohol   B. smoking   C. opiates   D. stimulants

4. A sleep cycle generally lasts about _____ minutes.
   A. 30   B. 60   C. 90   D. 120

5. Some psychologists have suggested that the seat of consciousness is _____.
   A. meditation   C. hypnosis
   B. working memory   D. long-term memory

6. _____ is a sleep disorder that is characterized by loud snoring and periods of cessation of breathing, resulting in the sleeper awaking and gasping for breath.
   A. Sleep apnea   C. Insomnia
   B. Narcolepsy   D. Cataplexy

7. The internal "biological clock" that controls the pattern of human physiological processes appears to be _____.
   A. set on a twenty-four-hour cycle   C. coordinated by cells in the thalamus
   B. identical in all humans   D. unaffected by natural cycles of light and dark

8. Psychoanalysts scrutinize the _____ content of dreams for clues about the _____ content.
   A. latent; manifest   C. manifest; latent
   B. conscious; preconscious   D. preconscious; conscious

9. The reason you are able to walk, chew gum, and breathe simultaneously is due to _____.
   A. preconscious processes   C. nonconscious processes
   B. conscious processes   D. working memory

10. Dr. Jones flew from New York City to Honolulu for the APA conference. She had trouble sleeping after she arrived. This was most likely caused by _____.
   A. a disruption in her circadian rhythms   C. a change in alpha wave patterns
   B. excitement about being in Hawaii   D. disruptions in REM sleep

COMPREHENSIVE REVIEW TEST

1. Who likened ordinary waking consciousness to a flowing stream that carries ever-changing sensations, perceptions, thoughts, memories, feelings, motives, and desires?
   A. John Watson   B. Sigmund Freud   C. William James   D. Francis Crick

2. Hilgard believed that hypnosis worked as a(n) _____.
   A. altered state   B. dissociated state   C. hallucination   D. conscious awareness

3. Which of the following is likely to occur occasionally in premature babies?
   A. Sleep apnea   B. Narcolepsy   C. Insomnia   D. Night terrors

4. _____ is a sleep disorder that is characterized by sudden REM sleep attacks and loss of muscle control.
   A. Sleep apnea   B. Narcolepsy   C. Insomnia   D. Epilepsy

5. Alcohol is most accurately classified as a _____.
   A. depressant   B. hallucinogen   C. stimulant   D. non-addictive drug

6. Studies have found meditation to be associated with all of the following EXCEPT _____.
   A. increased density of the amygdala   C. a decrease in stress hormones
   B. a reduction in anxiety   D. increased size of the hippocampus

7. Sleep paralysis occurs during _____ sleep.
   A. Stage 4   B. Stage 3   C. Stage 2   D. REM

8. Joey is in his deepest stage of sleep about half an hour after sleep onset. An EEG of his brain waves would most likely indicate _____ waves.
   A. delta   B. theta   C. beta   D. alpha

9. Which of the following is associated with weight gain and a shortened life span?
   A. Jet lag   B. REM rebound   C. Narcolepsy   D. Sleep debt

10. Most experts would define hypnosis as a state of awareness characterized by all of the following EXCEPT _____.
    A. deep relaxation   C. focused attention
    B. a unique EEG signature   D. heightened suggestibility

11. Which of the following drugs has been shown to cause widespread brain damage?
    A. Cocaine   B. Heroin   C. Cannabis   D. Methamphetamine

12. All of the following are medical uses for opiates EXCEPT _____.
    A. relieving pain
    B. reducing diarrhea
    C. reducing intraocular pressure
    D. suppressing coughs

13. What is the most common sleep disorder?
    A. Insomnia   B. Sleep apnea   C. Narcolepsy   D. Night terrors

14. Endocannabinoids are chemically similar to which drug?
    A. PCP   B. MDMA   C. THC   D. LSD

15. The preconscious is essentially the same as _____.
    A. long-term memory
    B. working memory
    C. the unconscious
    D. sensory memory

CRITICAL THINKING ESSAYS

1. Students often forego sleep because of multiple responsibilities—or just because there is something more "fun" to do. Using what you have learned in this chapter, make an argument for getting a good night's sleep. Use correct terminology.

2. In what ways are meditation and hypnosis similar?

CHAPTER 9
Motivation and Emotion

Make flashcards using the following terms or, even better, develop mnemonics (memory strategies) to help you remember the different concepts and terms. Use the definitions in the margins of this chapter for help. Numbers refer to page numbers in the textbook.

anorexia nervosa (378)
biological drive (370)
bulimia nervosa (378)
Cannon-Bard theory (398)
collectivism (367)
developmental level of analysis (373)
display rules (390)
drive theory (370)
emotion (388)
emotional intelligence (400)
extrinsic motivation (365)
false positive (406)
fixed-action patterns (369)
flow (368)
functional level of analysis (373)
hierarchy of needs (372)
homeostasis (370)
individualism (367)

instinct theory (369)
intrinsic motivation (365)
inverted U function (396)
James-Lange theory (398)
lateralization of emotion (394)
motivation (365)
need (370)
need for achievement (n Ach) (365)
overjustification (367)
polygraph (406)
proximal level of analysis (373)
sensation seekers (397)
set point (377)
sexual orientation (385)
sexual response cycle (382)
two-factor theory (399)

Lecture Assistant *for Chapter 9*

Tear this outline out and bring it with you to class in order to facilitate your note taking.
Spend more time listening to the lecture and less time writing!

Chapter Opening Problem: Motivation is largely an internal and subjective process. How can we determine what motivates people like Lance Armstrong to work so hard at becoming the best in the world at what they do?

9.1 WHAT MOTIVATES US?

Core Concept 9.1 =

- *Motivation* =

A) Why People Work: McClelland's Theory =

- *Extrinsic motivation* =

- *Intrinsic motivation* =

- *Need for achievement (n Ach)* =

1) <u>I/O Psychology: Putting Achievement Motivation in Perspective</u> =

2) <u>A Cross-Cultural View of Achievement</u> =
- *Individualism* =

- *Collectivism* =

B) The Unexpected Effects of Rewards on Motivation:

1) <u>Overjustification</u> =
- *Overjustification* =

2) <u>When Do Rewards Work?</u> =

C) Psychology Matters: Using Psychology to Learn Psychology =

- *Flow =*

9.2 HOW ARE OUR MOTIVATIONAL PRIORITIES DETERMINED?

Core Concept 9.2 =

A) Instinct Theory:

- *Instinct theory =*

- *Fixed-action patterns =*

B) Drive Theory:

- *Biological drive =*

- *Drive theory =*

- *Need =*

- *Homeostasis =*

C) Freud's Psychodynamic Theory:

  o *Id =*

  o *Eros =*

  o *Thanatos =*

D) Maslow's Hierarchy of Needs:

- *Hierarchy of needs =*

E) Putting It All Together—A New Hierarchy of Needs:

- *Functional level of analysis =*

- *Proximal level of analysis =*

- *Developmental level of analysis =*

F) Psychology Matters: Determining What Motivates Others =

9.3 WHERE DO HUNGER AND SEX FIT INTO THE MOTIVATIONAL HIERARCHY?

| Core Concept 9.3 | =

A) Hunger: A Homeostatic Drive *and* a Psychological Motive =

1) The Multiple-Systems Approach to Hunger =

- *Set point =*

2) Eating Disorders =

- *Anorexia nervosa =*

- *Bulimia nervosa =*

3) Obesity and Weight Control =

4) The Problem of Will Power and Chocolate Cookies =

- o *Self-control (impulse control) =*

B) Sexual Motivation: An Urge You Can Live Without =

1) The Scientific Study of Sexuality =

- *Sexual response cycle (4 phases) by Masters and Johnson =*
  - a)_____
  - b)_____
  - c)_____
  - d)_____

2) An Evolutionary Perspective on Sexuality =

C) **Psychology Matters: The What and Why of Sexual Orientation** =

- *Sexual orientation* =

1) Origins of Sexual Orientation =

2) Not a Disorder =

9.4 HOW DO OUR EMOTIONS MOTIVATE US?

Core Concept 9.4 =

A) **What Emotions Are Made Of:**

- *Emotion* =

- Four Main Components =

   a)_____

   b)_____

   c)_____

   d)_____

   o *Somatic marker* =

B) **What Emotions Do for Us:**

C) **Counting the Emotions:**

   o *Basic emotions* =

D) **Cultural Universals in Emotional Expression** =

- *Display rules* =

E) Psychology Matters: Gender Differences in Emotion Depend on Biology *and* Culture =

9.5 WHAT PROCESSES CONTROL OUR EMOTIONS?

Core Concept 9.5 =

A) The Neuroscience of Emotion:

1) Emotions in the Unconscious =

- o   *Fast response system =*

- o   *Implicit memory =*

2) Conscious Emotional Processing =

- o   *Explicit memory =*

3) The Cerebral Cortex's Role in Emotion =

- • *Lateralization of emotion =*

4) Emotions Where the Cortex Meets the Limbic System =

- o   *Ventromedial prefrontal cortex (VMPFC) =*

5) The Autonomic Nervous System's Role in Emotion =

6) Emotional Chemistry =

B) Arousal, Performance, and the Inverted U:

- • *Inverted U function =*

- • *Sensation seekers =*

C) Theories of Emotion: Resolving Some Old Issues

1) Do Our Feelings Come from Physical Responses? =

- • *James-Lange theory =*

2) <u>Do Our Feelings Come from Cognitions?</u> =

- *Cannon-Bard theory* =

3) <u>When the Situation Gets Complicated: The Two-Factor Theory</u> =

- *Schachter's two-factor theory* =

D) How Much Conscious Control Do We Have Over Our Emotions?

1) <u>Developing Emotional Intelligence</u> =

- *Emotional intelligence* =

    Four Components of Emotional Intelligence:

    a)_____ c)_____
    b)_____ d)_____

    a) <u>The Predictive Power of Emotional Intelligence</u> =

        o *The "marshmallow test"* =

    b) <u>The Nature and Nurture of Emotional Intelligence</u> =

2) <u>Let It Out: A Dangerous Myth</u> =

E) Psychology Matters: Detecting Deception =

F) Critical Thinking Applied: Do Lie Detectors Really Detect Lies? =

- *Polygraph* =

- *False positive* =

What Motivates Us?

1. Define "motivation."

Why People Work: McClelland's Theory

2. *Underline the word(s) in parentheses that will make each statement correct. (Both options may be correct!)*

   A. The desire to attain a difficult, but desired, goal is referred to as (TAT/*n Ach*).

   B. (External/Internal) motivation is the desire to engage in an activity for its own sake.

   C. The Thematic Apperception Test is used to measure (job burnout/need for achievement).

   D. I/O psychologists have found that higher job satisfaction is associated with (increased productivity/decreased absenteeism).

   E. In the U.S. and Canada, (collectivism/individualism) is emphasized; in Western European countries, (collectivism/individualism) is emphasized.

   F. (Collectivist/Individualist) cultures value group honor and loyalty, whereas (collectivist/individualist) cultures value personal achievement and distinction.

   G. People high in *n Ach* are more likely than those with low *n Ach* to (work hard/have high IQ scores).

3. What three types of needs do individuals have at work?

   A. _____ B. _____ C. _____

The Unexpected Effects of Rewards on Motivation

4. Define the term "overjustification." Under what conditions does it occur?

5. What are the three different ways that rewards can affect motivation?

   A. _____

   B. _____

   C. _____

Psychology Matters: Using Psychology to Learn Psychology

6. What does Czikszentmihali call the state of mind people possess when totally absorbed in an activity and thus unaware of the passage of time or of events occurring around them?

Answer: _____

How Are Our Motivational Priorities Determined?

7. *Fill in the blanks with the correct information.*

_____ theory is the idea that organisms are born with a set of biologically based behaviors that promote survival. Researchers prefer the term "_____" to "instincts." According to _____ theory, a _____ produces a state of energy or tension, called a _____. The organism is then motivated to reduce that _____ to return to a balanced condition known as _____. However, this theory does not explain the fact that organisms are sometimes motivated to _____ stimulation: for example, by bungee jumping.

8. *Match each term with its best description(s) by placing the letter corresponding to the term in the space next to its description. (Terms may be used more than once.)*

TERMS
A. Need   B. Biological Drive   C. Intrinsic motivation   D. Extrinsic motivation

DESCRIPTIONS
_____ You enjoy the challenge of doing Sudoku puzzles.
_____ A biological imbalance that threatens survival
_____ You are thirsty.
_____ You mountain bike because you find it to be a lot of fun.
_____ You study hard because you want an A in the class to increase your GPA.
_____ A bird builds a nest and begins to perform a display routine to attract a mate.
_____ You volunteer at the children's center because you like all the attention you get.

9. List and briefly describe each of the five steps in Maslow's hierarchy of needs.

A.   _____

B.   _____

C.   _____

D.   _____

E.   _____

10. What need, beyond self-actualization, did Maslow later add to his theory? Describe it.

11. *Fill in the blanks of this concept map with the correct information.*

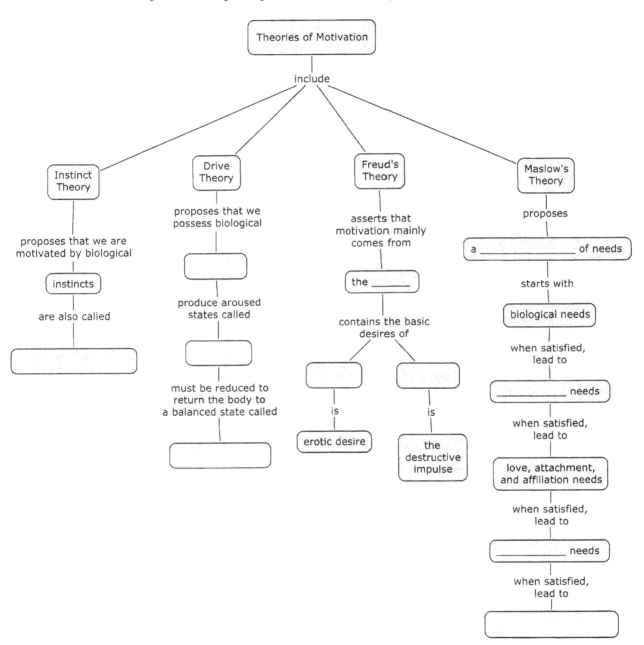

12. This site by Dr. C. George Boeree gives a thorough description of Maslow's theory:
http://webspace.ship.edu/cgboer/maslow.html

13. List at least one criticism of each theory of motivation.

   A. Instinct_____

   B. Drive_____

   C. Maslow's _____

14. *Fill in the blank next to each definition with the correct level of analysis.*

   A. _____ Stimuli in the organism's immediate environment that can change its motivational priorities

   B. _____ Changes related to an organism's age-related progression that might affect its motivational priorities

   C. _____ Concerns the adaptive purpose of a motive in terms of the organism's survival and reproductive success

15. *Indicate whether each statement is True (T) or False (F) by circling the appropriate letter after the statement.*

   A. The hierarchy of needs proposed by evolutionary psychologists has mating and parenting at the pinnacle of the hierarchy.　　　T F

   B. Evolutionary psychologists believe that creativity is not a separate motive, but instead is actually the expression of reproductive motives.　　　T F

   C. According to the text, most psychologists would likely agree that our motives have a "default" hierarchy that is essentially the same for everyone.　　　T F

   D. According to the text, most psychologists would likely agree that a person's motivational hierarchy is very rarely influenced by proximal stimuli.　　　T F

Psychology Matters: Determining What Motivates Others

16. What did Alfred Adler mean by the term "social interest"?

Where Do Hunger and Sex Fit into the Motivational Hierarchy?

Hunger: A Homeostatic Drive *and* a Psychological Motive

17. Describe the multiple-systems approach to hunger.

18. This site of the U.S. Surgeon General provides many links to informational pages including information on how to calculate your BMI and the negative health consequences of obesity. http://www.surgeongeneral.gov/topics/obesity/

19. *Indicate whether each statement is True (T) or False (F) by circling the appropriate letter after the statement.*

    A. Brain research shows that the hypothalamus and brain stem have central roles in hunger.   T F

    B. The "set point" refers to the stomach's feeling of fullness or emptiness.   T F

    C. The hormone leptin signals when the set point has been reached.   T F

    D. The brain's reward system gives us preferences for sweet and low-fat food.   T F

    E. Studies show that extreme exercise suppresses hunger.   T F

    F. Both animals and humans tend to eat more when they feel threatened.   T F

    G. Anorexia nervosa has the highest death rate of any recognized mental disorder.   T F

    H. Bulimia nervosa is associated with depression.   T F

    I. Bulimia is characterized by periods of binge eating followed by purging.   T F

    J. Those with anorexia can suffer from osteoporosis and shrinkage of brain tissue.   T F

    K. Those with bulimia can damage their esophagus and teeth.   T F

    L. Approximately 20 percent of Americans are now classified as obese.   T F

    M. The best odds for most people trying to lose weight come from cognitive-behavioral therapies.   T F

20. The National Institute of Mental Health has a helpful website devoted to educating people about eating disorders. Visit: http://www.nimh.nih.gov/health/publications/eating-disorders/complete-index.shtml

The Problem of Will Power and Chocolate Cookies

21. *Indicate whether each statement is True (T) or False (F) by circling the appropriate letter after the statement.*

    A. Individuals who resisted temptation were more likely than a control group to be successful on a subsequent word problem or coordination task.   T F

B. Compared to a control group, people who were asked to engage in self-control had higher blood-sugar levels after the task.   T F

C. Researchers speculate that exerting "will power" depletes energy.   T F

D. Psychologists tend to prefer the term "will power" over the term "self-control."   T F

Sexual Motivation: An Urge You Can Live Without

22. List and describe Masters and Johnson's four stages of the human sexual response cycle.

A. _____

B. _____

C. _____

D. _____

23. *Underline the word(s) in parentheses that will make each statement correct. (Both options may be correct!)*

A. The first major scientific study of human sexuality was conducted by (Kinsey/Masters and Johnson) in the mid-twentieth century.

B. Kinsey and his colleagues collected data on human sexuality through the use of (interviews/observation).

C. The National Health and Social Life Survey conducted during the 1990s involved (interviews/observations) of thousands of American adults, with (52/79) percent of individuals recruited for the study agreeing to participate.

D. The research of Masters and Johnson focused on the (physiology/psychology) of sex.

E. (Kinsey/Masters and Johnson) found that men and women have very (different/similar) patterns of (biological/psychological) sexual response.

F. Research shows that many (men/women) can have multiple orgasms in a short time period.

G. Research demonstrates that (men/women) tend to respond more slowly but often remain aroused longer than (men/women) do.

H. According to the (social learning/evolutionary) perspective, the goal of both sexes is to have as many offspring as possible; however, the (mating strategies/gender roles) that have developed over time are different for males and females.

24. According to Peplau, what are four crucial differences between men and women in their sexual responses?

A. _____

B. _____

C. _____

D. _____

25. The following is the home site for the Kinsey Institute. You can explore what the Institute does and what they have learned by visiting:
http://www.kinseyinstitute.org/research/ak-data.html

Sex, Hunger, and the Hierarchy of Needs

26. In the evolution-based needs hierarchy, where do Kenrick et al. put the motive for sex?

Psychology Matters: The What and Why of Sexual Orientation

27. *Underline the word(s) in parentheses that will make each statement correct. (Both options may be correct!)*

A. The incidence of homosexuality among females is about (twice/half) that of males.

B. (Transsexualism/Transvestism) refers to a sexual fetish in which one cross-dresses.

C. (Transsexualism/Transvestism) is not predictive of homosexuality.

D. Research shows that family configurations and parenting styles (are/aren't) related to the sexual orientation a child develops.

E. Research indicates that the (more/fewer) older brothers a boy has, the more likely he will have a homosexual orientation.

F. Studies show that sexual orientation in adults (is/isn't) related to testosterone levels.

G. Up until the (1970s/1980s), the diagnostic manual of the American Psychiatric Association listed homosexuality as a mental disorder.

H. Homosexual behavior is quite common in animals, particularly in (gorillas/bonobos).

I. Research shows (differences/no differences) in the adjustment or development of children raised by heterosexual or homosexual parents.

J. Research on homosexuality is (experimental/correlational), so it can't assess causality.

28. NEED A BREAK?

To get a better understanding of motivation and emotion, visit MyPsychLab.

How Do Our Emotions Motivate Us?

29. According to Core Concept 9.4, what two main functions do emotions serve?

A. _____

B. _____

What Emotions Are Made Of

30. What are the four intersecting components of emotion?

A. _____

B. _____

C. _____

D. _____

31. What is a "somatic marker," and with what component of emotion is it associated?

32. How do mirror neurons relate to the components of emotion?

What Emotions Do for Us

33. Explain the differences between "approach" emotions and "avoidance" emotions.

Approach _____

Avoidance _____

34. How do emotions help us make decisions?

Counting the Emotions

35. *Circle the basic (primary) emotions identified by Ekman, underline the ones identified by Plutchik, and draw an X through the ones identified by Izard.*

Contempt	Awe	Contentment	Anger
Pride	Sadness	Fear	Ambivalence
Surprise	Remorse	Bliss	Happiness/Joy
Disgust	Acceptance	Anxiety	Anticipation

Cultural Universals in Emotional Expression

36. Give two pieces of research evidence for the biological underpinnings of basic emotions.

A. _____

B. _____

37. What are "display rules?" Give an example.

Psychology Matters: Gender Differences in Emotion Depend on Biology *and* Culture

38. *Complete the following paragraph about gender and emotions.*

_____ are permissible ways of showing emotion in a particular society, and they usually differ for males and females. However, in terms of overall emotional expressiveness, there is no _____ difference. _____ differ in emotional expression much more than do the genders. For example, in _____ and _____, men hide their feelings of sadness more often than women do, but in _____, _____, _____, and _____ the reverse is true. In _____ cultures, such as many Asian countries, both genders restrain their emotional expressions.

What Processes Control Our Emotions?

The Neuroscience of Emotion

39. *Indicate whether each statement is True (T) or False (F) by circling the appropriate letter after the statement.*

   A. The emotion system that operates mainly unconsciously is a slow response system.   T F

   B. The fast response emotion system is highly linked to implicit memory.   T F

   C. Explicit memory is linked mainly to the fast response emotion system.   T F

   D. The slow response emotion system can easily learn responses via classical conditioning.   T F

40. *Fill in the table below with information about the roles that specific nervous systems or brain components play in generating emotions.*

STRUCTURE	ROLES/FUNCTIONS
A. _____	The _____ division usually dominates in pleasant emotions. An emergency will activate the _____ division.
B. Cerebral Cortex	The small area of cortex where reason and emotion meet is the _____. This area of cortex has connections with both the _____ and the _____. The fact that the left and right hemispheres are associated with different emotions is referred to as the _____ of emotion. In general, the _____hemisphere specializes in negative emotions and the _____hemisphere specializes in positive emotions.
C. Endocrine System (Hormones)	The hormone _____ is abundant with feelings of anger, and _____ is the hormone produced in fear.
D. _____	The _____ plays an important role in fear. It includes "fight-or-flight" emotional responses.

Arousal, Performance, and the Inverted U

41. Explain the "inverted U function" concerning the relationship between arousal and performance. What other factors can affect it and in what ways?

Theories of Emotion: Resolving Some Old Issues

42. *Match each theory of emotion with its best description by placing the letter corresponding to the theory in the blank next to the description. (Theories may be used more than once.)*

THEORIES
A. James-Lange   B. Cannon-Bard   C. Two-factor (Schachter's)

DESCRIPTIONS
_____ emotional feeling and internal physiological responses occur simultaneously
_____ physical responses underlie our emotions
_____ emotion depends on an appraisal of both our internal physical state and the external
      situation
_____ "We feel sorry because we cry."

How Much Control Do We Have Over Our Emotions?

43. According to Salovy and Grewal, what are four components of emotional intelligence?

      A. _____

      B. _____

      C. _____

      D. _____

44. Describe Mischel's "marshmallow test." What does it predict?

45. *Fill in the blanks with the correct information.*

Goleman believes that emotional intelligence (EI) is not fixed by heredity, but instead it

can be _____. If EI training is added to the curriculum of schools, he

believes it will result in improved _____, increased

_____, and perhaps even gains in _____.

However, Lieberman and Rosenthal point out that emotional intelligence may just be another

name for _____, which does have a biological component.

46. Researchers John D. Mayer, Peter Salovey, and David R. Caruso have extensively researched emotional intelligence. Visit Dr. Mayer's website to find out about their model of emotional intelligence, how it differs from Goleman's, their measure, and other information. http://www.unh.edu/emotional_intelligence/

47. What are some of the public myths about anger? What does research show about them?

Psychology Matters: Detecting Deception

48. *Underline the word(s) in parentheses that will make each statement correct. (Both options may be correct!)*

   A. The (fewer/more) observations of a person's behavior, the more likely it is that you'll be able to detect deception.

   B. When someone is deceiving you by giving you false information, his or her deception may be detected through (constriction/dilation) of the pupils and (less/more) constrained gesturing.

   C. In terms of nonverbal communication, it is easier to control the (body/face) than the (body/face).

   D. Looking a person "straight in the eye" is a reasonably good indicator of truth-telling, but only when dealing with people who usually (lie/tell the truth).

   E. People are (more/less) accurate in telling liars from truth-tellers among people in their own culture.

Critical Thinking Applied: Do Lie Detectors Really Detect Lies?

49. Explain what a polygraph is.

50. Discuss at least four problems with using a polygraph to detect lying.

PRACTICE TEST #1

1. In terms of the lateralization of emotion, the right hemisphere specializes in _____ emotions.
   A. negative   B. positive   C. basic   D. secondary

2. All of the following are considered by researchers to be components of emotion EXCEPT
   _____.
   A. physiological arousal   C. behavioral expression
   B. cognitive interpretation   D. cultural labeling of the feelings

3. You are hiking in the mountains when you unexpectedly encounter a wild dog that bares its
   teeth at you. Immediately, your _____ kicks into gear.
   A. autonomic nervous system   C. emotion-focused system
   B. problem-focused system   D. parasympathetic nervous system

4. As a graduate student, you are collaborating with your professors to study the need for
   achievement. One of the measures you're using is the _____, in which participants are asked
   to tell stories in response to a series of ambiguous pictures.
   A. ROR   B. TAT   C. ACH   D. TOT

5. Smelling freshly baked cookies can suddenly make you feel hungry. Which level of analysis best
   relates to this example?
   A. Proximal   C. Motivational
   B. Developmental   D. Functional

6. "We feel sorry because we cry" represents the _____ theory.
   A. LeDoux   B. James-Lange   C. two-factor   D. Cannon-Bard

7. The hormone that is most closely associated with fear is _____.
   A. melatonin   B. noradrenaline   C. serotonin   D. epinephrine

8. In Maslow's hierarchy of needs, the _____ needs are just above the attachment needs.
   A. belonging   B. biological   C. esteem   D. self-actualization

9. Collectivist cultures value _____ achievement over _____ achievement.
   A. individual; group   C. extrinsic; intrinsic
   B. intrinsic; extrinsic   D. group; individual

10. After the danger has passed and you calm down, you know that your _____ nervous system
    was at work.
    A. somatic   B. sympathetic   C. central   D. parasympathetic

PRACTICE TEST #2

1. Which level of analysis relates specifically to the evolutionary purposes of motives?
   A. Proximal
   B. Developmental
   C. Motivational
   D. Functional

2. Dylan tends to do his best skateboarding in tournaments when he's excited, rather than overly excited or too calm. His experience can be explained best by _____.
   A. intrinsic motivation
   B. homeostasis
   C. flow
   D. the inverted U function

3. Which hormone is more abundant in anger?
   A. Dopamine   B. Epinephrine   C. Serotonin   D. Norepinephrine

4. You were outside playing basketball for three hours. You became really thirsty, and rushed inside to drink a quart of water. Your behavior can best be explained by _____ theory.
   A. instinct   B. drive   C. Freud's   D. locus of control

5. Freud believed that in the depths of the unconscious mind are two basic desires known as

   _____.
   A. eros and lanatos
   B. oros and thanatos
   C. eros and thanatos
   D. oros and lanatos

6. _____ are what govern the Japanese custom of controlling how they show their emotions.
   A. Emotional show rules
   B. Display rules
   C. Cultural exhibit rules
   D. Ekman rules

7. The lateralization of emotion refers to the finding that _____.
   A. most emotions are processed in the left hemisphere
   B. most emotions are processed in the right hemisphere
   C. the left hemisphere influences positive emotions, while the right influences negative ones
   D. the right hemisphere influences positive emotions, while the left influences negative ones

8. Freud's theory is the only major theory of motivation that takes a _____ approach.
   A. theoretical   B. psychological   C. developmental   D. comprehensive

9. Larry loved to wash the car until his parents paid him a dollar to do so, regardless of how well he cleaned the car. Now he doesn't enjoy doing the activity. This is most likely the result of

   _____.
   A. intrinsic motivation
   B. overjustification
   C. talent overload
   D. work overload

10. Goleman has argued that including training in emotional intelligence in the school curriculum can do all of the following EXCEPT _____.
    A. improve relationships   C. eliminate cliques
    B. improve academic achievement   D. increase self-respect

PRACTICE TEST #3

1. "We cry when we notice we feel sorry inside and are involved in a sad situation" represents the _____ theory.
   A. LeDoux   B. James-Lange   C. two-factor   D. Cannon-Bard

2. Sarah has always thought she was fat, even when she was only twelve years old. She starves herself in order to get as thin as she can. It is likely that Sarah has _____.
   A. starvation syndrome   C. bulimia nervosa
   B. anorexia nervosa   D. failure to thrive

3. The brain's reward system gives us preferences for _____ and _____ food.
   A. sweet; high-fat   C. sweet; low-fat
   B. salty; high-fat   D. salty; low-fat

4. Which of the following is the best example of a drive?
   A. Hunger   B. Anger   C. Money   D. The need for achievement

5. You admit that you like your job but that the main reason that you work is because you get paid every week. Your motivation is mostly _____.
   A. deferred   B. intrinsic   C. extrinsic   D. primary

6. Theodore enjoys crossword puzzles because they are challenging and fun. This demonstrates _____.
   A. intrinsic motivation   C. the two-factor theory
   B. flow   D. self-transcendence

7. Someone such as Ghandi or Mother Teresa would most likely reach the _____ level of Maslow's theory of motivation.
   A. safety needs   C. esteem needs
   B. attachment and affiliation needs   D. self-transcendence

8. Plutchik would explain your experience of "love" as _____.
   A. a blend of two primary emotions   C. an adaptive evolutionary response
   B. one of the ten basic emotions   D. one part of the love-hate pair

9. During the _____ phase of the sexual response cycle, the clitoris swells and the penis becomes erect.
   A. orgasm   C. excitement
   B. resolution   D. plateau

10. Freud believed that motivation mainly came from the _____.
    A. ego   B. superego   C. id   D. ego-ideal

COMPREHENSIVE REVIEW TEST

1. According to Salovy and Grewal, all of the following are components of emotional intelligence EXCEPT _____.
   A. perceiving emotions in others   C. using one's emotions for solving problems
   B. regulating one's own emotions   D. knowing that emotions can occur unconsciously

2. In terms of nonverbal communication, which part of the body is the easiest to control?
   A. Hands   B. Face   C. Legs   D. Arms

3. The Thematic Apperception Test is used to measure _____.
   A. intrinsic motivation   C. id and superego impulses
   B. need for achievement   D. flow

4. Dave is an artist and becomes completely consumed with his painting so that he is unaware of what's going on around him and loses track of time. Dave is most likely experiencing _____.
   A. a need for achievement   C. flow
   B. sensation seeking   D. self-actualization

5. According to Masters and Johnson, all of the following are phases of the sexual response cycle EXCEPT the _____ phase.
   A. plateau   B. orgasm   C. excitement   D. revolution

6. The term "fixed-action pattern" is another way of saying _____.
   A. drive   B. instinct   C. motive   D. need

7. In Maslow's theory, which need is most conceptually similar to Erikson's idea of generativity?
   A. Esteem   C. Self-actualization
   B. Self-transcendence   D. Attachment and affiliation

8. In the movie *Romancing the Stone*, two people share a harrowing adventure and misattribute the arousal of being in the situation for attraction to each other. This plot is an example of _____.
   A. the James-Lange theory   C. the two-factor theory
   B. the Incentive theory   D. the Ekman-Plutchik hypothesis

9. Which of the following statements is TRUE?
   A. The hormone leptin helps signal when the body's set point has been reached.
   B. It is generally best to vent your anger rather than keep it bottled up.
   C. Homosexual individuals have higher levels of testosterone than do heterosexual individuals.
   D. The emotional fast-response system operates mainly at a conscious level.

10. Bingeing and purging is characteristic of which eating disorder?
    A. Obesity   B. Bulimia   C. Nervosa   D. Anorexia

11. According to drive theory, the body's physiology needs to return to a state called _____.
    A. homeostasis   B. the set point C. flow D. motivated readiness

12. According to Peplau, all of the following are crucial differences between men and women EXCEPT
    _____.
    A. men, on average, show more interest in sex than women do
    B. sex is more often linked with aggression for men than for women
    C. women's sexuality has less plasticity than does men's sexuality
    D. women are more likely to view sex as part of an emotionally committed relationship

13. All of the following motivational patterns for work, based on people's needs, are ones that
    McClelland identified—EXCEPT the need for _____.
    A. affiliation   B. achievement C. power   D. autonomy

14. Mischel's "marshmallow test" with four-year-olds showed that _____.
    A. girls have more self-control than boys do
    B. children able to wait for two marshmallows became adolescents who did better in school
    C. children who chose to immediately have a marshmallow were good at deception
    D. most children became upset during the test and chose a marshmallow immediately

15. The James-Lange theory of emotion would say that if you see a bear in the woods and start
    running away in fear, _____.
    A. your fear happens because you are running away
    B. you are running away because of your fear
    C. your interpretation of the situation causes both your fear and your running away
    D. you are clearly not a sensation-seeking individual

CRITICAL THINKING ESSAYS

1. Keeping in mind what you have learned in this chapter about achievement motivation and incentives, propose one way in which incentives can be effectively used to increase motivation in the workplace and one way in which incentives could undermine motivation.

2. Discuss the use of the polygraph in court proceedings. Include research on its use and include both its strengths and its limitations.

CHAPTER 10
Personality: Theories of the Whole Person

Before You Read . . . Term Identification

Make flashcards using the following terms or, even better, develop mnemonics (memory strategies) to help you remember the different concepts and terms. Use the definitions in the margins of this chapter for help. Numbers refer to page numbers in the textbook.

archetype (436)
basic anxiety (438)
collective unconscious (436)
collectivism (418)
dispositional theory (421)
disposition (417)
eclectic (456)
ego (430)
ego defense mechanism (431)
Electra complex (431)
extraversion (437)
family systems theory (445)
five-factor theory (423)
fixation (431)
fundamental attribution error (449)
fully functioning person (440)
humanistic theories (428)
humors (420)
id (430)
identification (431)
implicit personality theory (447)
individualism (418)
introversion (437)
libido (429)
locus of control (443)
mindset (448)
MMPI-2 (424)
Myers-Briggs Type Indicator (MBTI) (426)
Neo-Freudian (436)

neurotic needs (438)
observational learning (442)
Oedipus complex (431)
personal unconscious (436)
personality (414)
personality process (417)
personality type (426)
person-situation controversy (454)
phenomenal field (440)
positive psychology (442)
projective test (432)
psychic determinism (434)
psychoanalysis (429)
psychoanalytic theory (429)
psychodynamic theory (428)
psychosexual stages (430)
reciprocal determinism (443)
redemptive self (448)
reliability (425)
repression (431)
Rorschach Inkblot Technique (433)
self-actualizing personality (440)
self-narrative (448)
social-cognitive theories (428)
superego (430)
Thematic Apperception Test (TAT) (433)
traits (422)
unconscious (429)
validity (425)

Lecture Assistant *for Chapter 10*

Tear this outline out and bring it with you to class in order to facilitate your note taking.
Spend more time listening to the lecture and less time writing!

- *Personality =*

Chapter Opening Problem: What influences were at work to produce the unique behavior patterns, high achievement motivation, and consistency over time and place that we see in the personality of Mary Calkins?

10.1 WHAT FORCES SHAPE OUR PERSONALITIES?

Core Concept 10.1 =

A) Biology, Human Nature, and Personality =

B) The Effects of Nurture: Personality and the Environment =

C) The Effects of Nature: Dispositions and Mental Processes:

- *Disposition =*

- *Personality process =*

D) Social and Cultural Contributions to Personality =

- *Individualism =*

- *Collectivism =*

E) Psychology Matters: Explaining Unusual People and Unusual Behavior =

10.2 WHAT PERSISTENT PATTERNS, OR DISPOSITIONS, MAKE UP OUR PERSONALITIES?

- *Humors =*

Core Concept 10.2 =

- *Dispositional theory =*

A) Personality and Temperament:

- o   *Temperament =*

1) <u>Temperament from Transmitters</u>?

2) <u>Tempered with a Bit of Learning</u>?

B) Personality as a Composite of Traits:

- *Traits =*

1) <u>The "Big Five" Traits: The Five-Factor Theory</u> =

- *Five-factor theory =*

- o   *Factor analysis =*

- o   *Bipolar dimensions =*

The Big Five Traits Are:

- o   *Openness to experience =*

- o   *Conscientiousness =*

- o   *Extraversion =*

- o   *Agreeableness =*

- o   *Neuroticism =*

2) <u>Assessing Traits with Personality Inventories</u> =

- o *NEO Personality Inventory (NEO-PI)* =

- • *Minnesota Multiphasic Personality Inventory (MMPI-2)* =

- • *Reliability* =

- • *Validity* =

3) <u>Evaluating the Temperament and Trait Theories</u> =

C) Psychology Matters: Finding Your Type =

- • *Personality type* =
- • *Myers-Briggs Type Indicator (MBTI)* =

1) <u>Uses of the MBTI</u> =

2) <u>What Does Research on the MBTI Tell Us about Personality Types</u>?

10.3 DO MENTAL PROCESSES HELP SHAPE OUR PERSONALITIES?

Core Concept 10.3 =

- • *Psychodynamic theory* =
- • *Humanistic theories* =
- • *Social-cognitive theories* =

A) Psychodynamic Theories: Emphasis on Motivation and Mental Disorder =

1) Freud and Psychoanalysis =

- *Psychoanalysis =*

- *Psychoanalytic theory =*

  a) The Freudian Unconscious =

  - *Unconscious =*

  b) Unconscious Drives and Instincts =

  - *Libido =*

    o *Eros =*

    o *Thanatos =*

  c) The Structure of the Personality =

  - *Id =*

  - *Superego =*

    o *Ego ideal =*

  - *Ego =*

  d) The Influence of Early Experience on Personality Development =

  - *Psychosexual stages =*

  - *Oedipus complex =*

  - *Identification =*

  - *Electra complex =*

  - *Fixation =*

e) <u>Ego Defenses</u> =

- *Ego defense mechanisms* =

- *Repression* =

    o *Denial* =

    o *Rationalization* =

    o *Reaction formation* =

    o *Displacement* =

    o *Regression* =

    o *Sublimation* =

    o *Projection* =

f) <u>Projective Tests: Diagnosis via a Defense Mechanism</u> =

- *Projective test* =

- *Rorschach Inkblot Technique* =

- *Thematic Apperception Test (TAT)* =

g) <u>Psychic Determinism</u> =

- *Psychic determinism* =

h) <u>Evaluating Freud's Work</u> =

2) <u>Freud as Unscientific</u> =

3) <u>Retrospective but not Prospective</u> =

4) The Neo-Freudians =

- *Neo-Freudian* =

a) Carl Jung: Extending the Unconscious =

- *Personal unconscious* =

- *Collective unconscious* =

- *Archetype* =

  o *Principle of opposites* =

- *Introversion* =

- *Extroversion* =

b) Karen Horney: A Feminist Voice in Psychodynamic Psychology =

- *Basic anxiety* =

- *Neurotic needs* =

c) Other Neo-Freudian Theorists =

B) Humanistic Theories: Emphasis on Human Potential and Mental Health =

1) Abraham Maslow and the Healthy Personality =

- *Self-actualizing personality* =

  o *Hierarchy of needs* =

2) Carl Rogers's Fully Functioning Person =

- *Fully functioning person* =

2) <u>Carl Rogers's Fully Functioning Person (continued)</u> =

- *Phenomenal field* =

  o *Unconditional positive regard* =

3) <u>Evaluating the Humanistic Theories</u> =

- Positive psychology =

C) Social-Cognitive Theories: Emphasis on Social Learning =

1) <u>Observational Learning and Personality: Bandura's Theory</u> =

- *Observational learning* =

- *Reciprocal determinism* =

2) <u>Locus of Control: Rotter's Theory</u> =

- *Locus of control* =

3) <u>Evaluating the Social-Cognitive Approach to Personality</u> =

D) Current Trends: The Person in a Social System =

- *Family systems theory* =

E) Psychology Matters: Using Psychology to Learn Psychology =

10.4 WHAT "THEORIES" DO PEOPLE USE TO UNDERSTAND THEMSELVES AND OTHERS?

Core Concept 10.4 =

A) Implicit Personality Theories =

- *Implicit personality theory* =

B) Self-Narratives: The Stories of Our Lives =

- *Self-narrative* =

- *Redemptive self* =

  o *Generative* =

C) The Effects of Culture on Our Views of Personality:

1) Individualism, Collectivism, and Personality =

- *Fundamental attribution error* =

D) Psychology Matters: The Personality of Time =

E) Critical Thinking Applied: The Person-Situation Controversy =

- *Person-situation controversy* =

What Forces Shape Our Personalities?

1. Write a general definition of the term "personality."

Biology, Human Nature, and Personality

2. *Complete the following paragraph with the correct information.*

Responding to painful, threatening, or unhappy situations by striking at the nearest target

is what Freud called _____ of aggression. Sometimes we also call it

_____, after an ancient Hebrew ritual of symbolically transferring sins.

This human tendency seems to be built into our _____.

The Effects of Nurture: Personality and the Environment

3. *Underline the word(s) in parentheses that will make each statement correct. (Both options may be correct!)*

   A. Heredity accounts for roughly (half/a fourth) of our characteristics.

   B. Many personality theorists emphasize the importance of (early childhood/early adolescent) experiences.

   C. In general, first-born children are more likely than later-born children to (make people laugh/have a career that requires intellect).

   D. Walter Mischel believes that (inborn/environmental) influences are more important than (inborn/environmental) influences.

The Effects of Nature: Dispositions and Mental Processes

4. Explain the differences between "dispositional theories" and "process theories" of personality.

Social and Cultural Contributions to Personality

5. Compare and contrast the concepts of "individualism" and "collectivism."

6. What difference in shyness has been found between Asian-Americans and Jewish-Americans, and what is the most likely cause for this difference?

Psychology Matters: Explaining Unusual People and Unusual Behavior

7. *Fill in the following table to explain the general emphasis of the three different perspectives concerning personality.*

Perspective	Emphasis
A. Psychodynamic theories	
B. Humanistic theories	
C. Social-cognitive theories	

What Persistent Patterns, or *Dispositions*, Make up Our Personalities?

8. Differentiate among the following terms. Under what general heading can they all be placed?

Trait: _____

_____

Type: _____

_____

Temperament: _____

_____

General heading: _____

9. *Complete the following paragraph with the correct information*

According to Hippocrates, a person's temperament resulted from the balance of four fluids, or _____, secreted by the body. He believed that someone with a _____ temperament was angry due to yellow bile. A _____, or depressed, temperament supposedly was due to black bile. A cheerful, or _____, temperament was due to strong, warm blood, Hippocrates thought. Finally, if the body's dominant fluid was mucus, the person would have an unemotional, or _____, temperament.

Personality and Temperament

10. *Indicate whether each statement is True (T) or False (F) by circling the appropriate letter after the statement.*

   A. "Temperament" is defined as the personality dispositions learned very early in childhood through interactions with caregivers and the environment.   T F

   B. A fundamental brain area known to regulate personality is the temporal lobes.   T F

   C. Biological dispositions affect our basic personalities.   T F

   D. Modern psychology has replaced the idea of humors with the idea of hormones.   T F

   E. Kagan has discovered that newborns who remain calm in response to new stimulation become, over the next several months, shy or introverted children.   T F

   F. About 20 percent of newborns are highly responsive and excitable.   T F

   G. The percentage of shy college-aged students is higher than the percentage of shy children.   T F

Personality as a Composite of Traits

11. List the pairs (bipolar dimensions) that comprise the "Big Five" traits.

A. _____ _____   C. _____ _____

B. _____ _____   D. _____ _____

E. _____ _____

12. *In the table below, give the name of the "Big Five" trait that best fits the example.*

Example	Trait Name
Tanya loves to try new things, so she does a lot of traveling.	A.
Jerry prefers to do things alone rather than with others.	B.
David always checks the figures on his spreadsheet at least three times before submitting it to his boss.	C.
Jocelyn will worry everything that can go wrong, even when things are going right for her.	D.
Susana is always willing to lend a sympathetic ear when someone is having a hard time.	E.

13. *Underline the word(s) in parentheses that will make each statement correct. (Both options may be correct!)*

A. The five-factor theory was developed using the statistic called (regression/factor) analysis.

B. An extremely high score for any of the Big Five traits (is/isn't) necessarily good.

C. In general, the five-factor model (has/doesn't have) validity across cultures.

D. The MMPI-2 has good (validity/reliability).

E. The (NEO-PI/MMPI-2) assesses a person's Big Five personality traits.

F. The Minnesota Multiphasic Personality Inventory was developed to assess a person's (Big Five traits/serious mental problems).

G. Trait theories (describe/explain) behavior.

H. The Big Five traits (predict/explain) important things such as health and success in (academics/interpersonal relationships).

I. Tests have (reliability/validity) if they truly measure what they're supposed to measure.

Psychology Matters: Finding Your Type

14. *Indicate whether each statement is True (T) or False (F) by circling the appropriate letter after the statement.*

A. The Myers-Briggs Type Indicator is a measure of personality traits.　　　　T F

B. The MBTI derives from Jung's theory of personality.　　　　T F

C. The MBTI is often used in the business world.　　　　T F

D. Research shows that the MBTI is highly related to job success.　　　　T F

E. The Myers-Briggs Type Indicator assigns a person to a four-dimensional personality type based on the dimensions of Introversion-Extroversion, Thinking-Feeling, Sensation-Intuition, and Judgment-Perception.　　　　T F

F. The MBTI shows good reliability.　　　　T F

Do Mental *Processes* Help Shape Our Personalities?

16. *Fill in the blanks with the correct information.*

To understand the psychological forces underlying a person's personality traits, we must turn to _____ theories. The _____ theories focus on people's motives, often unconscious ones, as well as the influence of past experiences. The _____ theories emphasize the influence of learning, perception, and social interaction. _____ theories focus on consciousness and one's present, subjective reality.

Psychodynamic Theories: Emphasis on Motivation and Mental Disorder

17. *Fill in the blanks of this table with the correct information about Freud's ideas concerning unconscious drives and energy and the behaviors that result from those drives.*

Drive or Energy	Definition	Behaviors
A. _____	Unconscious sex drive	Sex, dancing, work, cooking, studying, drawing, body building
B. Thanatos		
C. Libido		Sex, dancing, work, cooking, studying, drawing, body building

18. *Underline the word(s) in parentheses that will make each statement correct. (Both options may be correct!)*

A. According to Freud, (Thanatos/Eros) is contained within the (id/ego).

B. The part of the personality, according to Freud, that acts most like an impulsive child is the (id/ego), and the part that acts as a moderator between the other parts of the personality is the (ego/superego).

C. Freud believed that the (ego/superego) includes the (conscience/ego-ideal).

D. In Freud's theory of psychosexual stages, the first stage is the (anal/oral) stage and the last is the (genital/phallic) stage.

E. According to Freud's theory, a person who is excessively neat, compulsive, and stubborn would be viewed as having (a fixation/an identification) in the (anal/phallic) stage.

F. In Freud's theory, a little boy who has an erotic attraction toward his mother is experiencing the (Electra/Oedipus) complex.

G. The psychosexual stage in which a child derives immature sexual gratification through masturbation is the (phallic/genital) stage.

H. According to Freud, arrested psychological development due to difficulties early in life is known as (fixation/repression).

I. Most psychologists today (accept/reject) Freud's ideas about psychosexual development.

J. The Freudian process in which a person tries to become like the same-sex parent is called (identification/the Oedipus complex).

K. Freud believed that the ego uses (psychosexual stages/defense mechanisms) to deal with conflict between the id and superego, and that all of these operate at the (preconscious/unconscious) level.

L. Freud's theory is referred to as (psychoanalytic/humanistic) theory, and his system of therapy is known as (hypnosis/psychoanalysis).

19. *Match each term with its best example(s) by placing the letter corresponding to the term in the space next to its example. (Terms may be used more than once.)*

TERMS

A. Displacement	C. Denial	E. Sublimation	G. Reaction formation
B. Rationalization	D. Regression	F. Projection	

EXAMPLES

_____ Attiq, who is unconsciously furious at his wife for not paying attention to him, brings her flowers and tells her how much he adores her.

_____ Richard is alcoholic, but insists that he doesn't have a problem with alcohol.

_____ Jennie is attracted to her male colleague at work. When she gets home, she accuses her husband of having an affair.

_____ Tim has channeled his passion into wonderful sculptures of the human body.

_____ Tanisha spends the whole day at work frustrated at her boss and finds herself yelling at her dog when she gets home.

_____ Twenty-year-old Caroline deals with her break-up by curling up on her bed, hugging her teddy bear, and crying uncontrollably.

_____ Kevin is a highly successful and respected football player due to his aggressive play.

_____ Rita smokes marijuana daily and says that it's no big deal, because it's not a "hard-core" drug and it's legal in some countries.

20. To find out more about Freud and psychoanalysis, visit the Freud Museum's site at:
http://www.freud.org.uk/

21. Define "projective test." Then compare and contrast the Rorschach Inkblot Technique and the Thematic Apperception Test (TAT).

22. NEED A BREAK?
To get a better understanding of personality theories, visit MyPsychLab.

23. Explain "psychic determinism."

24. What are four criticisms of Freudian theory?

A. _____

B. _____

C. _____

D. _____

25. What are "neo-Freudians"?

26. Describe the two issues over which Carl Jung broke with Freud.

A. _____

B. _____

27. This site by Dr. C. George Boeree describes Carl Jung's life and theory.
http://webspace.ship.edu/cgboer/jung.html

28. *Fill in the blanks of the following concept map about Jung's theory.*

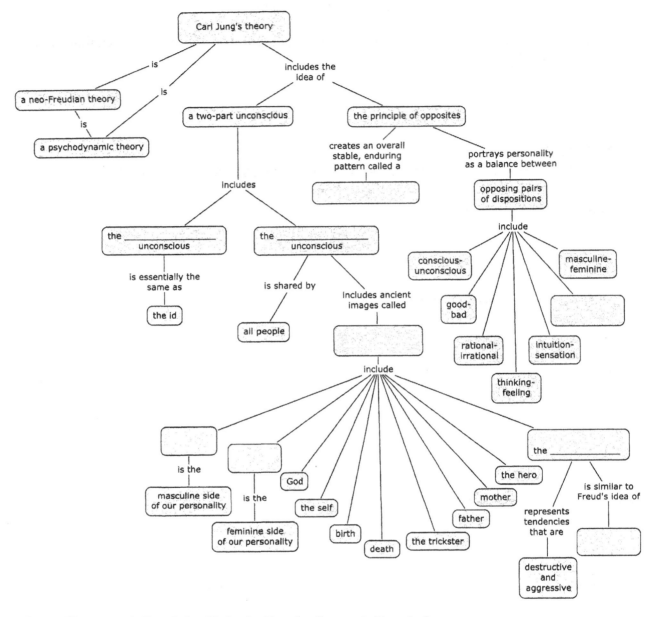

Karen Horney: A Feminist Voice in Psychodynamic Psychology

29. *Indicate whether each statement is True (T) or False (F) by circling the appropriate letter after the statement.*

A. Horney believed, along with Freud, that females suffer from penis envy.   T F

B. According to Horney, personality is determined mainly by early childhood experiences.   T F

C. Horney believed that normal growth involves the complete development
of social relationships and of one's potential.   T F

D. According to Horney's theory, mental disorder and adjustment problems
are caused by basic needs.   T F

E. Horney referred to one's sense of uncertainty and isolation as "basic anxiety."   T F

F. According to Horney, neurotic needs are abnormal desires people develop.   T F

G. Unlike Freud's theory, Horney's theory has a strong scientific foundation.   T F

30. Horney believed that there are ten different neurotic needs people may develop. List six of those ten neurotic needs.

A. _____   D. _____

B. _____   E. _____

C. _____   F. _____

31. According to Horney's theory, what are the three common patterns of attitudes and behavior that people use to deal with basic anxiety? Explain each.

Common Pattern	Explanation
A.	
B.	
C.	

32. Dr. C. George Boeree's site gives a great overview of Karen Horney and her theory. Visit:
http://webspace.ship.edu/cgboer/horney.html

Humanistic Theories: Emphasis on Human Potential and Mental Health

33. *Fill in the blanks with the correct information.*

Abraham Maslow referred to the humanistic perspective as psychology's

_____ to contrast his ideas with those of the psychoanalytic and behaviorist

perspectives. He believed that unfulfilled, "deficiency" needs in his hierarchy can produce

_____. However, those individuals who feel free to fulfill their potentialities

are who Maslow called _____.

Carl Rogers called the healthy personality the _____. He believed that such an individual has a self-concept that is both _____ and _____. Rogers insisted that psychology recognize the importance of an individual's perceptions and feelings, which he called the _____. The subjective experience, he believed, is part of the _____. According to Rogers, for positive growth, we need people in our lives who give us _____, which is love without conditions attached.

34. Explain the characteristics that Maslow believed are possessed by "self-actualizing personalities."

35. What are four criticisms of humanistic theories?

    A. _____

    B. _____

    C. _____

    D. _____

36. What is "positive psychology," and how is it similar to and different from humanistic psychology?

Social-Cognitive Theories: Emphasis on Social Learning

37. *Fill in the blanks with the correct information.*

    Albert Bandura believes that people are not just driven by rewards and punishments, but also by their _____, which don't have to come from direct experience but instead from _____ others. Thus, other people act as _____ that we either accept or reject, depending on whether they were rewarded or punished. However, Bandura cautions that personality is not all learned behavior. Instead, to understand the whole person we must understand the continual

interactions among _____, _____, and the _____.
This interaction is what Bandura calls _____.

Julian Rotter's theory says that the way we act depends on our sense of personal
_____, which he calls _____. His theory is both a
_____ theory and a _____ theory. Scores on his scale correlate
with people's _____ and _____. Research shows that
_____ are more likely to exercise, whereas _____ are more likely
to suffer from depression.

38. To find out much more about Bandura's life and theory, visit Dr. C. Boeree's website at:
http://webspace.ship.edu/cgboer/bandura.html

Current Trends: The Person in a Social System

39. Describe three important current trends in personality theory.

A. _____
B. _____
C. _____

40. For further exploration of personality theories and research being done on the topic, visit:
http://www.personalityresearch.org

Psychology Matters: Using Psychology to Learn Psychology

41. In terms of locus of control, which locus is generally more detrimental to college success?

Answer: _____

What "Theories" Do People Use to Understand Themselves and Others?

42. What do psychologists call the "folk theories" that individuals have about personality?

Answer: _____

Implicit Personality Theories

43. Identify and explain four different problems with implicit theories of personality.

A. _____   C. _____

B. _____ D. _____

Self-Narratives: The Stories of Our Lives

44. *Fill in the blanks with the correct information.*

According to McAdams, a component of personality that is just as important as motives, emotions, and social relationships is a person's _____, which is the story of one's _____ over time. In American culture, the _____ self is common, particularly in adults who possess what Erikson termed _____.

The Effects of Culture on Our Views of Personality

45. Define the "fundamental attribution error," and explain how it relates to collectivism and individualism.

46. To investigate how individualism and collectivism are relevant to education, visit: http://www.wested.org/online_pubs/lcd-99-01.pdf

Psychology Matters: The Personality of Time

47. *Underline the word(s) in parentheses that will make each statement correct. (Both options may be correct!)*

   A. The Zimbardo Time Perspective Inventory has (five/seven) factors.

   B. Having a (present/future) orientation is highly positively correlated with Conscientiousness.

   C. (Openness/Conscientiousness) is the only personality trait directly linked to biological mortality.

   D. Research in Lithuania shows that Neuroticism is positively correlated with (Past-Negative/Present-Fatalistic) Time Perspective.

Critical Thinking Applied: The Person-Situation Controversy

48. Explain the "person-situation controversy" and the evidence on both sides of this debate. Then, describe Mischel's ideas about the three factors that together explain a person's behavior.

PRACTICE TEST #1

1. All of the following are noted psychodynamic personality theorists EXCEPT _____.
   A. Freud   B. Mischel   C. Horney   D. Jung

2. Thinking-feeling and sensation-intuition are two of the bipolar dimensions included in _____.
   A. the Big Five   B. Rotter's theory   C. the MMPI-2   D. the Myers-Briggs test

3. The major goal of trait and type personality theories is to _____.
   A. create a test to evaluate personality   C. describe current personality characteristics
   B. predict future behavior of people   D. explain abnormal behavior in a person

4. The "fully functioning person" is an important concept in _____ theory.
   A. Jung's   B. Rogers's   C. Maslow's   D. Horney's

5. Jack believes that the root of all behavior comes from forces in his unconscious. He is a
   proponent of the _____ theory of personality.
   A. cognitive   B. humanistic   C. trait   D. psychodynamic

6. Freud saw personality as a continuing struggle between the _____ and the _____.
   A. id; ego   B. ego; superego   C. id; superego   D. id; real world

7. The assessment technique in which an individual is asked to interpret ambiguous stimulus is called a(n)
   _____ test.
   A. projective   B. objective   C. subjective   D. retrospective

8. Which of the following tests is a projective technique?
   A. The TAT   C. The NEO-PI
   B. The Myers-Briggs Type Indicator   D. The MMPI

9. Our internal story of our self-concept over time is referred to as our _____.
   A. ego-ideal   B. redemptive self   C. generativity D. self-narrative

10. According to Horney, the signs of mental disorder involve ten different _____.
    A. basic needs   B. basic anxieties   C. neurotic needs   D. neurotic anxieties

PRACTICE TEST #2

1. Karla went to the grocery store to purchase food for a special dinner. The clerk gave her change for a twenty-dollar bill instead of for a ten-dollar bill. When Karla decided to return the extra change, a Freudian would say her _____ was functioning.
   A. conscious   B. id   C. ego   D. superego

2. Jung theorized that we each have a(n) _____ unconscious, which is shared by all humans.
   A. personal   B. archetype   C. interactive   D. collective

3. Miles is very rigid about how everything in his schedule works. His desk must be perfectly arranged, and he gets upset if anything upset his schedule. Freud would say that Miles has a(n) _____ stage fixation.
   A. oral   B. anal   C. genital   D. latent

4. _____ theories focus on consciousness and one's present, subjective reality.
   A. Humanistic   B. Social-cognitive   C. Psychodynamic   D. Implicit

5. Mary decides to cheat on her final exam so that she can pass her class. She says, "Everyone cheats, so it's okay." Mary is using the defense mechanism of _____.
   A. denial   B. repression   C. rationalization   D. reaction formation

6. Caleb received a speeding ticket that will cost him $100.00. After he got home and looked at the ticket, he kicked his car's tires several times. Caleb is using the defense mechanism of _____.
   A. regression   B. sublimation C. displacement   D. rationalization

7. Angela works hard to earn high marks on her papers and exams. Rotter would say that Angela has a(n) _____ locus of control.
   A. internal   B. external   C. positive   D. intrinsic

8. Jay seems to be very conscientious at work, but he often is lackadaisical at home and fails to complete his chores. Whose personality theory would best explain his behavior?
   A. Freud   B. Maslow   C. Bandura   D. Jung

9. Personality is best described as _____.
   A. a description of the uniqueness of individuals
   B. the characteristic patterns of behavior that are constant across time
   C. qualities that are influenced by different situations and across time
   D. a sense of who you are—the self—that is innate

10. The _____ assesses a person's Big Five personality traits.
   A. NEO-PI   B. MMPI-2   C. ZTPI   D. MBTI

PRACTICE TEST #3

1. The "shadow," the "hero," and "anima" are _____.
   A. traits   B. archetypes   C. temperaments   D. psychosexual stages

2. Abraham Maslow's theory focuses on a lifelong process of striving to realize one's potential that is known as _____.
   A. humanism   B. sublimation   C. potential selfism   D. self-actualization

3. According to Horney, all of the following are ways to deal with basic anxiety EXCEPT _____.
   A. moving away from others   C. moving toward others
   B. moving against others   D. moving together with others

4. Which of the following is a strength of the humanistic approach?
   A. It is comprised of clear, testable concepts
   B. It explains the influence of environmental variables
   C. It explains the power of the unconscious
   D. It emphasizes the role of the self in behavior

5. The interaction between behavior, cognition, and the environment is what Bandura called _____.
   A. collectivism   B. the self-narrative   C. situationism   D. reciprocal determinism

6. Sally watched her older sister get out of doing her chores by whining to their parents. When it was time for Sally to do her chores, she whined about the work to her mother. Sally's behavior is reflective of _____ theory.
   A. Freud's   B. Horney's   C. Bandura's   D. Maslow's

7. A test that measures what it says it measures is said to have _____.
   A. validity   B. reliability   C. truth   D. precision

8. One of the criticisms of the social-cognitive theories is that they _____.
   A. are not based on research   C. emphasize rational information processing
   B. don't include therapeutic techniques   D. are not as comprehensive as other theories

9. In family systems theory, the emphasis is on _____.
   A. groups   B. individuals   C. interactions   D. communication

10. Your classmate trips as she walks into your theater class. You decide she must be a really clumsy person. This best exemplifies _____.
    A. the fundamental attribution error   C. reciprocal determinism
    B. an implicit personality theory   D. the phenomenal field

COMPREHENSIVE REVIEW TEST

1. The results of Kagan's work suggest that _____ has a biological basis.
   A. trait theory   B. locus of control   C. temperament   D. collectivism

2. Harvey is a biological psychologist who is interested in personality. He most likely attributes individual differences to _____.
   A. genes   B. hormones   C. humors   D. neurotransmitters

3. Each of the following is one of the "Big Five" EXCEPT _____.
   A. extraversion   B. neuroticism C. optimism   D. conscientiousness

4. The MMPI-2 is a personality assessment that is partly based on _____ theory.
   A. trait   B. social learning   C. psychodynamic   D. implicit personality

5. Mariellen is very dependable and exercises caution when making decisions. According to the five-factor theory, Mariellen is strong in _____.
   A. openness   B. extraversion   C. neuroticism D. conscientiousness

6. An exemplary personality test or inventory must have _____.
   A. clarity   B. constancy   C. reliability   D. theory-based references

7. Jung's idea of "the shadow" is similar to Freud's idea of _____.
   A. the ego   B. Thanatos   C. Eros   D. the superego

8. Freud believed that _____.
   A. situational variables dictate how people respond in a given circumstance
   B. people learn behaviors and ways of interacting by watching others
   C. all acts are determined by motives, not by chance
   D. people are reinforced by significant others and tend to repeat behaviors that are reinforced

9. All of the following are true of type and trait theories EXCEPT _____.
   A. they don't explain how personality develops
   B. they assume that personality traits are fixed or static
   C. they are considered to be process theories of personality
   D. they are viewed by some as oversimplifying human nature

10. Carl Rogers insisted that psychology recognize the importance of an individual's perceptions and feelings, which he called the _____.
    A. phenomenal field   C. self-narrative
    B. self-actualized personality   D. subjective archetype

11. What does Bandura call the process in which cognitions, behavior, and the environment mutually influence each other?
   A. Reciprocal determinism
   B. Locus of control
   C. Phenomenal field
   D. Causal direction

12. In Rogers's view, for healthy personality development, individuals need _____.
   A. reciprocal determinism
   B. positive self-narratives
   C. unconditional positive regard
   D. psychic determinism

13. The Myers-Briggs Type Inventory _____.
   A. is one of the best tools to use for diagnosing mental illness
   B. has questionable reliability and limited usefulness
   C. helps people to recognize their primary "Big Five" trait
   D. is a projective assessment tool

14. All of the following statements about implicit personality theories are true EXCEPT _____.
   A. they affect people's perceptions and judgments about others' personalities
   B. in general, impressions of others tend to be biased
   C. they are influenced by the theorist's culture of origin
   D. they are most concerned with normal personality functioning and development

15. Many psychologists use parts of different personality theories, rather than a single theory in its entirety. This is referred to as _____.
   A. a stable personality theory
   B. the fundamental attribution error
   C. an eclectic theory
   D. unconditional positive regard

CRITICAL THINKING ESSAYS

1. Discuss the person-situation controversy and how it relates to other concepts and theories you've learned about in this chapter.

2. Compare and contrast the humanistic theories of Maslow and of Rogers. How would the field of positive psychology improve these theories?

CHAPTER 11
Social Psychology

Before You Read . . . Term Identification

Make flashcards using the following terms or, even better, develop mnemonics (memory strategies) to help you remember the different concepts and terms. Use the definitions in the margins of this chapter for help. Numbers refer to page numbers in the textbook.

Abu Ghraib prison (503)
Asch effect (466)
autokinetic effect (469)
bullying (505)
bystander intervention problem (479)
chameleon effect (465)
cognitive dissonance theory (487)
cohesiveness (470)
conformity (466)
dehumanization (495)
diffusion of responsibility (480)
discrimination (493)
dispositionism (463)
expectancy-value theory (486)
fundamental attribution error (FAE) (490)
groupthink (470)
heroes (475)
in-group (482)
matching hypothesis (486)
out-group (482)
prejudice (493)

principle of proximity (484)
reward theory of attraction (484)
romantic love (489)
scapegoating (494)
Schlesinger Report (504)
script (464)
self-disclosure (485)
self-serving bias (491)
similarity principle (485)
situationism (463)
social context (461)
social distance (493)
social neuroscience (470)
social norms (464)
social psychology (461)
social reality (483)
social role (463)
Stanford Prison Experiment (500)
stereotype threat (497)
system power (500)
triangular theory of love (489)

Lecture Assistant *for Chapter 11*

Tear this outline out and bring it with you to class in order to facilitate your note taking.
Spend more time listening to the lecture and less time writing!

Chapter Opening Problem: What makes ordinary people harm other people as they did in this shocking experiment?

- *Social psychology* =

- *Social context* =

11.1 HOW DOES THE SOCIAL SITUATION AFFECT OUR BEHAVIOR?

Core Concept 11.1 =

- *Situationism* =

- *Dispositionism* =

A) Social Standards of Behavior:

1) Social Roles and Social Norms =

- *Social role* =

- *Social norms* =

2) Schemas and Scripts =

- *Schema* =

- *Script* =

3) Social Norms Influence Students' Political Views =

B) Conformity:

- *Chameleon effect* =

1) The Asch Effect: A Minority of One in a Challenging Majority =

  - *Asch effect* =

  - *Conformity* =

2) Cultural Differences in Conformity =

  - *Nonconformity* =

  - *Anticonformity* =

3) The Autokinetic Effect =

4) Conformity and Independence Light Up the Brain Differently =

  - *Social neuroscience* =

    - *Illusion of personal invulnerability* =

5) Groupthink =

C) Obedience to Authority:

1) Milgram's Research Revisited =

    - *Fundamental attribution error* =

2) Variations On an Obedience Theme =

3) Heroic Defiance =

  - *Heroes* =

4) Cross-Cultural Tests of Milgram's Research =

5) Why Do We Obey Authority? =

6) Some Real World Extensions of the Milgram Obedience to Authority Paradigm =

D) The Bystander Problem: The Evil of Inaction

- o Kitty Genovese =

1) Contrived Emergencies =

- *Bystander intervention problem* =

- *Diffusion of responsibility* =

2) Need Help? Ask for It! =

E) Psychology Matters: On Being "Shoe" at Yale U.

11.2 CONSTRUCTING SOCIAL REALITY: WHAT INFLUENCES OUR JUDGMENTS OF OTHERS?

Core Concept 11.2 =

A) Interpersonal Attraction:

1) Reward Theory: We (Usually) Prefer Rewarding Relationships =

- *Reward theory of attraction* =

2) Proximity =

3) Similarity =

4) Self-Disclosure =

5) Physical Attractiveness =

6) Exceptions to the Reward Theory of Attraction =

- *Matching hypothesis =*

- *Expectancy-value theory =*

7) Attraction and Dissonance =

- *Cognitive dissonance =*

B) Loving Relationships:

- *Romantic love =*

- *Triangular theory of love =*

C) Making Cognitive Attributions:

1) The Fundamental Attribution Error (FAE) =

2) Biased Thinking about Yourself =

- *Self-serving bias =*

3) <u>Universal Dimensions of Social Cognition: Warmth and Competence</u> =

4) <u>Cross-Cultural Research on the Need for Positive Self-Regard</u> =

E) Prejudice and Discrimination

- *Prejudice* =

- *Discrimination* =

1) <u>Causes of Prejudice</u> =

    a) <u>Dissimilarity and Social Distance</u> =

- *Social distance* =

    b) <u>Economic Competition</u> =

    c) <u>Scapegoating</u> =

    d) <u>Conformity to Social Norms</u> =

    e) <u>Media Stereotypes</u> =

    f) <u>Dehumanization</u> =

- *Dehumanization* =

2) <u>Combating Prejudice</u> =

    a) <u>New Role Models</u> =

    b) <u>Equal Status Contact</u> =

c) The Jigsaw Classroom =

d) Legislation =

3) Stereotype Threat =

F) Psychology Matters: Stereotype Lift and Values Affirmations

11.3 HOW DO SYSTEMS CREATE SITUATIONS THAT INFLUENCE BEHAVIOR?

Core Concept 11.3 =

* *System power* =

A) The Stanford Prison Experiment:

B) Chains of System Command:

1) The Situation and the System at Abu Ghraib Prison =

2) The Systems Lesson =

3) Using Psychology to Understand the Abuses at Abu Ghraib =

* *Schlesinger Report* =

C) Preventing Bullying by Systemic Changes and Reframing =

1) What Does Bullying Look Like Today? =

D) Psychology Matters: Using Psychology to Learn Psychology

1) Social Validation =

2) Authority =

3) The Poison Parasite Argument =

E) Critical Thinking Applied: Is Terrorism "A Senseless Act of Violence, Perpetuated by Crazy Fanatics"?

As You Read . . . Practice Activities

---

1. Identify the three major themes of social psychology.

A. _____

B. _____

C. _____

2. The Social Psychology Network is the largest online compilation of information about social psychology. Visit:

http://www.socialpsychology.org

How Does the Social Situation Affect Our Behavior?

3. Define "situationism" and "dispositionism." How do these concepts relate to the "power of the situation"?

Social Standards of Behavior

4. *Match each term with its best description(s) by placing the letter corresponding to the term in the space next to its description. (Terms may be used more than once.)*

TERMS

    A. Social role   B. Schema   C. Social norm   D. Script

DESCRIPTIONS

_____ An unwritten rule for appropriate attitudes and behaviors in a given setting

_____ A cluster of related concepts that provides a general conceptual framework

_____ A socially defined pattern of behavior that is expected of individuals in a given setting or group

_____ Knowledge about the sequence of events and actions that are expected in a particular social setting

_____ May result from a person's own interests, or may be imposed on a person

_____ Can be a broad guideline or quite specific

5. In what two main ways do people adjust to joining a new group and learning its social norms?

A. _____

B. _____

Conformity

6. In general, under what four circumstances is a person more likely to conform?

A. _____

B. _____

C. _____

D. _____

7 *Fill in the blanks of the following concept map with the correct information.*

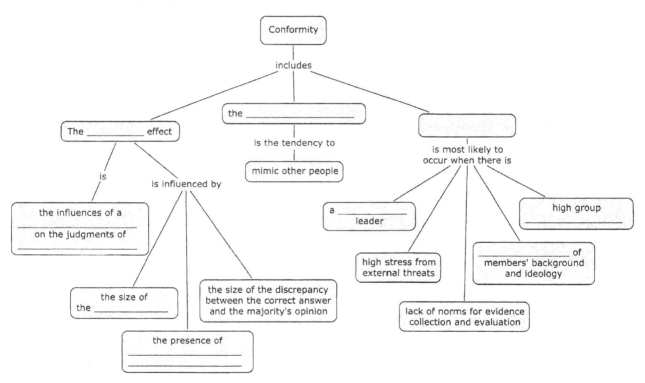

8. The Solomon Asch Center focuses on Asch's work and how his findings are used today. Visit:
http://aschcenter.blogs.brynmawr.edu/

9. *Identify the conditions that promote groupthink by checking the correct ones.*

A. _____ a large-sized group   G. _____ a collectivistic orientation

299

B. _____ insulation of the group   H. _____ lack of norms concerning procedures
C. _____ an important task to do   I. _____ homogeneity of backgrounds
D. _____ high group cohesiveness   J. _____ high stress from external sources
E. _____ low group cohesiveness   K. _____ time pressures to solve the problem
F. _____ directive leadership   L. _____ using many sources of independent evidence

10. *Underline the word(s) in parentheses that will make each statement correct. (Both options may be correct!)*

A. In Asch's original study, (one-third/two-thirds) of participants conformed to group pressure, whereas (one-third/two-thirds) did not conform.

B. Conformity research that used fMRI scans of participants' brains showed that brain areas having to do with (emotions/planning) were particularly active when participants made judgments that (were consistent and conformed to/were independent and against) the incorrect majority group's judgments. This study is an example of (sociobiology/social neuroscience) research.

C. The (autokinetic/Asch) effect was used in a study by (Sherif/Milgram) and involved participants' tendency to follow the group (norm/script).

D. In the Asch effect, people conform because of (normative/informational) influences.

E. The U.S. Senate Intelligence Committee cited (the Asch effect/groupthink) as one of the processes involved in the federal government's 2003 decision to wage preemptive war against Iraq.

F. The autokinetic effect is (perceptual illusion/measure of obedience).

G. An aspect of groupthink is (collective rationalization/examining few alternatives).

H. Cross-cultural studies of the Asch effect have shown a higher degree of nonconformity in (American/Japanese) students than in (American/Japanese) students.

Obedience to Authority

11. *Indicate whether each statement is True (T) or False (F) by circling the appropriate letter after the statement.*

A. When Milgram asked 40 psychiatrists to predict the percentage of American citizens who would go to each of the 30 levels in his experiment, the psychiatrists estimated that about 7 percent would go all the way to the end.　　　T F

B. One reason that the 40 psychiatrists underestimated the percentage of Americans who would go all the way to the end of Milgram's experiment was that their psychiatric training led them to rely to heavily on the dispositional perspective.　　T F

C. In a 2010 television show in France that simulated the Milgram study, 80 Percent of participants gave the maximum level of electric shock.　　T F

D. In Milgram's study, participants always agreed to give shocks if the Learner said he wanted to be shocked.　　T F

E. To obtain maximum obedience in Milgram's study, the Teachers should first observe someone else administering the final shock level.　　T F

F. In Milgram's study, participants were more likely to give high levels of shock when the Experimenter filled in for the Learner.　　T F

G. The "Experimenter" in Milgram's study was Milgram himself.　　T F

H. "Heroes" are people who are able to resist situational forces and instead remain true to their personal values.　　T F

I. Replications of Milgram's study in other cultures showed higher rates of obedience in Australia than in South Africa.　　T F

J. Milgram found less obedience in the Teacher when the Learner was nearby rather than remote.　　T F

12. The following site summarizes the work of Stanley Milgram:
http://www.stanleymilgram.com/

The Bystander Problem: The Evil of Inaction

13. Explain what happened in the real-life case of Kitty Genovese. What social psychological concept was exemplified in her case?

14. *Fill in the blanks with the correct information.*

　　Latané and Darley developed a series of studies to investigate the
_____ problem. They discovered that the speed of response by the participants in the study depended on the _____ they thought were present. The _____ people the participants thought were present, the slower the participants were to respond. Latané and Darley proposed that this behavior occurs because each person assumes that someone else will do something; in other word, the participants experience a _____ of _____. Another factor that likely plays a role in participants' inaction or slow responses is _____, because participants are looking to others for cues on how to behave.

15. What factor did Latané and Darley find was the best predictor of bystander intervention?

16. Discuss findings on whether or not training can counter the bystander intervention problem.

Need Help? Ask for It!

17. What three things can a person do to increase his or her chances of getting assistance from would-be helpers?

    A. _____

    B. _____

    C. _____

ychology Matters: On Being "Shoe" at Yale U

18. What social psychology concept was demonstrated by the example of being "Shoe" at Yale? How does this relate to the concepts of "in-group" and "out-group"?

Constructing Social Reality: What Influences Our Judgments of Others?

19. Define the term "social reality."

Interpersonal Attraction

20. *In the space next to its example, give the name of the specific factor that has been found to promote interpersonal attraction.*

    _____ A. Stacy and Kim share the same beliefs about religion, working, and even how to decorate a house.

    _____ B. Hal and Ruby were neighbors in their apartment building. Some friends were surprised when they announced their engagement.

    _____ C. Isabelle and Howard both were voted "Hottest" when they were in high school. In college, they both did modeling for local stores.

    _____ D. Cameron and Sam spend hours talking about their childhoods, their families, their fears, and their hopes for the future.

21. Explain the "reward theory of attraction." Does research support this theory?

22. Samantha has always thought that everyone in theater is very politically liberal; yet she meets an actor who is very conservative in his views. Samantha is now likely experiencing what social psychological concept?

Answer: _____

23. *Underline the word(s) in parentheses that will make each statement correct. (Both options may be correct!)*

A. Research shows that the best predictor of how well a person will be liked after a first meeting is (sincerity/physical attractiveness).

B. (Men/Women) are more influenced by physical attractiveness than are (men/women).

C. The reward theory of attraction states that attraction is a form of (social learning/biological responsiveness).

D. Physically attractive people are viewed by others as being more (intelligent/vain) than individuals with average looks.

E. The public favors physically attractive (male/female) politicians.

F. The (matching hypothesis/cognitive dissonance theory) refers to the finding that people end up with friends or partners who have their same level of (attractiveness/education).

G. A recent study on the matching hypothesis demonstrates that researchers also need to take into account (social desirability/self-worth).

H. People with low self-esteem generally feel a stronger commitment to a relationship when their partner thinks (poorly/highly) of them.

I. (Expectancy-value/Cognitive dissonance) theory proposes that people decide whether to pursue a relationship by weighing the worth they see in the other person with the perceived likelihood of success in the relationship.

J. A main way of reducing cognitive dissonance is by changing one's (behavior/thoughts).

K. Research indicates that cognitive dissonance has more power to change individuals' attitudes in (Japan/the U.S.) than in (Japan/the U.S.).

24. *Fill in the blanks with the correct information.*

In general, _____ theory says that when people's thoughts and behaviors are in conflict, people often _____ the conflict by changing their thinking to fit their behavior in order not to appear _____ or _____. This theory explains why we tend to _____ or _____ responsibility for our bad decisions, hurtful acts, and unwise decisions.

Loving Relationships

25. *Fill in the blanks with the correct terms.*

    A. Robert Sternberg has developed the _____ theory of love.

    B. According to Sternberg, the three components of love are _____, _____, and _____.

    C. Sternberg refers to _____ as one's dedication to putting the relationship first in one's life.

    D. The type of love that involves all three components is called _____ love.

26. *In the space next to each example, give the name of the type of love or attraction exhibited.*

A. _____ Darnell and Pekisha are good friends. They talk about their childhood experiences, personal fears, and goals. They are not sexually attracted to each other and have many other friends they spend time with as well.

B. _____ Sarah just melts at the sight of Tomas and can't stop thinking about him. She constantly daydreams about kissing him.

C. _____ Ty and Jordan are sexually attracted to each other and confide in each other. However, they put many other things in their life before their relationship.

D. _____ Jack and Pat have been together for fifty-three years. Their sex life is essentially nonexistent, yet they enjoy spending time together, sharing their feelings and ideas and having new adventures.

27. What four main factors are necessary for a relationship to stay healthy and to thrive?

    A. _____   C. _____

    B. _____   D. _____

Making Cognitive Attributions

28. Compare and contrast the "fundamental attribution error" and the "self-serving bias."

29. What are the two universal dimensions of human social cognition?

   A. _____ B. _____

30. When plotted on a graph, levels of warmth and competence result in four different quadrants. Explain how we tend to view people who fall into each of these four quadrants.

31. How does the motivation to seek positive self-regard vary depending on culture? What role does the development of a self-critical focus play?

32. NEED A BREAK?
   To get a better understanding of social psychology, visit MyPsychLab.

Prejudice and Discrimination

33. Distinguish between prejudice and discrimination. How are the two concepts related?

34. What six causes of prejudice have been studied by social psychologists?

   A. _____ D. _____
   B. _____ E. _____
   C. _____ F. _____

35. *Indicate whether each statement is True (T) or False (F) by circling the appropriate letter after the statement.*

    A. Viewing other people as less than human is known as "scapegoating."   T F

    B. Economic competition between groups often contributes to prejudice.   T F

    C. The greater the perceived social distance, the more likely one is to view members of the out-group as social equals.   T F

    D. According to the text, the source of prejudice and discrimination that is perhaps most pervasive is conformity to social norms.   T F

    E. The 1994 massacre of the Tutsi people by the Hutus showed the power of dehumanization.   T F

    F. The "jigsaw classroom" is a technique used to measure conformity.   T F

    G. Role models may serve better to prevent prejudice than to get rid of it.   T F

    H. Contact with people from an out-group is an effective way to erase prejudice.   T F

36. What four main strategies for reducing prejudice do the authors of the text discuss? Which of the four tends to be the least effective?

    A. _____   B. _____

    C. _____   D. _____

              LEAST EFFECTIVE = _____

37. What is "stereotype threat"? Give an example.

Psychology Matters: Stereotype Lift and Values Affirmations

38. *In the space next to its example, give the name of the social psychology concept.*

    _____ Tia performs well on a test of emotional sensitivity—a characteristic that she has heard is much more developed in women than in men.

39. What are "values affirmations," and how are they related to performance?

How Do Systems Create Situations That Influence Behavior?

40. Define "system power."

The Stanford Prison Experiment

41. Compare and contrast the Stanford Prison Experiment and Milgram's experiment.

Stanford Prison Experiment	Milgram's Experiment

42. Visit this site for in-depth information on the Stanford Prison Experiment, including photos.

http://www.prisonexp.org/

Chains of System Command

43. What important social psychology lessons can be learned from the abuses that occurred at Abu Ghraib prison?

44. *Underline the word(s) in parentheses that will make each statement correct. (Both options may be correct!)*

   A. (Systems/Situations) are created by (systems/situations).

   B. To address societal problems, your authors support a (public health/expectancy-value) model.

   C. Milgram's obedience study was about the effects of (system/individual) power and the Stanford Prison Study was about the effects of (system/individual) power.

45. According to the *Schlesinger Report* concerning Abu Ghraib prison, what six main social psychology concepts contributed to the abuses committed by ordinarily humane individuals?

   A. _____   C. _____   E. _____

   B. _____   D. _____   F. _____

46. *Indicate whether each statement is True (T) or False (F) by circling the appropriate letter after the statement.*

   A. In a large-scale British study of bullying, 73 percent of students reported being bullied, being a perpetrator of bullying, or witnessing bullying.　　　T F

   B. Boys are more often targets of bullying than are girls.　　　T F

   C. Girls use physical bullying less frequently than boys do.　　　T F

   D. Physical appearance is the most common reason that students are bullied.　　　T F

   E. Perceived or actual sexual orientation is one of the most common reasons that students are bullied.　　　T F

   F. Kids with the highest social status are usually the ones who are bullies.　　　T F

Psychology Matters: Using Psychology to Learn Psychology

47. *Fill in the blanks to explain the three subtle forms of persuasive pressure we all may encounter.*

Form of Persuasive Pressure	Explanation
A. Poison Parasite Argument	
B. _____	
C. Social Validation	

Critical Thinking Applied:
Is Terrorism "A Senseless Act of Violence, Perpetrated by Crazy Fanatics"?

48. Based on what you've learned about social psychology and critical thinking, how would you respond to the statement that "terrorism is a senseless act of violence, perpetrated by crazy fanatics"?

PRACTICE TEST #1

1. Sarah dresses like her favorite actress. This tendency to mimic is called the _____ effect.
   A. imitation   B. chameleon   C. simulation   D. impersonation

2. The tragic case of Kitty Genovese raised public awareness of the problem of _____.
   A. social control   B. bystander apathy   C. situationism   D. social perception

3. A _____ is the socially defined pattern of behavior that is expected of people in a certain situation.
   A. social norm   B. social context   C. schema   D. social role

4. Darla believes that it is people's innate qualities that determine how they behave. This reflects the concept of _____.
   A. innatism   B. interactionism   C. dispositionism   D. situationism

5. Asch studied the concept of _____.
   A. conformity   B. obedience   C. influence   D. agreement

6. Sternberg's theory of love includes all of the following components EXCEPT _____.
   A. passion   B. intimacy   C. commitment   D. similarity

7. You understand that as a student, you come into class, sit down, take out your books, paper, and pen, and get ready to take notes. You listen to the teacher and ask questions. You don't leave until time is up or the teacher permits it. That is your _____ of being in a college class.
   A. social norm   B. schema   C. script   D. responsibility

8. Social psychologists believe that the primary determinant of individual behavior is _____.
   A. the nature of the social situation in which the behavior occurs
   B. the individual's personality and disposition
   C. the individual's life history of learning, and his or her values and beliefs
   D. the nature and type of interpersonal relationships that the individual is having at the time

9. Jerry has a job interview after school, so he comes to class in a suit and tie. His friends and acquaintances poke fun at him because he has _____.
   A. committed social interference   C. refused to join the group ritual
   B. violated social norms   D. given into the bystander effect

10. The unwritten rules for group behavior are called social _____.
    A. schemas   B. scripts   C. norms   D. models

PRACTICE TEST #2

1. Gerry got an A in psychology, but a C in calculus. He attributed his psychology grade to his hard work and his calculus grade to the teacher's unfair tests. Gerry is exhibiting _____.
   - A. the self-serving bias
   - B. cognitive dissonance
   - C. the fundamental attribution error
   - D. an ascription error

2. The idea that somehow other people are more responsible for their own behavior than we are for ours is referred to as the _____.
   - A. dissimilarity effect
   - B. external attribution theory
   - C. fundamental attribution error
   - D. learned helplessness bias

3. Research shows that we can effectively combat prejudice by all of the following means EXCEPT _____.
   - A. new role models
   - B. talking about it
   - C. equal status contact
   - D. legislation

4. We tend to like people who like us, with whom we exchange gifts, and with whom we can share interests. This demonstrates what is called the _____ theory of attraction.
   - A. exchange
   - B. similarity
   - C. reward
   - D. compensation

5. Conformity research that used fMRI scans of participants' brains showed that brain areas having to do with _____ were particularly active when participants made judgments that were independent and against the incorrect majority group's judgments.
   - A. planning
   - B. emotions
   - C. self-control
   - D. decision making

6. Julie thought all football players were stupid. Then she met the quarterback Bert, a top scholar with a 4.0 GPA. According to social psychologists, Julie then experienced _____.
   - A. cognitive dissonance
   - B. social distance
   - C. the Asch effect
   - D. out-group prejudice

7. Chris and Pat have been dating for two years. They were both voted best-looking in their senior class. Their relationship demonstrates the _____ hypothesis.
   - A. similarity
   - B. attractiveness
   - C. charisma
   - D. matching

8. All of the following have been found to be sources of reward in relationships EXCEPT _____.
   - A. similarity
   - B. proximity
   - C. self-disclosure
   - D. prosperity

9. The best predictor of bystander intervention is _____.
   - A. ethnicity of the bystanders
   - B. ethnicity of the victim
   - C. the location of the emergency
   - D. the number of bystanders

10. The U.S.'s involvement in the Vietnam War was ultimately ascribed to _____.
    - A. groupthink
    - B. social pressure
    - C. incompetence
    - D. the Asch effect

PRACTICE TEST #3

1. Prejudice is a(n) _____, whereas discrimination is a(n) _____.
   A. behavior; attitude
   B. attitude; behavior
   C. schema; script
   D. script; schema

2. Patel and Nitya share secrets, openly discuss their emotions, and are strongly sexually attracted to each other. According to Sternberg's theory, which type of love do they have?
   A. Complete   B. Romantic   C. Companionate   D. Infatuation

3 We tend to feel pity or sympathy for individuals we perceive as _____ in warmth and _____ in competence.
   A. low; low   B. high; high   C. low; high   D. high; low

4. Sally tripped on the rug when she entered the dorm. She blamed this on the rug being slippery. When Stuart did the same thing, she called him clumsy. This is representative of _____.
   A. the proximity bias
   B. cognitive dissonance
   C. the fundamental attribution error
   D. an ascription error

5. All of the following increase the likelihood of getting help from would-be helpers EXCEPT _____.
   A. asking for help
   B. reducing the situation's ambiguity
   C. being in the vicinity of older people
   D. identifying specific individuals to give help

6. An individual is less likely to conform to a majority opinion when _____.
   A. he or she has an ally in dissenting
   B. the group is cohesive
   C. a judgment task is ambiguous or unclear
   D. the person's responses are given in public

7. The term "social _____" refers to our subjective interpretations of other people and of our relationships with them.
   A. norms   B. psychology   C. distance   D. reality

8. The Asch study primarily examined the impact of _____.
   A. a group majority on the judgments of an individual
   B. an individual's opinion on a unanimous group decision
   C. a researcher's presence upon group decisions
   D. a group's size upon the judgment of an individual

9. _____ is blaming an innocent person or group for one's own troubles and then discriminating against or abusing that person or group.
   A. Groupthink   B. Dehumanization   C. Bullying   D. Scapegoating

10. Research shows that if someone is in trouble, _____ will be the best determinant as to whether they are likely to get help from others.

    A. the age of the person in trouble   C. the gender of the person in trouble

    B. the size of the group present   D. the seriousness of the problem

COMPREHENSIVE REVIEW TEST

1. Conformity is best defined as the tendency _____.
    A. to adopt the behavior and attitudes of others
    B. to be influenced by private expectations of how others will act
    C. to behave in ways that don't match your attitudes
    D. to assist those who are unfamiliar with customs and expectations

2. Based on Milgram's experiment, we can conclude that people are most likely to be obedient under all of the following conditions EXCEPT when _____.
    A. a peer models obedience   C. the victim was remote from the subject
    B. the authority figure was challenged   D. the authority figure had higher relative status

3. All of the following are forms of subtle persuasive pressure EXCEPT _____.
    A. social validation   C. cognitive dissonance
    B. authority   D. the poison parasite argument

4. Raoul drinks a lot of alcohol although he knows he's hurting his health. He tells himself that it's better than being a drug addict and he's not hurting anybody, so he continues to drink. Raoul is demonstrating _____.
    A. the fundamental attribution error   C. the Asch effect
    B. cognitive dissonance   D. scapegoating

5. The two universal dimensions of human social cognition are _____ and _____.
    A. competence; warmth   C. collectivism; individualism
    B. rewards; costs   D. attraction; respect

6. The type of love that involves commitment and intimacy but no passion is called _____ love.
    A. empty   B. consummate   C. companionate   D. abstinent

7. All of the following are factors that have been found to promote attraction EXCEPT _____.
    A. proximity   B. similarity   C. attributions   D. self-disclosure

8. The case of Kitty Genovese resulted in research about what social psychology phenomenon?
    A. The Asch effect   C. The self-serving bias
    B. Cognitive dissonance   D. The bystander intervention problem

9. In the original Asch study, what proportion of people conformed?
    A. two-thirds   B. one-fourth   C. one-third   D. one-half

10. All of the following have been found to be effective in preventing or reducing prejudice EXCEPT _____.
    A. role models   B. education   C. jigsaw classroom   D. equal status contact

11. The U.S. Senate Intelligence Committee cited _____ as one of the processes involved in the decision to wage war against Iraq.
    A. groupthink   B. the Asch effect   C. the FAE   D. the self-serving bias

12. Knowledge about the sequence of events and actions that are expected in a particular social setting is referred to as a _____.
    A. schema   B. social role   C. social norm D. script

13. All of the following have been found to promote groupthink EXCEPT _____.
    A. lack of directive leadership   C. lack of norms concerning procedures
    B. high group cohesiveness   D. homogeneity of group members

14. The best predictor of how well a person will be liked after a first meeting is his or her _____.
    A. friendliness   B. self-disclosure   C. happiness   D. physical attractiveness

15. The autokinetic effect was used to study _____.
    A. attributions   B. obedience   C. conformity   D. scripts

CRITICAL THINKING ESSAYS

1. Explain the findings of the Asch studies and the bystander intervention studies. Then, tell what we've learned from these studies about the situationism versus dispositionism debate.

2. What factors contribute to prejudice, and what strategies are most and least effective for reducing prejudice?

CHAPTER 12
Psychological Disorders

Before You Read . . . Term Identification

Make flashcards using the following terms or, even better, develop mnemonics (memory strategies) to help you remember the different concepts and terms. Use the definitions in the margins of this chapter for help. Numbers refer to page numbers in the textbook.

affective disturbances (517)
agoraphobia (531)
antisocial personality disorder (543)
anxiety disorder (530)
attention-deficit hyperactivity disorder (542)
autism (541)
bipolar disorder (529)
borderline personality disorder (543)
conversion disorder (534)
delusion (517)
depersonalization (546)
depersonalization disorder (536)
diathesis-stress hypothesis (540)
dissociative amnesia (535)
dissociative disorders (535)
dissociative fugue (536)
dissociative identity disorder (536)
DSM-IV (524)
dyslexia (542)
ecological view (546)
generalized anxiety disorder (531)
hallucination (517)

hypochondriasis (535)
insanity (523)
labeling (546)
learned helplessness (529)
major depression (526)
medical model (519)
mood disorder (526)
narcissistic personality disorder (543)
neurosis (525)
obsessive-compulsive disorder (533)
panic disorder (531)
personality disorder (542)
phobia (532)
preparedness hypothesis (533)
psychopathology (517)
psychosis (525)
rumination (529)
schizophrenia (537)
seasonal affective disorder (SAD) (528)
shyness (544)
somatoform disorders (534)

Lecture Assistant *for Chapter 12*
Tear this outline out and bring it with you to class in order to facilitate your note taking.
Spend more time listening to the lecture and less time writing!

Chapter Opening Problem: Is it possible to distinguish mental disorders from merely unusual behavior? That is, are there specific signs that clearly indicate a mental disorder?

- *psychopathology =*

12.1 WHAT IS PSYCHOLOGICAL DISORDER?

- *Hallucination =*

- *Delusion =*

- *Affective disturbances =*

Core Concept 12.1 =

A) Changing Concepts of Psychological Disorder:

1) The Medical Model =

- *Medical model =*

2) Psychological Alternatives to the Medical Model =

3) The Biopsychology of Mental Disorder =

B) Indicators of Abnormality

- *Etiology =*

C) A Caution to Readers =

D) Psychology Matters: The Plea of Insanity

- *Insanity* =

12.2 HOW ARE PSYCHOLOGICAL DISORDERS CLASSIFIED IN THE *DSM-IV*?

- DSM-IV =

Core Concept 12.2 =

A) Overview of the *DSM-IV* Classification System:

- *Neurosis* =

- *Psychosis* =

1) Five-Dimensional Diagnosis: The Multiaxial System =

2) Controversy Surrounding the *DSM-IV* =

B) Mood Disorders:

- *Mood disorder* =

1) Major Depression =

- *Major depression (major depressive disorder)* =

  a) Incidence =

  - *Dysthymia* =

  b) Cross-Cultural Comparisons =

  c) Causes of Depression =

d) <u>Sunlight and Depression</u> =

- *Seasonal affective disorder (SAD)* =

e) <u>Psychological Factors</u> =

- *Rumination* =

- *Learned helplessness* =

f) <u>Who Becomes Depressed?</u> =

2) <u>Bipolar Disorder</u> =

- *Bipolar disorder (manic-depressive disorder)* =

C) Anxiety Disorders:

- *Anxiety disorder* =

1) <u>Generalized Anxiety Disorder</u> =

2) <u>Panic Disorder</u> =

- *Agoraphobia* =

3) <u>Phobic Disorder</u> =

- *Phobia* =

- *Preparedness hypothesis* =

4) <u>Obsessive-Compulsive Disorder (OCD)</u> =

- o *Obsession* =

- o *Compulsion* =

D) Somatoform Disorders:

- *Somatoform disorders =*

1) <u>Conversion Disorder</u> =

2) <u>Hypochondriasis</u> =

E) Dissociative Disorders:

- *Dissociative disorders =*

1) <u>Dissociative Amnesia</u> =

2) <u>Dissociative Fugue</u> =

3) <u>Depersonalization Disorder</u> =

4) <u>Dissociative Identity Disorder</u> =

F) Schizophrenia:

- *Schizophrenia =*

1) <u>Major Types of Schizophrenia</u> =

2) Possible Causes of Schizophrenia =

- *Diathesis-stress hypothesis* =

G) Developmental Disorders:

1) Autism =

2) Dyslexia =

3) Attention-Deficit Hyperactivity Disorder (ADHD) =

H) Personality Disorders:

- *Personality disorder* =

1) Narcissistic Personality Disorder =

2) Antisocial Personality Disorder =

3) Borderline Personality Disorder =

I) Adjustment Disorders and Other Conditions: The Biggest Category of All =

J) Gender Differences in Mental Disorders =

K) Psychology Matters: Shyness

- *Shyness* =

12.3 WHAT ARE THE CONSEQUENCES OF LABELING PEOPLE?

- *Labeling* =

Core Concept 12.3 =

A) Diagnostic Labels, Labeling, and Depersonalization

- *Depersonalization* =

B) The Cultural Context of Psychological Disorders =

- *Ecological view* =

C) Psychology Matters: Using Psychology to Learn Psychology

D) Critical Thinking Applied: Insane Places Revisited—Another Look at the Rosenhan Study

What Is a Psychological Disorder?

1. Briefly describe the study that David Rosenhan and his colleagues conducted on mental hospitals. What did they discover from this study?

2. *Underline the word(s) in parentheses that will make each statement correct. (Both options may be correct!)*

    A. Another term for psychopathology is mental (illness/disorder).

    B. According to the World Health Organization, about (45/450) million people around the world suffer from mental disorders.

    C. Around the world, (depression/anxiety) caused more disability among people aged fifteen to forty-four than any other cause except HIV/AIDS.

    D. According to the (psychological/medical) model, mental problems are diseases.

    E. The (psychological/medical) model views psychological disorder as an interaction between biological, cognitive, developmental, and (socio-cultural/behavioral) factors.

    F. Psychological disorders are an exaggeration of (normal/abnormal) responses.

    G. It's best to think of psychological disorder as (a separate category of mental health/part of a continuum).

3. Describe the three most common symptoms associated with severe psychopathology.

Symptoms	Descriptions
A. _____	
B. _____	
C. _____	

Changing Concepts of Psychological Disorder

4. *Underline the word(s) in parentheses that will make each statement correct. (Both options may be correct!)*

    A. Around 400 B.C., the Greek physician Hippocrates stated that abnormal behavior has (physical/supernatural) causes.

    B. In the (ancient world/Middle Ages), psychopathology was believed to be caused by (demons and spirits/an imbalance of humors).

    C. The (psychological/medical) model resurfaced during the late (seventeenth/eighteenth) century.

    D. A modern analysis of the Salem witch trials has concluded that the girls believed to be witches were probably suffering from poisoning caused by a (tree root/fungus).

5. Why do many modern psychologists believe that the medical model is problematic? Give at least three reasons.

    A. _____

    B. _____

    C. _____

6. *Fill in the blanks with the correct information.*

    The _____ approach includes several of psychology's major perspectives and is an alternative to the _____ model. Albert Bandura's idea of _____ is typical of this approach in that it proposes that behavior, _____, and social/environmental factors all influence each other.

    However, despite most psychologists' concerns about the medical model, they don't deny the influences of _____ on thinking and behavior. The Human _____ Project has provided specialists in the field of _____ genetics the opportunity to search for genes associated with specific disorders. Most experts believe that psychological disorders are likely to be caused by _____ genes interacting with influences in the _____.

7. Compare the medical model and the psychological model of psychological disorder.

Indicators of Abnormality

8. What are the five indicators of abnormality?

A. _____ B. _____ C. _____

D. _____ E. _____

9. *Match each indicator of abnormality with its best example(s) by placing the letter corresponding to the indicator in the space next to its example. (Terms may be used only once.)*

INDICATORS OF ABNORMALITY
A. Distress   C. Unpredictability   E. Unconventionality
B. Maladaptiveness   D. Irrationality

EXAMPLES
_____ Jackson sleeps in most mornings and ambles into work two hours late. Consequently, he gets fired. This has happened at least ten times, but he is not concerned, because he is sure that things will take care of themselves.
_____ Jerrell and his business partners decide to run through the snow naked just for fun.
_____ Mei-Ling spends her days working at the job she has held for ten years. One day she goes into the office and throws her computer out of the window.
_____ Michael spends hours talking on the phone to his brother who died four years ago.
_____ Kelly has been feeling sad for several weeks. Lately she has begun to think about ending her life by jumping off of a bridge.

10. *Indicate whether each statement is True (T) or False (F) by circling the appropriate letter after the statement.*

A. When trying to label a behavior as abnormal, clinicians are less confident in their labels when two or more indicators are present.   T F

B. Over 300 specific variations of psychopathology are described in the *DSM-IV*.   T F

C. The *DSM-IV* is used only by psychiatrists.   T F

A Caution to Readers

11. What caution is given to readers of this chapter by your textbook authors?

Psychology Matters: The Plea of Insanity

12. *Underline the word(s) in parentheses that will make each statement correct. (Both options may be correct!)*

    A. The plea of insanity is a (psychological/legal) term.

    B. The term "insanity" can refer to (psychosis/mental retardation).

    C. The insanity plea occurs in less than (1/5) percent of criminal cases.

    D. The insanity plea was used unsuccessfully in the murder case of (Jeffrey Dahmer/Charles Manson).

13. Legally, a crime requires what two elements? How does the insanity plea relate to these two elements?

How Are Psychological Disorders Classified in the *DSM-IV*?

14. What does the acronym *DSM-IV* stand for?

15. The *DSM-IV* groups just about all forms of psychopathology into categories based on what two types of symptoms?

    A. _____   B. _____

Overview of the *DSM-IV* Classification System

16. Give the former and current definitions of "neurosis" and "psychosis."

17. *Fill in the blanks with the correct information.*

    A. The *DSM-IV* was first published in the year _____ by the American _____

       Association and was then revised in the year _____.

    B. The *DSM-IV* has huge economic power because it is used by _____

       companies to determine what psychological treatments they will _____.

C. The term _____ was removed from the fourth edition of the *DSM* and was replaced by the term "disorder."

D. In the *DSM-IV*, the term _____ is used mainly for loss of contact with reality.

E. The *DSM-IV* is closely aligned with the _____ model.

F. The *DSM-IV* has no diagnosis of _____.

G. The *DSM-IV* assesses patients on _____ different dimensions (i.e., axes).

H. The Global Assessment of Functioning Scale is used for Axis _____ assessments.

18. Explain three different issues that have surfaced in the controversy surrounding the *DSM-IV*.

Mood Disorders

19. *Underline the word(s) in parentheses that will make each statement correct. (Both options may be correct!)*

A. Major depression is a type of (mood/affective) disorder.

B. Bipolar disorder used to be called (dysthymia/manic-depressive disorder).

C. Cross-cultural studies show that (depression/anxiety) is the most prevalent form of disability around the world.

D. One of every (fifty/one hundred and fifty) depression sufferers commits suicide.

E. When a person attributes negative effects to something he or she cannot control or change, this is called (rumination/learned helplessness).

F. Cultures that have (high/low) rates of divorce or marital separation have high rates of depression.

G. Research has linked depression to lower brain wave activity in the (left/right) (frontal/temporal) lobe.

H. Recent neuroimaging studies have linked depression to an area of the (cerebral cortex/hippocampus) called Area (25/51), where the area shows up "hot" in (depressed/nondepressed) individuals.

I. Dysthymia is a more (mild/severe) form of depression than major depression.

20. What is "rumination" and how does it relate to depression?

21. *Fill in the table below with the correct information about seasonal affective disorder.*

What It Is	When It Occurs	Hormone Involved	How It's Treated

22. What two main reasons have been proposed for why women have a higher incidence of depression than men do?

A. _____

B. _____

23. How do researchers know that unipolar depression and bipolar depression are two separate types?

24. This National Mental Health Association provides information to help with screening for depression. Visit the following site:
   http://www.depression-screening.org/

Anxiety Disorders

25. *Fill in the blanks in the following table about phobias.*

Name of Phobia	Description
A.	Fear of normal situations involving interactions with other people
B. Agoraphobia	
C.	Fear of closed-in spaces
D. Ophidiophobia	
E.	Fear of heights

26. The major differences among the anxiety disorders have to do with what two aspects of anxiety?

      A. _____   B. _____

27. *Match each term with its description(s) by placing the letter corresponding to the term in the space next to its description. (Terms may be used more than once.)*

TERMS
A. Generalized anxiety disorder   C. Panic disorder
B. Phobic disorder   D. Obsessive-compulsive disorder

DESCRIPTIONS
_____ Anxiety is persistent, pervasive, and not tied to a specific object or event.
_____ Consists of a persistent and irrational fear
_____ Is related to the preparedness hypothesis.
_____ Anxiety comes in waves, with periods of relative calm in between.
_____ Involves repetitive, purposeful acts done to reduce anxiety
_____ Anticipatory anxiety often develops in conjunction with it.
_____ Often involves deep motor control areas of the brain

28. This international foundation's website brings together information and research about obsessive-compulsive disorder (OCD). Visit:
http://www.ocfoundation.org/

Somatoform Disorders

29. What are "somatoform disorders"? How do they differ from "psychosomatic disorders"?

30. *Identify the following examples of somatoform disorders by writing the name of the disorder in the blank next to the example.*

      A. _____ Genevieve did not see the trains collide, but she heard the awful noise of the engines smashing together. Now she cannot hear anything, although her doctors cannot find anything wrong with her ears.

      B. _____ Barry watches many medical shows on television. He is sure that he has some dreaded disease, so he visits doctor after doctor, trying to get a diagnosis.

31. *Indicate whether each statement is True (T) or False (F) by circling the appropriate letter after the statement.*

      A. "Glove anesthesia" is a form of sensory loss in hypochondriasis.   T F

      B. David Oakley suggests that a common brain mechanism underlies conversion disorder and hypnosis, and that conversion disorder should therefore be called an *auto-suggestive disorder* rather than a somatoform disorder.   T F

      C. Hypochondriasis is a type of psychosomatic disorder.   T F

      D. Somatoform disorders occur only in about 6 percent of the population.   T F

      E. Hypochondriasis used to be called "hysteria."   T F

      F. The term "conversion disorder" is related to Freudian theory.   T F

      G. Conversion disorder is more common in economically undeveloped regions than in industrialized countries.   T F

Dissociative Disorders

32. *Match each term with its description(s) by placing the letter corresponding to the term in the space next to its description. (Terms may be used more than once.)*

TERMS
A. Dissociative amnesia   C. Dissociative identity disorder
B. Dissociative fugue   D. Depersonalization disorder

DESCRIPTIONS
_____ Formerly called multiple personality disorder
_____ Involves a loss of memory, loss of identity, and fleeing from one's home
_____ Is highly related to posttraumatic stress disorder
_____ Often accompanied by OCD and certain personality disorders
_____ Involves "out-of-body" experiences and the sense that one is observing oneself

33. What is the common factor in all of the dissociative disorders?

      ANSWER: _____

34. What are three different explanations for the existence of dissociative identity disorder?

A. _____

B. _____

C. _____

35. Compare and contrast the concepts of "multiple personality," "split personality," and "schizophrenia."

36. The Internet Mental Health site is maintained by a Canadian physician and contains information about psychological disorders, as well as discussion groups about the disorders. http://www.mentalhealth.com/

Schizophrenia

37. *Identify the type of schizophrenia by writing its name in the space next to its best example.*

A. _____ This patient has a history of schizophrenia, but has no current symptoms. His thinking is mildly disturbed. The disease may be entering remission.

B. _____ This patient has incoherent speech, hallucinations, and delusions. She may talk to imaginary people.

C. _____ This patient may have delusions of persecution or grandiosity. These delusions are illogical and not well organized.

D. _____ This patient has symptoms of each type of schizophrenia, but the symptoms do not fit into a clear category.

E. _____ This patient may remain motionless for hours or days, and often holds a rigid, statue-like position.

38. What are the differences between "positive symptoms" and "negative symptoms" of schizophrenia? What evidence supports this distinction? What problems are there with this distinction?

39. Explain the "diathesis-stress hypothesis" concerning the cause of schizophrenia.

40. *Fill in the blanks by describing the supporting evidence for the three possible biological causes of schizophrenia.*

Possible Cause	Supporting Evidence
A. Neurotransmitters	
B. Brain structures	
C. Genetics	

41. The Schizophrenia Society of Canada has provided information on schizophrenia to the public for over twenty-five years. Visit its excellent website at:
http://www.schizophrenia.ca/

Developmental Disorders

42. *Underline the word(s) in parentheses that will make each statement correct. (Both options may be correct!)*

A. (Dyslexia/Autism) involves problems with (activity level/language), social interactions, and "reading" other people.

B. Some research evidence links (dyslexia/autism) with (mirror neurons/toxic materials).

C. It is estimated that one in (500/5000) children develop some form of autism, that one in (5/50) children has some degree of dyslexia, and that 3 percent to (5 percent/12 percent) of school-aged children have attention-deficit hyperactivity disorder.

D. (English/Italian) speakers are more likely than (English/Italian) speakers to develop dyslexia.

E. Individuals with (autism/ADHD) have a poorly developed theory of mind.

43. This is the site for Children and Adults with Attention Deficit/Hyperactivity Disorder (CHADD), an organization devoted to helping those with ADHD.
http://www.chadd.org

44. The following website (created by Russell A. Dewey, PhD) provides a comprehensive set of links to other sites about psychological disorders.
http://www.psywww.com/resource/selfhelp.htm

Personality Disorders

45. *Match each term with its best example(s) by placing the letter corresponding to the term in the space next to its example. (Terms may be used more than once.)*

TERMS
A. Borderline personality disorder   B. Antisocial personality disorder

C. Narcissistic personality disorder

EXAMPLES

_____ Pamela is thirty-seven years old, and her entire adult life she has constantly talked about her accomplishments, daydreamed about gaining status and power, and felt entitled to special privileges. She shows very little empathy toward others.

_____ Sixty-year-old Jeff is charming, funny, and bright. He easily lies, cheats, and cons other people, but feels no guilt or shame for doing so.

_____ Ever since her teenage years, Elaine has impulsively shopped, has been unpredictable, angry, and moody in her all her relationships, and has engaged in self-scratching to the point of leaving scars on her body.

_____ Fourteen-year-old Margarite abuses animals and destroys people's property. She's been caught a few times, but always is indifferent to what is said or done to her.

46. The Mayo Clinic gives a good overview of several different personality disorders. Visit:
http://www.mayoclinic.com/health/personality-disorders/DS00562

Adjustment Disorders and Other Conditions: The Biggest Category of All

47. Briefly discuss adjustment disorders, what they include, and how prevalent they are.

48. NEED A BREAK?
To get a better understanding of psychological disorders, visit MyPsychLab.

49. Fill in the blanks of the following concept map with the correct information.

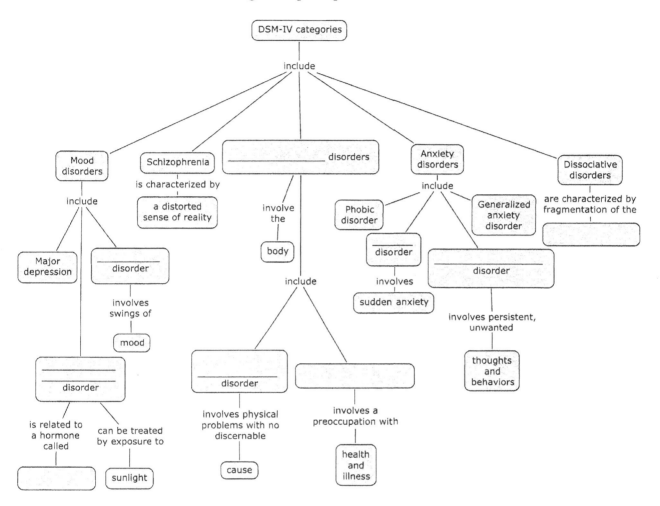

Gender Differences in Mental Disorders

50. Which disorders are more prevalent in men, and which are more prevalent in women? How might social norms contribute to these differences?

51. What brain difference might contribute to the gender difference found for many disorders?

Psychology Matters: Shyness

52. Explain shyness and how it relates to psychological disorder.

What Are The Consequences of Labeling People?

Diagnostic Labels, Labeling, and Depersonalization

53. What are three potential negative consequences of labeling a person as mentally disturbed?

A. _____   B. _____

C. _____

The Cultural Context of Psychological Disorder

54. What is the "ecological model" of psychological disorder, and what evidence supports this model?

55. According to Kleinman and Cohen, what are the three persistent myths related to culture and psychological disorder?

A. _____

B. _____

C. _____

Critical Thinking Applied: Insane Places Revisited—Another Look at the Rosenhan Study

56. Rosenhan's study called into question the reliability of psychiatric diagnoses and whether mental disorder can be distinguished from normalcy. Discuss four criticisms leveled at Rosenhan's study and conclusions. Then, discuss how Rosenhan countered these criticisms.

Criticisms of Rosenhan	Rosenhan's Responses to Criticisms
A	
B.	
C.	
D.	

57. What factors did Rosenhan believe contributed to the impersonal, non-therapeutic environment of mental hospitals?

PRACTICE TEST #1

1. The "pseudopatients" in Rosenhan's study exhibited what following abnormal behavior once admitted?
   A. Talking to themselves
   B. Walking in circles
   C. Taking notes
   D. Flapping their arms

2. What two types of symptoms does the *DSM-IV* use to classify individuals?
   A. Objective and subjective
   B. Intrinsic and extrinsic
   C. Cognitive and affective
   D. Mental and behavioral

3. In 400 B.C., Hippocrates believed that psychopathology was caused by _____.
   A. witchcraft   B. biology   C. bad parenting   D. demons and spirits

4. All of the following are indicators of psychopathology EXCEPT _____.
   A. false beliefs   B. delusions   C. extreme moods   D. hallucinations

5. Daniel is delusional, has hallucinations, and sits rigidly for hours without moving. He would most likely be diagnosed as having _____.
   A. catatonic schizophrenia
   B. bipolar disorder
   C. somatoform schizophrenia
   D. dissociative fugue

6. All of the following are disorders more common in women than in men EXCEPT _____.
   A. major depressive disorder
   B. schizophrenia
   C. bipolar disorder
   D. anxiety disorders

7. Janet's therapist believes that her phobia came about as a result of her mother's decision to reward her fear of public speaking by soothing her with ice cream and candy. Her therapist most likely is a proponent of the _____ perspective.
   A. social   B. cognitive   C. behavioral   D. psychodynamic

8. Doreen laughs uncontrollably at funerals. She is exhibiting the psychopathology indicator of
   _____.
   A. distress   B. maladaptiveness   C. irrationality D. unpredictability

9. Your friend Sam was so overwhelmed with anxiety that he could not bring himself to take the Graduate Record Exam. He is displaying the indicator of abnormality called _____.
   A. distress   B. maladaptiveness   C. irrationality D. unpredictability

10. The *DSM-IV* categorizes disorders based on _____.
    A. symptoms
    B. causes
    C. both symptoms and causes
    D. symptoms, causes, and treatment options

PRACTICE TEST #2

1. Which *DSM-IV* category covers disorders in which an individual is overly concerned with issues of physical health?
   A. Dissociative disorders
   B. Affective disorders
   C. Somatoform disorders
   D. Personality disorders

2. All of the following are current *DSM-IV* diagnostic categories EXCEPT _____.
   A. anxiety disorders
   B. neurotic disorders
   C. dissociative disorders
   D. mood disorders

3. The *DSM* was developed primarily by _____.
   A. internists   B. psychologists   C. psychiatrists   D. social workers

4. The current edition of the *DSM* has gotten rid of the term _____, which refers to a relatively common pattern of self-defeating behavior.
   A. neurosis   B. distress   C. insanity   D. lunacy

5. All of the following would be classified under the *DSM-IV* category of mood disorders EXCEPT _____.
   A. depression
   B. bipolar disorder
   C. schizophrenia
   D. seasonal affective disorder

6. All of the following are considered indicators of psychopathology EXCEPT _____.
   A. irrationality
   B. distress
   C. unpredictability
   D. behavior different from the norm

7. Evidence suggests that the direct biological triggering mechanism for panic disorder lies in the _____.
   A. genes   B. brain stem   C. limbic system   D. endocrine system

8. Lorraine's mother passed away after a long illness. Lorraine was quite sad for several months following her mother's death. When she was still in that state a year later, her friends were concerned that she might be suffering from _____.
   A. major depression
   B. conversion disorder
   C. bipolar disorder
   D. anxiety disorder

9. A particular form of depression related to sunlight deprivation is known as _____.
   A. clinical depression
   B. seasonal affective disorder
   C. sunlight deprivation disorder
   D. winter latitude disorder

10. More women than men are diagnosed with depression. One model suggests that women are more vulnerable because of their tendency towards a(n) _____ response.
    A. ruminative   B. hormonal   C. irrational   D. helplessness

PRACTICE TEST #3

1. Patty went to a therapist because her behavior was causing her anxiety. Some days she was quite depressed. At other times she would go on spending sprees and stay up for three days straight. Her therapist most likely diagnosed her with _____.
   A. panic disorder   B. anxiety disorder   C. bipolar disorder   D. schizophrenia

2. At the mall, Lisa finds herself suddenly unable to catch her breath, feels that her heartbeat is irregular, and experiences an overwhelming sense of doom. These feelings last for just a few minutes. Lisa is most likely suffering from _____.
   A. social phobia   C. compulsive disorder
   B. learned helplessness   D. panic disorder

3. Which of the following statements about depression is FALSE?
   A. Women report higher rates of depression than men do.
   B. Depression is more common in countries with low divorce rates than in countries with high divorce rates.
   C. Depression is linked with rumination.
   D. Dysthymia is a milder form of depression than major depressive disorder.

4. Which statement about shyness is TRUE?
   A. Shyness is a social disorder listed in the *DSM-IV*.
   B. Shy children grow up to be shy adults.
   C. Shyness is considered to be an anxiety disorder.
   D. Shyness can develop into a social phobia.

5. Rupert has trouble going to social events because he refuses to use the bathroom anywhere except at his own house. He is most likely suffering from _____.
   A. panic disorder   C. major depression
   B. obsessive-compulsive disorderD. a social phobia

6. Harvey has an idea for a soap opera story in which a character who witnesses a murder then loses his vision for no physical reason. Harvey is going to have the character develop _____.
   A. anxiety disorder   C. hypochondriasis
   B. obsessive-compulsive disorderD. conversion disorder

7. Usually the fugue state lasts for _____.
   A. about a year   B. minutes or hours   C. less than an hour   D. a few hours or days

8. Seasonal affective disorder is linked to the hormone called _____.
   A. epinephrine   B. glutamate   C. melatonin   D. monosodium

340

9. Sam felt as though he was constantly in a dream or "out of his body." He would most likely be diagnosed with _____.
   A. depersonalization disorder
   B. dissociative amnesia
   C. schizophrenia
   D. dissociative fugue

10. Individuals with dissociative identity disorder frequently report a history of _____.
   A. viral infections
   B. a parent with mental illness
   C. sexual abuse
   D. anger management problems

COMPREHENSIVE REVIEW TEST

1. In the *DSM-IV*, an Axis II diagnosis relates to _____.
   A. long-standing problems   C. relevant medical problems
   B. the primary clinical diagnosis   D. a global assessment of functioning

2. Neil lines his windows with tinfoil because he fears the government is listening to his conversations. He will not talk on a public phone for the same reasons. Neil would likely be diagnosed with _____ schizophrenia.
   A. paranoid B. catatonic   C. disorganized D. undifferentiated

3. Research on the causes of schizophrenia have focused on the neurotransmitter _____.
   A. serotonin   B. glutamate   C. melatonin   D. acetycholine

4. Kathryn reads about diseases, and is sure she has many of them. She makes appointments with doctors, but they can find nothing physically wrong with her. Kathryn may have _____.
   A. conversion disorder   C. dissociative disorder
   B. catatonic schizophrenia   D. a somatoform disorder

5. Children with autism generally exhibit all of the following symptoms EXCEPT _____.
   A. theory of mind deficiencies   C. language difficulties
   B. social isolation   D. hyperactivity

6. Jen has been having trouble concentrating, making decisions, and finishing her schoolwork since her boyfriend started dating her roommate. Jen would most likely be diagnosed with _____.
   A. conversion disorder   C. adjustment disorder
   B. dissociative fugue   D. obsessive-compulsive disorder

7. Layal feels she has no control over events in her life and can do nothing to change her situation. Layal is exhibiting _____.
   A. rumination   C. unpredictability
   B. learned helplessness   D. delusions

8. Iris has an intense fear of being in small rooms that resulted from her being punished as a child by being locked in a closet. This explanation is most supportive of the _____ approach.
   A. humanistic   B. behavioral   C. cognitive   D. biological

9. Raphael constantly thinks about his problems and failures in life and currently has depression. Which approach suggests that Raphael's negative thoughts are the cause of his depression?
   A. Biological   B. Humanistic   C. Behavioral   D. Cognitive

10. While walking in the corridor of an inpatient psychiatric unit, you say "Hello, how are you?" to a patient and he responds by saying: "Fine, like rainbows! They go swimming on their way without concern about drowning." The most likely diagnosis for this patient is _____.
A. dysthymia
C. schizophrenia
B. antisocial personality disorder
D. panic disorder

11. A psychologist who believes that schizophrenia arises from the interaction of a genetic predisposition and an environmental trigger supports the _____.
A. double-bind model
C. interventionist view
B. diathesis-stress hypothesis
D. nature/nurture theory

12. Jimmy has been diagnosed with dyslexia. To effectively help him overcome this problem, he is most likely receiving which of the following treatments?
A. Medication   B. Reading program   C. Physical therapy   D. Special eyeglasses

13. _____ used to be called "multiple personality disorder."
A. Dissociative identity disorder
C. Depersonalization disorder
B. Conversion disorder
D. Schizophrenia

14. Ahmed has an intense fear of open spaces, so he always stays at home. It is likely he has _____.
A. acrophobia   B. claustrophobia   C. agoraphobia   D. ophidiophobia

15. Which of the following statements about the insanity plea is true?
A. Insanity is clearly defined in the *DSM-IV*.
B. It is a legal term that only a court can officially apply.
C. It is successful in only two out of every thousand criminal cases.
D. It is applied only to illegal acts and to the intent to commit such acts.

CRITICAL THINKING ESSAYS

1. Explain some of the gender differences in the incidence of different types of psychological disorders. Then, discuss the possible reasons for these gender differences.

2. You are at a party when you get into a debate about the insanity plea. Describe the myths about the use of the insanity plea and respond to these myths based on what you have learned in this chapter.

CHAPTER 13
Therapies for Psychological Disorders

Before You Read . . . Term Identification

Make flashcards using the following terms or, even better, develop mnemonics (memory strategies) to help you remember the different concepts and terms. Use the definitions in the margins of this chapter for help. Numbers refer to page numbers in the textbook.

active listener (576)
analysis of transference (564)
antianxiety drugs (580)
antidepressants (578)
antipsychotics (578)
aversion therapy (570)
behavior modification (568)
behavior therapy (568)
biomedical therapy (560)
client-centered therapy (565)
cognitive therapy (566)
cognitive-behavioral therapy (571)
combination therapy (586)
community mental health movement (583)
contingency management (570)
deinstitutionalization (583)
electroconvulsive therapy (ect) (582)
empirically supported treatment (591)
exposure therapy (569)
group therapy (567)

humanistic therapy (565)
insight therapy (562)
Neo-Freudian psychodynamic therapy (564)
paraprofessional (560)
participant modeling (571)
positive psychotherapy (ppt) (573)
psychoanalysis (562)
psychological therapy (560)
psychosurgery (581)
rational-emotive behavior therapy (572)
reflection of feeling (565)
self-help support groups (567)
stimulants (580)
systematic desensitization (569)
tardive dyskinesia (578)
therapeutic alliance (557)
therapeutic community ()
therapy (556)
token economy (571)
transcranial magnetic stimulation (583)

Lecture Assistant *for Chapter 13*

Tear this outline out and bring it with you to class in order to facilitate your note taking.
Spend more time listening to the lecture and less time writing!

Chapter Opening Problem: What is the best treatment for Derek's depression: psychological therapy, drug
therapy, or both? More broadly, the problem is this: How do we decide
among the available therapies for any of the mental disorders?

- *Therapy =*

13.1 WHAT IS THERAPY?

Core Concept 13.1 =

A) Entering Therapy:

B) The Therapeutic Alliance and the Goals of Therapy:

1) <u>What Are the Components of Therapy?</u> =

- *Therapeutic alliance =*

Three General Steps of Therapy:
a)_____

b)_____

c)_____

2) <u>Who Does Therapy?</u> =

C) Therapy in Historical and Cultural Context:

1) <u>History of Therapy</u> =

2) <u>Modern Approaches to Therapy</u> =

- *Psychological therapy =*

- *Biomedical therapy =*

3) <u>Disorder and Therapy in a Cultural Context</u> =

D) Psychology Matters: Paraprofessionals Do Therapy, Too

- *Paraprofessional* =

13.2 HOW DO PSYCHOLOGISTS TREAT PSYCHOLOGICAL DISORDERS?

Core Concept 13.2 =

A) Insight Therapies:

1) <u>Freudian Psychoanalysis</u> =

- *Psychoanalysis* =

- *Analysis of transference* =

2) <u>Neo-Freudian Psychodynamic Therapies</u> =

3) <u>Humanistic Therapies</u> =

- *Client-centered therapy* =

- *Reflection of feeling (reflective listening)* =

4) Cognitive Therapies =

- *Cognitive therapy =*

5) Group Therapies =

    a) Self-Help Support Groups =

    b) Couples and Family Therapy =

B) Behavior Therapies:

- *Behavior modification (behavior therapy) =*

1) Classical Conditioning Therapies =

    a) Systematic Desensitization =

- *Exposure therapy =*

    b) Aversion Therapy =

2) Operant Conditioning Therapies =

    a) Contingency Management =

    b) Token Economies =

3) Participant Modeling: An Observational-Learning Therapy =

- *Participant modeling* =

  o *Symbolic modeling* =

C) Cognitive-Behavioral Therapy: A Synthesis

- *Cognitive-behavioral therapy* =

1) Rational-Emotive Behavior Therapy: Challenging the "Shoulds" and "Oughts" =

- *Rational-emotive behavior therapy (REBT)* =

2) Positive Psychotherapy (PPT) =

3) Changing the Brain by Changing the Mind =

D) Evaluating the Psychological Therapies:

1) Eysenck's Controversial Proclamation =

2) In Response to Eysenck =

3) New Questions =

E) Psychology Matters: Where Do Most People Get Help?

- *Active listener* =

13.3 HOW IS THE BIOMEDICAL APPROACH USED TO TREAT PSYCHOLOGICAL DISORDERS?

Core Concept 13.3 =

A) Drug Therapy:

1) <u>Antipsychotic Drugs</u> =

- *Antipsychotics* =

- *Tardive dyskinesia* =

2) <u>Antidepressants and Mood Stabilizers</u> =

    a) <u>Antidepressant Drugs</u> =

    b) <u>Controversy over SSRIs</u> =

    c) <u>Mood Stabilizers</u> =

        o *Lithium* =

3) <u>Antianxiety Drugs</u> =

    o *Barbiturates* =

    o *Benzodiazepines* =

4) <u>Stimulants</u> =

5) <u>Evaluating the Drug Therapies</u> =

B) Other Medical Therapies for Psychological Disorders:

1) <u>Psychosurgery</u> =

    o *Prefrontal lobotomy* =

2) <u>Brain-Stimulation Therapies</u> =

- *Electroconvulsive therapy (ECT)* =

- *Transcranial magnetic stimulation (TMS)* =

C) Hospitalization and the Alternatives =

1) <u>Deinstitutionalization and Community Mental Health</u> =

- *Deinstitutionalization* =

- *Community mental health movement* =

D) Psychology Matters: What Sort of Therapy Would You Recommend?

13.4 HOW DO THE PSYCHOLOGICAL THERAPIES AND BIOMEDICAL THERAPIES COMPARE?

- *Combination therapy* =

Core Concept 13.4 =

A) Depression and Anxiety Disorders: Psychological versus Medical Treatment =

1) <u>CBT versus Drugs</u> =

2) <u>ECT</u>=

B) Schizophrenia: Psychological versus Medical Treatment =

C) "The Worried Well" and Other Problems: Not Everyone Needs Drugs =

    1) <u>Early Intervention and Prevention Programs: A Modest Proposal</u> =

D) Psychology Matters: Using Psychology to Learn Psychology =

    1) <u>Learning as Therapy</u> =

    2) <u>Change Behavior, Not Just Thinking</u> =

E) Critical Thinking Applied: Evidence-Based Practice =

        o   *Evidence-based practice* =

    •   *Empirically supported treatment (EST)* =

What Is Therapy?

Entering Therapy

1. *Underline the word(s) in parentheses that will make each statement correct. (Both options may be correct!)*

    A. Practitioners using the medical model tend to use the term (client/patient) and view psychological disorders as (mental illnesses/problems in living).

    B. Access to therapy can be blocked by lack of (qualified therapists/finances).

    C. People usually enter therapy when they are (told by loved ones that they need help/unable to resolve a problem by themselves).

The Therapeutic Alliance and the Goals of Therapy

2. For what three reasons might it be more appropriate to seek help from a professionally trained therapist than to talk about problems with a sympathetic friend or family member?

    A. _____

    B. _____

    C. _____

3. What is meant by a "therapeutic alliance"?

4. Along with developing the relationship between therapist and client, what three steps are generally involved in the therapy process?

    A. _____

    B. _____

    C. _____

5. The American Counseling Association is one of the major organizations for professional counselors. Explore its website at:
    http://www.counseling.org/

6. *Fill in the table below with the correct information.*

Profession	Training	Areas of Expertise	Able to Prescribe Drugs?
A. Counseling psychologist			
B. Clinical psychologist			
C. Psychiatrist			
D. Psychoanalyst			
E. Psychiatric nurse practitioner			
F. Clinical social worker			
G. Pastoral counselor			

7. In what contexts can psychologists prescribe drugs for mental disorders? Explain the controversy concerning clinical and counseling psychologists being granted such prescription privileges.

Therapy in Historical and Cultural Context

8. What was the intended purpose of asylums for mentally ill individuals? What became the reality of such institutions?

   A) Intent: _____

   B) Reality: _____

9. What are the two main forms of psychotherapy? What third form was recently developed?

   A. _____   B. _____

   C. (Third form) _____

Psychology Matters: Paraprofessionals Do Therapy, Too

10. What are "paraprofessionals" and how do they compare to professionals in terms of therapeutic outcomes?

How Do Psychologists Treat Psychological Disorders?

Insight Therapies

11. *Indicate whether each statement is True (T) or False (F) by circling the appropriate letter after the statement.*

A. Insight therapies try to change how a person thinks or feels.   T F

B. All insight therapies assume that problems lie in the unconscious.   T F

C. Freud's ideas represent the mainstream of psychiatry.   T F

D. The goal of psychoanalysis is to reveal and interpret the content of the unconscious.   T F

E. According to Freud, the superego uses defense mechanisms to deal with conflict.   T F

F. The projection of parental attributes onto the therapist is called displacement.   T F

G. According to Freud, analysis of transference helps patients get rid of unconscious conflicts with parents.   T F

H. Freud used dream interpretation and free association to access the unconscious.   T F

I. Blocking a problem from consciousness is what Freud called repression.   T F

J. Neo-Freudian psychodynamic therapies have retained Freud's emphasis on motivation.   T F

12. Neo-Freudians made a break with Freud over what three main points?

    A. _____   B. _____

              C. _____

13. What do humanistic therapists believe motivates people?

14. How would a humanistic therapist attempt to help clients deal with their problems?

15. *Fill in the blanks with the correct information.*

Carl Rogers developed _____ therapy, in which clients are given a nurturing environment to help them work through their problems. Rogers believed that healthy development is blocked when a person's desire for a positive _____ conflicts with _____ from self and others. A main technique used by Rogerian therapists is _____ (also called _____), in which the therapist paraphrases the client's words back to the client, trying to capture the emotional tone as well.

16. This site by Dr. C. George Boeree gives a thorough description of Rogerian theory.
http://webspace.ship.edu/cgboer/rogers.html

17. What four main qualities did an APA task force find are shared by effective therapies?

A. _____   C. _____

B. _____   D. _____

18. *Underline the word(s) in parentheses that will make each statement correct. (Both options may be correct!)*

A. Cognitive therapies see (rational thinking/positive emotions) as the key to positive therapeutic changes.

B. Aaron Beck believes that depression occurs because of negative (self-talk/feedback from others).

C. Most commonly, group therapy approaches use a (behavioral/humanistic) perspective.

D. The Twelve Steps of Alcoholics Anonymous were developed based on (psychological theory/trial-and-error experiences of early support-group members).

E. Family therapy is effective in the treatment of (depression/anorexia nervosa).

Behavior Therapies

19. *In the table below, fill in the type of behavior therapy described in the scenario and then give a brief description of the technique.*

Scenario	Type of Therapy	Description
A. Jim has arachnophobia. His therapist handles a tarantula and encourages Jim to do so also.		
B. Jim is encouraged to close his eyes, breathe deeply, and imagine being in a room with many representatives of several species of large spiders.		
C. Dalia is terrified of snakes. Her therapist has her spend time in nature center where she touches and holds snakes.		
D. A kindergarten teacher only responds to the children when they say "please" before making a request.		
E. Emotionally disturbed teenagers can earn points for good behavior in school. Later they can exchange the points for food or privileges.		

20. *Match each behavior therapy with its theoretical basis by placing the letter corresponding to the theoretical basis in the space next to its behavior therapy. (Theoretical bases may be used more than once.)*

THEORETICAL BASIS
   A. Social learning theory   B. Operant conditioning   C. Classical conditioning

BEHAVIOR THERAPY
   _____ Systematic desensitization
   _____ Aversion therapy
   _____ Contingency management
   _____ Token economy
   _____ Participant modeling
   _____ Exposure therapy

Cognitive-Behavioral Therapy: A Synthesis

21. Explain what "rational-emotive behavior therapy" is. Who developed this technique?

22. What is "positive psychotherapy" and how does it differ from humanistic therapies?

23. *Fill in the blanks of the following concept map with the correct information.*

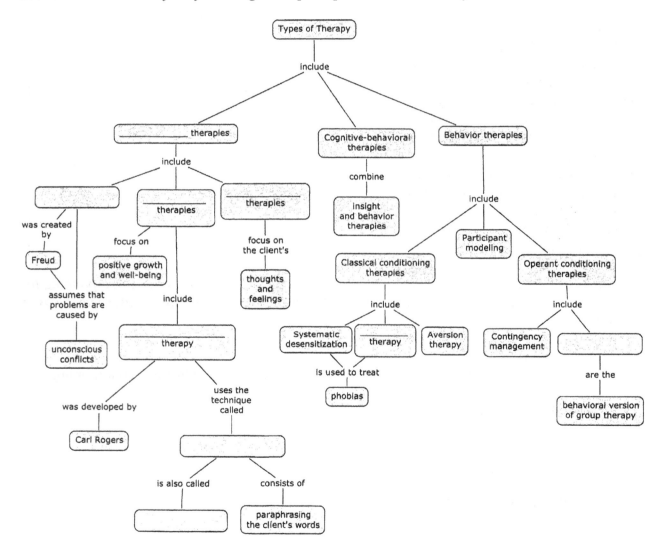

24. To read more about cognitive-behavioral therapy and find out how it is used to treat anxiety disorders, visit the following website:
   http://www.helpguide.org/mental/anxiety_therapy.htm

Evaluating the Psychological Therapies

25. What kinds of data are necessary to assess whether therapy is effective? Why aren't personal testimonials enough?

26. What study did Eysenck do in 1952, and what did he find? Why was this study controversial?

27. *Indicate whether each statement is True (T) or False (F) by circling the appropriate letter after the statement.*

   A. Studies assessing the effectiveness of psychotherapy have found that such therapy has effectiveness similar or superior to many medical practices.   T F

   B. Insight therapies are generally better than behavior therapies for treating anxiety disorders.   T F

   C. Eysenck's study was criticized for overestimating the improvement rate of individuals in the non-therapy control group.   T F

   D. Most therapies are effective in curing psychological disorders.   T F

Psychology Matters: Where Do Most People Get Help?

28. What three techniques are helpful to use when a friend or family member comes to you with a problem?

   A. _____

   B. _____

   C. _____

29. NEED A BREAK?
   To get a better understanding of therapies for psychological disorders, visit MyPsychLab.

How Is The Biomedical Approach Used to Treat Psychological Disorders?

Drug Therapy

30. *Indicate whether each statement is True (T) or False (F) by circling the appropriate letter after the statement.*

    A. Antipsychotic drugs are often called tranquilizers.   T F

    B. Most antipsychotic drugs work by reducing the activity of norepinephrine.   T F

    C. Antipsychotic drugs help reduce schizophrenia's "negative" symptoms.   T F

    D. Long-term antidepressant use can result in tardive dyskinesia.   T F

    E. Tardive dyskinesia is an incurable condition where there is loss of motor control.   T F

31. *Underline the word(s) in parentheses that will make each statement correct. (Both options may be correct!)*

    A. In animal studies, antidepressants stimulate the growth of (synapses/new neurons) in the (hippocampus/hypothalamus).

    B. Some antidepressants work by limiting the activity of the enzyme (MAO/GABA) so that more (norepinephrine/dopamine) is available.

    C. Recent research shows that the risk of antidepressants stimulating suicidal thoughts is less than (1e/5) percent.

    D. More prescriptions have been written for (antianxiety/antidepressant) drugs than there are people who have been diagnosed as clinically (anxious/depressed).

    E. A neuron's reabsorption of neurotransmitters after they've been released into the synapse is called (reuptake/reapportion).

    F. The chemical (lithium/thorazine) is an effective mood stabilizer in the treatment of (anxiety/bipolar disorder).

    G. (Stimulants/Barbiturates) are used to treat attention-deficit hyperactivity disorder.

    H. To reduce anxiety, many people take (barbiturates/benzodiazepines).

    I. (Barbiturates/Benzodiazepines) are sometimes called "minor tranquilizers."

    J. Barbiturates act as a (GABA/central nervous system) depressant and are dangerous if (taken in excess/combined with alcohol).

32. What are the three main classes of antidepressants and how does each work on the brain?

Class of Antidepressants	How It Works on the Brain
A.	
B.	
C.	

33. Discuss the arguments for and against the use of drug therapies.

<u>For Drug Therapies</u>   <u>Against Drug Therapies</u>

34. Visit the American Psychiatric Association website to gain more information about psychiatrists and their expertise.
<u>http://www.psych.org/</u>

Other Medical Therapies for Psychological Disorders

35. What is a "prefrontal lobotomy" and why was it done? What were the complications associated with this psychosurgery?

What a Prefrontal Lobotomy Is	Why It Was Done	Complications

36. What is electroconvulsive therapy (ECT)? For what conditions is ECT an appropriate treatment? Describe the new alternative treatment called TMS and why it is better than ECT.

37. What is the name of the technique in which a microelectrode is surgically implanted within the brain of a severely depressed person and then sends a constant trickle of electrical current to that brain area?

         ANSWER: _____

Hospitalization and the Alternatives

38. Discuss the challenges to American society related to deinstitutionalization. How has the community mental health movement attempted to address this issue?

39. The National Alliance on Mental Illness (NAMI) is an organization that provides support, education, and advocacy for mentally ill individuals and their families. Its excellent, informative website can be found at:
                    http://www.nami.org

Psychology Matters: What Sort of Therapy Would You Recommend?

40. What checklist of four main questions do your authors suggest for you to consider when trying to decide on a therapeutic approach?

    A. _____

    B. _____

    C. _____

    D. _____

41. What two main therapeutic approaches do your authors believe you should avoid?

    A. _____   B. _____

How Do the Psychological Therapies and Biomedical Therapies Compare?

42. Why has relatively little research been done on combination therapies?

43. *Indicate whether each statement is True (T) or False (F) by circling the appropriate letter after the statement.*

A. Combination therapies are the best therapies for "problems of living."   T F

B. A large number of people with psychological problems do not have *DSM-IV* disorders.   T F

C. Prozac is the world's most widely prescribed drug.   T F

D. Studies show that antidepressant drugs are generally more effective than cognitive-behavioral therapy for treating depression in the long-run.   T F

E. Studies show that cognitive-behavioral therapy is generally more effective than antidepressant drugs for treating depression in the short-run.   T F

F. CBT and antidepressants target different areas of the brain.   T F

G. The one study comparing ECT to antidepressants showed that ECT was more effective in reducing suicide attempts.   T F

H. Antidepressants affect the frontal cortex, whereas CBT affects the limbic system.   T F

I. Behavioral therapies are used more than drug therapies to treat schizophrenia.   T F

J. The "worried well" are those whose problems are not real.   T F

K. Research shows that exercise works just as well as medication in treating depression and anxiety.   T F

Critical Thinking Applied: Evidence-Based Practice

44. What is meant by "evidence-based practice" and "empirically supported treatments"? What are the arguments in favor of and in opposition to these?

PRACTICE TEST #1

1. Which of the following is a common element among the different forms of therapy?
   A. A relationship that focuses on removing the patient from existing social networks
   B. A relationship that focuses on improving behavior and mental processes
   C. A relationship that focuses on reinforcing existing behavioral patterns
   D. There is no common element among the therapies

2. One of the main techniques used by Rogerian therapists involves this type of listening to help clients understand their emotions.
   A. Reflective   B. Projective   C. Conditional   D. Unconditional

3. Grace has a severe phobia involving bridges. Her therapist decides to reduce her fears by driving her back and forth over long bridges. The therapist is using a type of _____.
   A. systematic desensitization   C. aversion therapy
   B. participant modeling   D. exposure therapy

4. Which of the following researchers claimed that psychotherapy is not effective?
   A. Jerome Frank   B. Hans Eysenck   C. Albert Ellis   D. Mary Cover Jones

5. Simon has a private practice and works with clients who have problems related to mood disorders. To help them, he prescribes antidepressant drugs. Simon is most likely a _____.
   A. psychologist   B. social worker   C. psychiatrist D. pastoral counselor

6. All of the following are primary goals of therapy EXCEPT _____.
   A. diagnosing what the problem is   C. making the patient into a different, better person
   B. identifying causes of the disorder   D. developing a treatment plan for the patient

7. Omar is a Freudian psychoanalyst. During a therapy session, his latest patient discusses her trouble with her mother in choosing a restaurant for dinner. Omar would look for the _____ reasons for the problems.
   A. conscious   B. unconscious   C. manipulative   D. intentional

8. _____ therapies are focused on the patient's self-concept, values, and needs.
   A. Humanistic   B. Behavioral   C. Biomedical   D. Psychodynamic

9. Explanations for psychological disorder vary by culture. Asian cultures see such disorders as _____.
   A. an early exposure to an unhealthy environment
   B. the result of specific disease processes
   C. abnormal genetics or neurotransmitter imbalances
   D. a disconnect between the group and the individual

10. All of the following are used to treat depression EXCEPT _____.
    A. SSRIs   B. tricyclics   C. amphetamines   D. MAO inhibitors

PRACTICE TEST #2

1. Paraprofessional counselors and licensed professionals have been found to be equivalent only in the realm of _____ therapy.
   A. insight   B. pastoral   C. behavioral   D. cognitive

2. A shared assumption of the insight therapies is that the distressed person needs to _____.
   A. develop an understanding of the underlying difficulties
   B. be given medication to help him or her cope with the difficulty
   C. spend years in therapy working on the difficulty
   D. delve into his or her relationship with both parents

3. All of the following are techniques that might be used by a Freudian therapist EXCEPT _____.
   A. dream analysis   C. free association
   B. reflective listening   D. interpretation

4. Lara has earned her M.D. and has completed her residency on an adolescent inpatient unit. When she opens her practice, she will be a _____.
   A. counseling psychologist   C. psychoanalyst
   B. psychiatric social worker   D. psychiatrist

5. Systematic desensitization is based on which theoretical perspective?
   A. Operant conditioning   C. Social learning theory
   B. Classical conditioning   D. Humanistic theory

6. Aaron is working with a client. His major technique involves client-centered therapy. Aaron is following the therapy approach of _____.
   A. Carl Rogers   B. Sigmund Freud   C. Aaron Beck D. Abraham Maslow

7. Cognitive psychologists believe that depression is the result of _____.
   A. negative self-talk   C. learned responses
   B. genetic predispositions   D. home situations

8. Some smoking cessation programs encourage smokers to smoke as many cigarettes as they possibly can while a noxious odor or event is occurring so they will develop negative reactions to cigarettes. This is the behavior modification technique called _____.
   A. flooding   C. aversion therapy
   B. contingency management   D. counterconditioning

9. A highly effective drug for treating bipolar disorder is _____.
   A. Prozac   B. Haloperidol   C. Lithium   D. Xanax

10. Behavioral therapists believe that both normal and abnormal behaviors develop _____.
    A. through a learning process   C. due to traumatic childhood events
    B. due to genetic makeup   D. because of dispositional influences

PRACTICE TEST #3

1. Natasha has a fear of snakes. Over a four-hour period, her therapist urges Natasha to imitate him as he first goes into a room in which there is a snake in a terrarium, then sits next to the terrarium, then moves the terrarium, then picks the snake out of the terrarium, and finally holds the snake. This type of treatment is called _____.
   A. systematic desensitization   C. participant modeling
   B. symbolic modeling therapy   D. exposure therapy

2. Neo-Freudian therapists retained Freud's emphasis on _____.
   A. the couch   B. motivation   C. childhood   D. sexual urges

3. Caitlyn is a behavioral therapist. She has a client who is deathly afraid of snakes. Caitlyn has her client watch a video of a child playing with pet snakes. This is a process called _____.
   A. aversion therapy   C. free association
   B. symbolic modeling   D. systematic desensitization

4. The behavioral version of group therapy is _____.
   A. the self-help group   C. contingency management
   B. rational-emotive therapy D. the token economy

5. Galena has been in psychoanalysis for several months and has been experiencing a great deal of anger toward her therapist lately. She feels the anger most when she talks about her mother. The therapist would most likely say that Galena is experiencing _____.
   A. resistance   B. transference   C. catharsis   D. repression

6. Rational-emotive therapy attempts to challenge _____.
   A. ideas about what one should do   C. feelings that last longer than they should
   B. the client environment   D. the client's memories of childhood

7. The two main types of psychotherapy are _____ and behavioral.
   A. medical   C. insight
   B. psychodynamic   D. cognitive

8. The category of drug most often used to treat ADHD is a(n) _____.
   A. depressant   B. antianxiety drug   C. stimulant   D. MAO inhibitor

9. _____ is a side effect of antipsychotic drugs that involves a disturbance of motor control of the facial muscles.
   A. Tardive dyskinesia   C. Delusional disorder
   B. Seizure disorder   D. Paralysis

10. Benzodiazepines and barbiturates fall into which class of drugs?
    A. Antianxiety drugs   C. Stimulants
    B. Antidepressants   D. Mood stabilizers

COMPREHENSIVE REVIEW TEST

1. John's therapist is trying to help him change the way he thinks about his recent divorce. What type of therapy is most likely to be used in this effort?
   - A. Social learning therapy
   - B. Cognitive therapy
   - C. Pastoral counseling
   - D. Psychoanalysis

2. All of the following are qualities that an APA task force found were shared by effective therapies EXCEPT _____.
   - A. empathy
   - B. confidence
   - C. feedback
   - D) positive regard

3. Dr. Caldwell is working with a client who is deathly afraid of spiders. Rather than use live spiders in the therapy process, Dr. Caldwell has her patient engage in relaxation and first imagine that he sees a spider across the room, then imagine the spider is closer, and eventually imagine holding the spider in his hand. She is using a technique known as _____.
   - A. contingency management
   - B. participant modeling
   - C. systematic desensitization
   - D. aversion therapy

4. According to Albert Ellis, all of the following statements are examples of faulty thinking EXCEPT which?
   - A. "I must be loved by everyone."
   - B. "Life is full of problems and I must find quick solutions to them."
   - C. "I can achieve happiness by simply enjoying myself each day."
   - D. "I should avoid all forms of criticism."

5. Antidepressant drugs generally work by _____.
   - A. reducing the amount of dopamine available at the synapses
   - B. increasing the amount of norepinephrine and/or serotonin
   - C. increasing the electrical activity in the limbic system
   - D. decreasing the amount of insulin in the bloodstream

6. According to an APA task force, all of the following qualities are shared by effective therapies EXCEPT _____.
   - A. feedback
   - B. empathy
   - C. genuineness
   - D. logic

7. According to your authors, the drug therapies to avoid for more than a short time are _____.
   - A. antipsychotics
   - B. minor tranquilizers
   - C. antidepressants
   - D. stimulants for ADHD

8. TMS is being investigated to use as a substitute for ECT because _____.
   - A. TMS is less expensive
   - B. TMS is quicker to administer
   - C. TMS is backed by research
   - D. TMS does not cause memory loss

9. The term "worried well" refers to people whose problems are _____.
   - A. problems in living
   - B. all in their head
   - C. a way to get attention
   - D. minor conditions listed in the *DSM-IV*

10. The effectiveness of therapy depends less on the _____ and more on the _____.
    A. competence of the therapist; degree to which the therapist is liked
    B. type of therapy used; quality of the relationship between client and therapist
    C. degree to which the therapist is liked; competence of the therapist
    D. quality of the relationship between client and therapist; type of therapy used

11. Antidepressants affect the _____, whereas CBT affects the _____.
    A. limbic system; frontal lobes   C. frontal lobes; limbic system
    B. hippocampus; temporal lobes   D. temporal lobes; hippocampus

12. Research shows that the best therapies for "problems in living" are _____ therapies.
    A. drug   B. psychological   C. combination   D. TMS

13. The two therapeutic approaches your authors suggest you should avoid are venting
    anger/aggression and long-term use of _____.
    A. TMS   B. antipsychotics   C. antianxiety drugs   D. behavior therapies

14. ECT has been shown to be an effective treatment for _____.
    A. phobias B. panic disorder   C. severe depression   D. schizophrenia

15. The community mental health movement _____.
    A. has led to increasing numbers of institutionalizations
    B. has never been completely funded
    C. has led to a reduction in the number of mentally ill homeless people
    D. has been proven to be less effective than treatment at fully staffed mental hospitals

CRITICAL THINKING ESSAYS

1. Theresa is absolutely terrified of elevators, because she's sure the cable will snap. Despite chronic pain from a knee injury she sustained while playing college soccer, she climbs the stairs all the way to the sixteenth floor of the building where her office is. Her physician has told her that she'll soon need knee-replacement surgery if she doesn't take better care of her knee.

    Theresa has decided to seek therapy to try to get rid of her fear of elevators. Based on what you've learned in the chapter, explain what a behavior therapist would likely do to help Theresa and what a cognitive therapist would likely do.

2. Discuss the pros and cons of drug therapies for psychological problems.

CHAPTER 14
Stress, Health, and Well-Being

Before You Read . . . Term Identification

Make flashcards using the following terms or, even better, develop mnemonics (memory strategies) to help you remember the different concepts and terms. Use the definitions in the margins of this chapter for help. Numbers refer to page numbers in the textbook.

acute stress (614)
alarm phase (616)
behavioral medicine (640)
benefit-finding (633)
burnout (607)
catastrophic event (601)
catharsis (633)
chronic stressor (606)
cognitive appraisal (600)
cognitive restructuring (631)
compassion fatigue (608)
compassion satisfaction (608)
coping (631)
coping strategy (630)
cortisol (617)
critical incident stress debriefing (633)
cytokines (618)
defending (630)
disenfranchised grief (605)
distress (600)
downward social comparison (632)
emotion-focused coping (631)
exhaustion phase (616)
externals (623)
fight-or-flight response (613)
general adaptation syndrome (GAS) (616)
grief (603)
hardiness (624)
hassle (609)
health psychology (640)
immunosuppression (617)
integration (604)
internals (623)

job engagement (607)
learned helplessness (624)
locus of control (623)
moderator (621)
narrative (602)
optimism (625)
oxytocin (617)
positive lifestyle choice (630)
posttraumatic stress disorder (ptsd) (605)
primary control (624)
problem-focused coping (631)
psychological debriefing (633)
psycho-neuroimmunology (618)
resilience (626)
resistance phase (616)
rumination (631)
secondary control (624)
sense-making (633)
social comparison (632)
Social Readjustment Rating Scale (609)
social support (635)
societal stressor (606)
stress (600)
stressor (600)
subjective well-being (SWB) (636)
targeted rejection (604)
telomeres (618)
tend-and-befriend (617)
terrorism (601)
traumatic stressor (601)
Type A (622)
upward social comparison (632)
vicarious traumatization (603)

Lecture Assistant *for Chapter 14*

Tear this outline out and bring it with you to class in order to facilitate your note taking.
Spend more time listening to the lecture and less time writing!

Chapter Opening Problem: Were the reactions and experiences of the 9/11 firefighters and others at the World Trade Center attacks typical of people in stressful situations? And what factors explain individual differences in the physical and psychological responses to stress?

14.1 WHAT CAUSES DISTRESS?

- *Stress =*

- *Stressor =*

- *Distress =*

  Core Concept 14.1 =

- *Cognitive appraisal =*

A) Traumatic Stressors:

- *Traumatic stressor =*

1) Catastrophe =

- *Catastrophic event =*

  a) A Natural Laboratory for Disaster =

  - *Terrorism =*

  b) Psychological Response to Catastrophe =

  Five Stages:
  1. _____
  2. _____
  3. _____
  4. _____
  5. _____

- *Narrative =*

c) <u>Trauma in the Media</u> =

  - *Vicarious traumatization* =

d) <u>Cultural Variations in Response to Catastrophes</u> =

2) <u>Personal Loss</u> =

- *Grief* =

- *Integration* =

  a) <u>Humiliation as Loss</u> =

    - *Targeted rejection* =

  b) <u>Disenfranchised Grief</u> =

3) <u>Posttraumatic Stress</u> =

- *Posttraumatic stress disorder (PTSD)* =

  a) <u>What are the Symptoms of PTSD?</u> =

  b) <u>PTSD in Combat Personnel</u> =

B) Chronic Stressors:

- *Chronic stressor* =

  1) <u>Societal Stressors</u> =

  2) <u>Burnout</u> =

    - *Job engagement* =

  3) <u>Compassion Fatigue (Secondary Traumatic Stress)</u> =

    - *Compassion satisfaction* =

4) <u>Major Life Events</u> =

- *Social Readjustment Rating Scale (SRRS)* =

5) <u>Daily Hassles</u> =

- *Hassle* =

C) Psychology Matters: Student Stress

14.2 HOW DOES STRESS AFFECT US PHYSICALLY?

- *Fight-or-flight response* =

Core Concept 14.2 =

A) Physiological Responses to Stress:

1) <u>The Fight-or-Flight Response</u> =

- *Acute stress* =

2) <u>The General Adaptation Syndrome</u> =

a) <u>The Alarm Phase</u> =

b) <u>The Resistance Phase</u> =

c) <u>The Exhaustion Phase</u> =

3) Tend and Befriend =

- *Cortisol* =

- *Oxytocin* =

B) Stress and the Immune System:

- *Immunosuppression* =

1) Psycho-Neuroimmunology =

2) Bi-Directional Links between the Brain and Body =

- *Cytokines* =

- *Telomeres* =

C) Psychology Matters: Cognitive Appraisal of Ambiguous Threats

14.3 WHO IS MOST VULNERABLE TO STRESS?

Core Concept 14.3 =

- *Moderator* =

A) Type A Personality and Hostility:

- *Type A* =

B) Locus of Control:

- *Locus of control* =

- *Internals* =

- *Externals* =

1) Locus of Control, Health, and Longevity =

2) Culture Affects Locus of Control =

- *Primary control =*

- *Secondary control =*

3) Is Locus of Control Innate, or Learned? =

- *Learned helplessness =*

C) Hardiness:

- *Hardiness =*

  Composed of Three Characteristics:

  1) _____
  2) _____
  3) _____

D) Optimism:

E) Resilience:

- *Coping ugly =*

- *"Ordinary magic" =*

F) Psychology Matters: Using Psychology to Learn Psychology

14.4 HOW CAN WE TRANSFORM NEGATIVE STRESS INTO POSITIVE LIFE STRATEGIES?

Core Concept 14.4 =

- *Coping strategy =*

- *Positive lifestyle choices =*

A) Psychological Coping Strategies:

1) <u>Defending versus Coping</u> =

- *Defending =*

- *Coping =*

2) <u>Problem-Focused and Emotion-Focused Coping</u> =

- *Problem-focused coping =*

- *Emotion-focused coping =*

- *Rumination =*

3) <u>Cognitive Restructuring</u> =

- *Social comparison =*
- *Downward social comparison =*
- *Upward social comparison =*

4) <u>Positive Emotions</u> =

5) <u>Finding Meaning</u> =

- *Sense making =*

- *Benefit finding =*

6) <u>Psychological Debriefing: Help or Hindrance</u> =

- *Psychological debriefing* =

- *Catharsis* =

    a) <u>Critical Incident Stress Debriefing (CISD)</u> =

    b) <u>Is CISD Effective?</u> =

B) Positive Lifestyle Choices: A "Two-for-One" Benefit to Your Health:

1) <u>Social Support</u> =

- *Social support* =

    a) <u>Benefits of Social Support</u> =

    b) <u>Supporters Reap What They Sow</u> =

2) <u>Exercise</u> =

3) <u>Nutrition and Diet</u> =

4) <u>Sleep and Meditation</u> =

C) Putting It All Together: Developing Happiness and Subjective Well-Being:

- *Subjective well-being (SWB) =*

Three Central Components of Subjective Well-Being:

1) _____

2) _____

3) _____

D) Psychology Matters: Behavioral Medicine and Health Psychology

- *Behavioral medicine =*

- *Health psychology =*

E) Critical Thinking Applied: Is *Change* Really Hazardous To Your Health?

What Causes Distress?

1. Differentiate between the terms "stress," "stressor," and "distress."

2. What is "cognitive appraisal," and why is it important for understanding stress?

Traumatic Stressors

3. *Indicate whether each statement is True (T) or False (F) by circling the appropriate letter after the statement.*

    A. Catastrophic events are traumatic stressors.   T F

    B. Loss of a loved one is a stressor, but is not classified as a traumatic stressor.   T F

    C. Survivors of terrorism tend to experience stress-related symptoms for longer periods of time than do survivors of natural disasters.   T F

    D. Narratives tend to help people find meaning in loss, which facilitates healing.   T F

    E. Psychologists generally feel that the grief process should not last more than one year.   T F

4. *Complete the following paragraph with the correct information.*

        Cohen and Ahearn identified five stages in the response to stressors such as natural disasters. Immediately after the event, people experience _____. They are unable to _____ what has happened. During the next phase, called _____, there is little awareness of what is going on. The third phase is called _____. People work together during this phase. In the fourth phase, survivors may experience a _____ or depletion of energy. The final period, _____, is a time of adapting to changes created by the disaster.

5. From the American Psychological Association, the following page features a wealth of information and links to other websites for coping with trauma.
    http://www.apa.org/helpcenter/recovering-disasters.aspx

6. What is "vicarious traumatization"? Give an example of this concept. How can you avoid such traumatization?

7. *Underline the word(s) in parentheses that will make each statement correct. (Both options may be correct!)*

   A. Grief psychologists recommend (closure/integration) for dealing with personal loss.

   B. (Closure/Integration) involves making a personal loss part of one's self.

   C. Studies show that people are more likely to suffer from depression when a partner (dies/rejects them) than when a partner (dies/rejects them).

   D. When others minimize your mourning and fail to sympathize, this is called (humiliation/disenfranchised) grief.

   E. (Confiding in others/Writing down one's feelings) has been found to help in coping with loss.

   F. Approximately one adult in (twelve/twenty) in the U.S. will experience posttraumatic stress disorder at some time in his or her life.

   G. (Men/Women) are more likely that (men/women) to develop symptoms of PTSD after experiencing a trauma.

   H. (African/Hispanic) Americans are more likely than non-Hispanic Caucasian Americans to develop PTSD.

   I. Victims of targeted rejection experience (more/less) depression than victims of other types of stressors.

   J. Research shows that many soldiers exposed to explosions—even when not directly hit by them—experience (social/cognitive) deficits.

8. List the symptoms of post-traumatic stress disorder.

9. The National Center for PTSD website has many links and much information on dealing with the aftermath of terrorist activity and other tragedies and disasters. Visit: http://www.ptsd.va.gov/

Chronic Stressors

10. How does a "chronic stressor" differ from a "traumatic stressor"?

11. What are the five chronic stressors that the text authors discuss?

    A. _____   B. _____

    C. _____   D. _____

            E. _____

12. *Match each term with its best description(s) by placing the letter corresponding to the term in the space next to its description. (Terms may be used more than once.)*

TERMS
  A. Burnout   C. Societal stressor   E. Daily hassle
  B. Compassion fatigue   D. Major life event

DESCRIPTIONS
    _____ Once again, Tina's children have not picked up their toys or put away their clothes, as she has repeatedly asked them to do.
    _____ Paul just welcomed his new baby into the world.
    _____ Bridget has worked the same job for ten years and has come to hate it.
    _____ Darnell once again has three exams on the same day.
    _____ Sangeeta works a minimum-wage job and has four children.
    _____ Janice has been counseling rape victims and finds that she is losing patience and empathy.
    _____ Mei-ki is constantly belittled by others because she is from China and does not yet speak fluent English.
    _____ Ricardo just started college.

13. Distinguish between burnout and compassion fatigue. What are the contributors to each of these forms of stress?

14. What is the opposite of job burnout? ANSWER: _____

15. What six areas of work life are associated with employee/workplace fit?

    A. _____ B. _____ C. _____

    D. _____ E. _____ F. _____

16. What five main suggestions have researchers made to caregivers to help them take action against compassion fatigue?

A. _____

B. _____

C. _____

D. _____

E. _____

17. *Indicate whether each statement is True (T) or False (F) by circling the appropriate letter after the statement.*

A. By definition, only negative events are stressful.   T F

B. The birth of a child is often associated with lower marital satisfaction.   T F

C. A reason to be cautious about interpreting scores on the Social Readjustment
   Rating Scale is that it cannot be applied cross-culturally.   T F

D. The fewer daily hassles people experience, the greater their sense of well-being.   T F

E. Having many health problems causes people to perceive minor annoyances
   as hassles.   T F

F. Daily hassles tend to be interpreted similarly by people in the same culture.   T F

Psychology Matters: Student Stress

18. What two qualities particularly characterize students who are most effective in preventing and coping with stress?

A. _____   B. _____

19. This site by the American Institute of Stress contains a great deal of research-based information about stress and managing stress.
   http://www.stress.org

How Does Stress Affect Us Physically?

20. Define the term "fight-or-flight response" and describe its evolutionary significance.

21. What are the pros and cons of the fight-or-flight response?

Physiological Responses to Stress

22. *Fill in the blanks with the correct information.*

    A sudden and temporary state of stress is called _____ stress. Almost instantaneously, reactions in our muscles, _____ nervous system, and _____ system allow us to make an efficient and effective response. The fight-or-flight response, however, can be problematic when we are faced with _____ stressors.

23. Explain what the General Adaptation Syndrome is and what its value is.

24. *Write the phase of the General Adaptation Syndrome in the space next to its best example.*

    A. _____ Jerry's wife of sixty years died recently. He has been suffering from a broken heart. Two weeks after his wife dies, Jerry dies in his sleep.

    B. _____ Joshua is driving on a snowy night with very low visibility. Finally, the snow lets up, and Joshua is able to drive more easily. He begins to breathe in a normal rhythm.

    C. _____ Sean is the first responder on the scene of an automobile accident. He pulls three people from a burning car without any assistance.

25. *Underline the word(s) in parentheses that will make each statement correct. (Both options may be correct!)*

    A. During the alarm phase, the (hippocampus/hypothalamus) sets off emergency messages to the (hormone system/sympathetic nervous system).

    B. During the alarm phase, (endorphins/serotonins) are released, which reduce the body's awareness of (digestive/pain) signals.

    C. During the resistance phase, a person's (red/white) blood cell count increases.

    D. Resistance displayed during the resistance phase applies to (the original stressor/a new stressor).

    E. In the exhaustion phase, the body requires (rest/rejuvenation).

F. One study showed that men had higher levels of (oxytocin/cortisol) than did women during stress.

26. Explain Shelly Taylor's "tend-and-befriend" model of stress. How do hormone studies support her theory?

Stress and the Immune System

27. *Fill in the blanks with the correct information.*

A. Impairment of the function of the immune system is called _____.

B. _____ is the study of the interrelationships between psychology, the immune system, and the nervous system.

C. _____ are proteins that fight infection and help communication between the immune system and the brain.

D. A way to assess the age of a cell is to measure the length of its _____.

E. _____ are protein complexes that cap the ends of chromosomes and protect against damage to _____.

F. A major factor that plays a role in the stress-illness relationship is a person's _____ of stressors.

G. When a stressor is experienced, the brain signals the adrenal glands to release a hormone called _____.

H. _____ can signal the brain to engage in social-behavioral withdrawal.

28. To understand more about psycho-neuroimmunology, visit the following APA website to read a brief article about fascinating research in this field.
http://www.apa.org/monitor/dec01/anewtake.aspx

Psychology Matters: Cognitive Appraisal of Ambiguous Threats

29. *Indicate whether each statement is True (T) or False (F) by circling the appropriate letter after the statement.*

A. Uncertainty can add to the stress of a situation.   T F

B. The U.S. government's color-coded warning system helped to reduce most citizens' stress about the threat of terrorist attacks.   T F

C. We must have concrete understanding of the nature of a threat in order
to make effective cognitive appraisals.   T F

Who Is Most Vulnerable To Stress?

30. *Fill in the blanks with the correct information.*

In the stress-illness relationship model discussed in the text, there are two opportunities

for intervention: one lies between _____ and stress, and the other occurs

between stress and _____. The first intervening factors are referred to as

_____, and most of them are variations on the concept of

_____, which has to do with one's perceptions.

Type A Personality and Hostility

31. *Put a check next to each behavior associated with Type A personality. Then, circle the ones
that are predictive of heart disease.*

_____ Perfectionism	_____ High activity	_____ Competitiveness
_____ Impatience	_____ Anger	_____ Achievement-oriented
_____ Hostility	_____ Time urgency	_____ Internal locus of control

32. *Underline the word(s) in parentheses that will make each statement correct. (Both options
may be correct!)*

A. The perfectionism characteristic of Type A personality is linked to (anxiety/depression).

B. Type A personality is associated with (heart disease/allergies).

C. Hostility is associated with higher levels of (oxytocin/cytokines).

D. Hostile people are more likely than other people to perceive (incompetence/threat) in a
situation.

E. (Antipsychotic medication/stress-management training) is effective in reducing the risk of
heart disease in Type A individuals.

Locus of Control

33. Explain the differences between "internals" and "externals" and how these differences relate
to stress and health.

34. NEED A BREAK?
To get a better understanding of stress, health, and well-being, visit MyPsychLab.

35. Explain the nursing home study concerning locus of control and what this study found.

36. In the table below, define "primary control" and "secondary control" and explain how they relate to culture and health.

Type of Control	Definition	Relation to Culture	Relation to Health
A. Primary			
B. Secondary			

37. *Fill in the blanks with the correct information.*

_____ is a passive resignation that follows recurring failure. It

was first identified in studies of _____ by _____ and his

colleagues. They found that animals that received inescapable shocks soon

_____ their attempts to avoid painful shocks.

Hardiness

38. Define the term "hardiness." Then, list and briefly describe the "three Cs" of hardiness.

Definition: _____

     A. _____

     B. _____

     C. _____

Optimism

39. What has research found concerning the relationship between optimism and health?

40. Selgman's research shows that optimistic thinking is associated with three attributions about negative events. What are those three attributions?

    A. _____

    B. _____

    C. _____

Resilience

41. Define the term "resilience" and discuss its relationship to other characteristics discussed in this chapter.

42. What does researcher Ann Masten mean by the term "ordinary magic"?

43. The American Psychological Association has a website and brochure titled *The Road to Resilience.* You can access it at the following site:
    http://www.apa.org/helpcenter/road-resilience.aspx

Psychology Matters: Using Psychology to Learn Psychology

44. Why is writing often an effective way of dealing with stress?

45. The National Association of School Psychologists has a helpful article concerning stress in adolescents and children and how they cope. Visit:
    http://www.nasponline.org/families/stress.pdf

How Can We Transform Negative Stress into Positive Life Strategies?

Psychological Coping Strategies

46. Distinguish between "defending" and "coping." What is the impact of each?

47. Differentiate between "problem-focused coping" and "emotion-focused coping."

8. *Fill in the blanks with the correct information.*

Mary gets a call about a problem at work that could have been avoided if everyone had done what she had asked. Before she goes to work, she takes a long, hot shower. She is using _____-focused coping. On the other hand, when John gets the same phone call, he begins to make a list of what needs to be done to correct the situation. John is using _____-focused coping.

49. *Fill in the blanks of the following concept map with the correct information.*

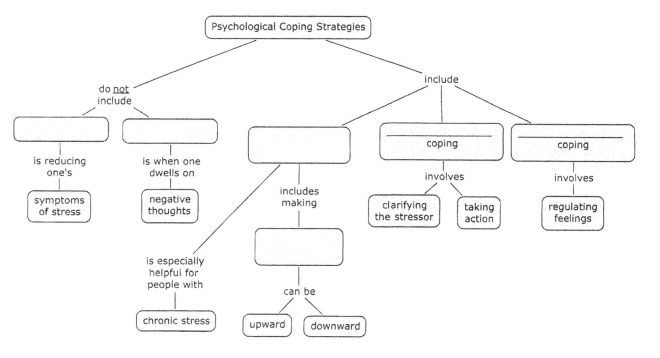

50. *Underline the word(s) in parentheses that will make each statement correct. (Both options may be correct!)*

   A. Researchers believe that (benefit-finding/sense-making) is a way to find meaning in loss.

   B. When faced with a loss, people usually first engage in (benefit-finding/sense-making).

   C. After caring for her dying mother, Janet eventually came to feel that the experience, though awful, allowed her the time to really get to know her mother. This exemplifies (benefit-finding/sense-making).

   D. (Psychological debriefing/Catharsis) is based on the assumption that it is psychologically healthier to express negative emotions than to keep them to oneself.

   E. Research shows that catharsis tends to (decrease/prolong) feelings of distress.

   F. Critical incident stress debriefing (has/has not) been shown to help victims of traumatic events.

   G. (Humor/Positive emotion) helps to reduce the effects of stress.

Positive Lifestyle Choices: A "Two-for-One" Benefit to Your Health

51. Define "social support" and explain the three specific benefits it provides individuals.

   Definition: _____

   A. _____ B. _____

                C. _____

52. What has research discovered about the role of physical affection in reducing stress?

53. *Indicate whether each statement is True (T) or False (F) by circling the appropriate letter after the statement.*

   A. Just thirty minutes of aerobic exercise per day can lower the risk of heart disease, stroke, and breast cancer.   T F

   B. Recent research shows that exercise can be as effective as antidepressant medication for depressed patients.   T F

   C. During exercise, we get an increase in endorphins and a decrease in serotonin.   T F

   D. Men are more likely than women to be conscious of good nutrition.   T F

E. Chronic sleep deprivation is linked to diabetes.   T F

F. Mindfulness-based stress reduction is a modern variation of Buddhist meditation.   T F

G. Research shows that meditation increases immune system functioning.   T F

Putting It All Together: Developing Happiness and Subjective Well-Being

54. According to experts, feelings of well-being require the satisfaction of what three different needs?

A. _____   B. _____

C. _____

55. Name and briefly describe the three central components of subjective well-being (SWB.)

Name	Description
A.	
B.	
C.	

56. *Indicate whether each statement is True (T) or False (F) by circling the appropriate letter after the statement.*

A. "Subjective well-being" essentially means the same thing as "self-esteem."   T F

B. Younger people tend to be happier than older people.   T F

C. African Americans report lower levels of happiness and higher levels of
   depression than do European Americans.   T F

57. To explore the topics of happiness and subjective well-being in more detail, go to the homepage of Dr. Ed Diener, Ph.D. and explore the various links. Visit:
http://internal.psychology.illinois.edu/~ediener/

Psychology Matters: Behavioral Medicine and Health Psychology

58. Discuss how health psychology and behavioral medicine are related, and what topics they tend to investigate.

Critical Thinking Applied: Is *Change* Really Hazardous to Your Health?

59. Evaluate the effectiveness of the Social Readjustment Rating Scale for demonstrating that stress is caused by too many life changes.

PRACTICE TEST #1

1. All of the following are phases of the General Adaptation Syndrome EXCEPT _____ .
   A. exhaustion   B. reactance   C. alarm   D. resistance

2. The emotional arousal caused by change and threat is known as _____ .
   A. a stressor   B. adaptation   C. fear   D. distress

3. Hostility is associated with higher levels of _____ .
   A. oxytocin   B. serotonin   C. cytokines   D. telomeres

4. The innate response that occurs when you are threatened or in danger is known as the _____ response.
   A. survival   B. fight-or-flight   C. endurance   D. stress

5. Research shows that subjective well-being includes all of the following EXCEPT _____ .
   A. feeling competent   C. having social connections
   B. having a sense of autonomy   D. earning a high level of income

6. Melissa watched the television coverage of the hurricanes in Florida for five days straight, eighteen hours a day. Although she lived far from where the hurricanes occurred, she experienced what researchers call _____ .
   A. vicarious traumatization   C. media stress
   B. disaster stress   D. saturation stress

7. The _____ suggests that chronic stressful conditions tend to produce disease-causing changes in the body.
   A. SRRS   C. fight-or-flight response
   B. General Adaptation Syndrome   D. alarm reaction

8. The pressures of work that last over time are a source of _____ stress.
   A. acute   B. traumatic   C. critical   D. chronic

9. Xiao moves to the United States from his native country of China to take a university teaching job. His new employer offers a cross-cultural adjustment outreach program to help reduce his exposure to _____ .
   A. daily hassles   C. burnout
   B. societal stressors   D. acute stress

10. Mr. Ionnati is a teacher who is beginning to lose his sense of concern for his students. Mr. Ionnati appears to be experiencing _____ .
   A. an acute stressor   C. burnout
   B. a societal stressor   D. job boredom

PRACTICE TEST #2

1. After being raped, Alice seemed to recover, and was not aware of feelings of victimization or betrayal. Months later, she realizes that she feels terribly anxious in interpersonal situations and is having frequent nightmares. This response is an example of _____.
   A. general adaptation syndrome
   B. posttraumatic stress disorder
   C. learned helplessness
   D. biological readjustment

2. The Social Readjustment Rating Scale shows _____ to be the most stressful life event.
   A. job change   B. job loss   C. spousal death   D. divorce

3. Learned helplessness usually results from a lack of _____.
   A. money   B. control   C. treatment   D. assistance

4. Behavioral medicine is the area of medicine that studies the connection between _____ and disease.
   A. subjective well-being
   B. patient lifestyle
   C. treatment regimens
   D. patient compliance

5. Some people are better able than others to cope with adversity and stress. This quality is known in psychology as _____.
   A. strength   B. power   C. energy   D. resilience

6. When Rick was under stress, his _____ nervous system was activated.
   A. somatic   B. sympathetic   C. skeletal   D. parasympathetic

7. Which kind of coping is particularly helpful for people experiencing chronic stress?
   A. Cognitive restructuring
   B. Emotion-focused coping
   C. Problem-focused coping
   D. Defending

8. The three Cs of hardiness include all of the following EXCEPT _____.
   A. challenge   B. commitment   C. command   D. control

9. What technique is especially suitable for people suffering from chronic stress and is based on a person learning to reappraise stressors as less uncertain and more within one's control?
   A. Rationalization
   B. Cognitive restructuring
   C. Primary appraisal
   D. Tangible support

10. You know that you have a really important job interview tomorrow. You focus on remaining calm and getting a good night's rest before the interview in the morning. You are using _____ coping.
    A. emotion-focused
    B. problem-focused
    C. job-resilient
    D. adaptive-focused

PRACTICE TEST #3

1. The psychologist most associated with the study of the stress response in females is _____.
   A. Hans Selye   B. Carol Gilligan   C. Shelley Taylor   D. John Holmes

2. Jason has been under a great deal of stress lately. He has also been getting sick a great deal. The chemical messenger most implicated in this stress/health connection is _____.
   A. serotonin.   B. testosterone.   C. acetycholine.   D. cytokines.

3. During the alarm phase, blood flow increases to all of the following area EXCEPT _____.
   A. the heart   B. the brain   C. the muscles D. the digestive system

4. Mary could not be in California to help her sister when her sister's husband had surgery; she had several restaurants deliver food instead. Mary is providing _____ support.
   A. emotional   B. tangible   C. informational   D. helpful

5. Joe has been unemployed for a year. During the first month, he went to many job interviews but had no offers. Gradually, he stopped looking at the want ads and visiting employment agencies. Now he gets up late, spends his day watching TV, and rarely goes out. Joe's behavior is likely the result of _____.
   A. cognitive restructuring   C. learned helplessness
   B. a Type B personality pattern   D. diminished hedonic capacity

6. _____ cap the end of chromosomes and protect against damage to DNA.
   A. Cytokines   B. Cortisols   C. Oxytocins   D. Telomeres

7. Optimistic thinking includes all of the following EXCEPT _____.
   A. finding the good in every situation   C. attributing unpleasantness to specific causes
   B. assuming pain is temporary   D. blaming problems on external conditions

8. In the _____ phase of the GAS, the body requires rest and rejuvenation.
   A. resistance   B. alarm   C. exhaustion   D. reconstruction

9. When stressed, Chris seeks out social support such as close friends and family. Chris's reactions support the _____ theory of stress.
   A. tend-and-befriend   C. fight-or-flight
   B. general adaptation syndrome   D. social comparison

10. All of the following are components of subjective well-being EXCEPT _____.
   A. frequent positive emotions   C. a relative absence of negative emotions
   B. a high degree of spirituality   D. satisfaction with one's current life

COMPREHENSIVE REVIEW TEST

1. Intervening factors between stressors and the experience of stress are called _____.
   A. translators   B. covariates   C. moderators   D. intermediaries

2. Studies of nursing home residents demonstrated the importance of personal _____ for good health, satisfaction, and longevity.
   A. control   B. support   C. values   D. challenges

3. Latrice believes that her achievements are due to her own hard work and capabilities. Latrice would most likely be classified as _____.
   A. resilient B. an internal   C. hardy   D. Type B

4. David is studying how psychological and physical stresses relate to the body's ability to fight off infections. Which of the following best describes David's area of research?
   A. The General Adaptation Syndrome   C. Behavioral medicine
   B. Psycho-neuroimmunology   D. The fight-or-flight response

5. During the alarm phase, the _____ sets off emergency messages to the endocrine system and the sympathetic nervous system.
   A. pituitary   B. cerebral cortex   C. hippocampus   D. hypothalamus

6. _____ control, more common in Western cultures, is taking action in order to try to control external events.
   A. Internal   B. Locus of   C. Primary   D. Secondary

7. What two factors do researchers believe are essential for dealing effectively with loss?
   A. Problem-focused coping and emotion-focused coping
   B. Hardiness and resilience
   C. Optimism and internal locus of control
   D. Sense-making and benefit-finding

8. Which of the following involves reducing the symptoms of stress or reducing one's awareness of those symptoms?
   A. Defending   B. Rumination   C. Acceptance   D. Emotion-focused coping

9. The characteristic of Type A personality that is most associated with heart disease is _____.
   A. impatience   B. irritability   C. hostility   D. perfectionism

10. Which of the following tends to prolong feelings of distress rather than reduce them?
    A. Upward social comparisons   C. Psychological debriefing
    B. Cognitive restructuring   D. Downward social comparisons

11. All of the following are stages in the psychological response to catastrophe EXCEPT _____.
    A. psychic numbness   C. communal effort
    B. letdown   D. denial

12. Erizon's dog died and he is depressed by the loss of his wonderful canine friend of twelve years. His family and friends tell him that "it was just a dog," and that he can go to the dog pound and get another one. They just can't understand why he is so upset by the death of an animal. Erizon is experiencing _____.
    A. vicarious traumatization
    B. disenfranchised grief
    C. critical incident stress debriefing
    D. learned helplessness

13. Which of the following statements about the Social Readjustment Rating Scale is TRUE?
    A. Having numerous stressors on the SRRS causes illness.
    B. The Social Readjustment Rating Scale lists forty-three life events.
    C. Women tend to score higher than men on the SRRS.
    D. A third variable may be impacting the frequency of life changes and the risk of illness.

14. Grief psychologists recommend _____ for dealing with personal loss.
    A. closure   B. integration   C. catharsis   D. psychological debriefing

15. _____ is a passive resignation that follows recurring failure.
    A. Type B personality
    B. Internal locus of control
    C. Learned helplessness
    D. Disenfranchised grief

CRITICAL THINKING ESSAYS

1. The campus health center has asked you to participate in a program on wellness and health. They have asked you to talk about the role of personality factors in stress management and health. Explain what you will tell the audience concerning research findings on this topic.

2. Discuss the research findings concerning the importance of a sense of personal control for health and well-being. Explain different kinds of control and discuss research findings having to do with control, stress, and well-being.

Appendix:
Answer Keys

1) mind; a field of study; the study of the mind
2) The broader definition of psychology is "the study of behavior and mental processes."
3) "Internal factors" are mental processes and "external factors" refer to observable behaviors.
4) A. experimental (research), B. teachers, C. applied
5) A. experimental, B. experimental, C. applied, D. Teachers of psychology, E. experimental
6) A. clinical or counseling, B. environmental, C. school, D. forensic, E. I/O, F. sports
8) A. F, B. F (many are researchers or teachers or in applied fields that have nothing to do with mental illness), C. T, D. F (they are MDs and trained to perform many medical procedures), E. F (that's the definition of psychology, not psychiatry), F. T, G. T. H. F (psychology is broader)
9) Psychiatrists have medical degrees and thus tend to have a medical view of their patients. With an M.D., they are able to prescribe drugs to their patients, too; therefore, they tend to treat people with more severe mental disorders. Psychologists are not all therapists or counselors. Many are researchers and/or teachers. Clinical and counseling psychologists work with people with mental illness, as do psychiatrists—yet psychologists generally don't have medical training and thus can't prescribe medications to people. Most psychologists have doctorates.
10) Pseudo-psychology is any set of practices or assertions about psychological factors that is not backed up by scientific research.
11) A. astrology (horoscopes), B. graphology (handwriting analysis), C. fortune telling
12) A. What is the source? B. Is the claim reasonable or extreme? C. What's the evidence? D. Could bias contaminate the conclusion? E. Does the reasoning avoid common fallacies? F. Does the issue require multiple perspectives?
13) A. What's the source? (The source is a man you don't know and a physician who may be getting paid for doing the ad.); Is the claim reasonable or extreme? (Losing forty pounds in one month is extreme weight loss.); What's the evidence? (It's only anecdotal evidence. There's no scientific data to back up the claims.)
B. Is the claim reasonable or extreme? (Claiming the psychic knew all about his past and present seems extreme.); What's the evidence? (It's anecdotal evidence, just based on your friend's experience that one time he visited the psychic.); Could bias contaminate the conclusion? (Your friend could have both emotional bias and confirmation bias.); Does the reasoning avoid common fallacies? (Your friend's idea that supposed knowledge about the past and present means that there is also knowledge about the future is not logical.)
C. What's the source? (It's an Internet article written by two people trying to sell their product.); Is the claim reasonable or extreme? (It seems extreme to say that there has been no violence of any kind at their school.); What's the evidence? (It's anecdotal evidence about their one school, and they provide no data to back up their claims of no violence at their school and that the anti-bullying program has caused the reduction in violence.); Could bias contaminate the conclusion? (The two authors could be emotionally involved in the topic or could only be paying attention to evidence that confirms their ideas.); Does the issue require

multiple perspectives? (It's simplistic to think that bullying is the only—or even the major—cause of school violence. Many other factors play a role.)

14) One person's experience cannot represent the experiences of others. What's true for one person is not necessarily true for other people.

15) Confirmation bias is when we pay attention to information that is consistent with our beliefs yet ignore information that is contrary to our beliefs. Thus, we cannot be objective and look at multiple perspectives, which are needed for critical thinking.

16) A. confirmation bias, B. anecdotal, C. emotional bias

18) A cognitive map (a mental map or a concept map) is a way of mentally organizing concepts so that they fit together in a meaningful, sensible way.

19) A. The ancient Greeks thought about consciousness and madness, and knew that emotions could distort thinking (even though they also thought emotions came from the heart, liver, and spleen). They also realized that perceptions are interpretations of the physical world.
B. Asian societies explored consciousness through Buddhism, yoga, and meditation.
C. African societies were developing theories about personality and mental disorders, and spiritual healers (shamans) developed therapies for those with such disorders.

20) A. Greek tradition, B. the Church

21) The Church believed that people should not be interested in the "world of the flesh." In addition, medieval Christians believed that the mind and soul are inseparable, and that the mind is a mystery that mortals should not try to solve.

22) A. biological, B. cognitive, C. behavioral, D. whole-person, E. developmental, F. sociocultural

23) Descartes believed that the body and mind are separate entities. Therefore, even though Christians believed that the mind should not be investigated, now scientists were free to investigate the workings of the body (because it was separate from the mind). Thus, the field of biology made many new discoveries.

24) medicine, biological science, neuroscience, Evolutionary, Darwin, natural selection

25) A. Wundt, Titchener, James, B. James, Dewey, C. Wundt, Titchener, D. Dewey

26) C, A, C, A, B, B

27) The periodic table simplified the relationships between elements and made them clear. This inspired Wundt to try to do the same for the study of the mind and to use the scientific method.

29) It emphasizes mental activities such as sensation, perception, memory, learning, and thinking. It also views the mind as similar to a computer.

30) Watson and others believed that only objective behavior can be studied scientifically.

31) The behavioral perspective looks at observable behavior and the ways in which stimuli in the environment can shape and modify those behaviors.

33) Psychologists include research psychologists, applied psychologists, and teachers of psychology. Almost half of all psychologists receiving a doctoral degree define themselves as clinical or counseling psychologists, who are applied psychologists trained to do therapy with clients and help treat mental disorders. Psychoanalysts, however, are psychiatrists and clinical psychologists who follow Freud's psychodynamic theory and his treatment method.

34) A, C, A, B, D, C, B

35) The "Big Five" refers to five main personality traits that people across the world tend to vary on: introversion/extroversion, anxiety/well-being, openness to new experiences, agreeableness, and conscientiousness. This is part of the Trait & Temperament perspective.

36) People change in predictable ways as the influences of heredity and environment unfold over time (i.e., people think and act differently at different times of their lives).

37) Cross-cultural psychologists study psychological processes in people of different cultures to look for similarities and differences between those cultures. Most psychological knowledge is from North America and Europe, so may not generalize to people in other cultures.

38) Culture is a complex blend of language, customs, beliefs, & values, shared by a group.

39) A. The biological perspective includes the evolutionary perspective and also ties in with the field of neuroscience. The focus is on biological processes & genes that may cause behavior.
B. The cognitive perspective is concerned with mental processes such as sensation, perception, memory, and thinking. Often the mind is viewed as similar to a computer.
C. The behavioral perspective is not concerned with mental processes, but instead focuses on observable behavior and how it can be influenced by stimuli in the environment.
D. The whole-person perspectives are those that try to explain an entire person rather than just certain aspects of behavior or thought. Psychodynamic psychology views the mind as filled with unconscious energies that are in conflict and that motivate human behavior. Humanistic psychology focuses not on conflicts, but instead on positive aspects of human nature. Trait & Temperament psychology is concerned with basic personality traits that occur across cultures and that tend to be stable within people.
E. The developmental perspective takes into account both nature and nurture, and sees people as changing in some predictable ways over the lifespan.
F. The sociocultural perspective recognizes the huge importance of the social environment, including culture, in people's behaviors and mental processes.

40) Mary Calkins was the first female president of the American Psychological Association (in 1905). Due to her gender, Harvard refused to give her the doctoral degree she had earned.

42) A. F (it's about 66 percent), B. F (that happened in 1905), C. F (it was only 12 percent)

45) A. T, B. F (a doctorate is almost always required), C. T

47) Psychology is a science; therefore, it uses the scientific method and empirical investigation. Pseudo-psychology does not use the scientific method; therefore, it is not a science. Instead, pseudo-psychology is based on biases, hope, anecdotal evidence, and gullibility.

48) A. theory, B. scientific method, C. empirical investigation, D. theory

49) A. It has the power to explain the facts. B. It has the ability to be tested.

50) A. First, develop a hypothesis (a testable prediction) and decide how you can test that hypothesis. Operational definitions will need to be developed.
B. Second, gather objective data. You do this by using empirical investigation, which is collecting evidence carefully and systematically.
D. Third, statistically analyze data to see whether your hypothesis is supported or rejected.
E. Fourth, expose your study to the scrutiny of the scientific community, through presentations or publications, so that other researchers can critique your study to look for any flaws or can try to replicate your study.

51) D, C, B, E, I, H, F, G, A

52) If a hypothesis is not falsifiable, then it cannot be tested using the scientific method.

53) Science can't answer questions that can't be empirically tested by the scientific method.
54) A. Type of teaching method, B. Scores on the final exam, C. The class getting the traditional lecture method, D. The class getting the new discussion method
55) Random assignment to groups (to the two classes) was left out. Thus, the two groups could have started out differently, so Dr. Vargas won't know whether any difference in final exam scores is due to the teaching method or to preexisting differences between the two classes.
56) A. hypothesis, B. both options are correct, C. replication, D. dependent variable, E. random assignment, F. operational definition
57) A. Experiments allow the researcher a lot of control and make it possible for them to assess causation. They can be costly and time-consuming, however.
B. Correlational studies need to be done when it's impossible or unethical to do an experiment. This design can assess whether or not there is a relationship between variables, but cannot assess causation. The researcher has less control than he or she would in an experiment.
C. Surveys are how one gathers data on what people think or feel—but people may lie, the questions may be unclear or biased, and social desirability bias may come into play.
D. Naturalistic observations are observing people in their natural environments. Thus, one can see how people really behave. However, the researcher won't know what the people are thinking or feeling. Plus, the researcher has very little control over other factors.
E. Case studies are in-depth studies of one or more people—most often, people who are highly unusual. However, this small sample size makes it unlikely that results can be generalized to others. There is also little control over variables, and there could be too much subjectivity.
58) A. F (experiments are), B. F (it's called a zero correlation), C. T, D. F (correlation does not necessarily mean causation), E. F (it's a very strong negative correlation), F. T, G. F (it's also known as the case-study method), H. F (it's called naturalistic observation)
59) correlation coefficient; zero correlation; positive correlation; negative correlation
60) A. expectancy bias, B. double-blind study, C. double-blind study, D. emotional bias, E. placebo, F. both options are correct, G. both options are correct
62) In a double-blind study, the participants do not know whether they are in the control group or the experimental group; therefore, they will not change their behaviors due to the knowledge about what group they belong to. The researcher also does not know which group any specific person belongs to, so this reduces the chance that the researcher will be influenced by his or her expectations (i.e., expectancy bias).
63) Pseudo-psychology does not use empirical investigation, but instead is based on confirmation bias, anecdote, hope, and gullibility. Empirical investigation is an essential feature of the scientific method. The scientific method has four basic steps, the first of which is to develop a hypothesis and to create operational definitions. The second step is to collect objective data; the third step is to statistically analyze the results. The fourth step is to publish, criticize, and replicate the results. Experiments include the dependent variable (outcome variable) and the independent variable (the one the researcher manipulates).
64) A. experiment; expectancy or confirmation bias can occur, so use a double-blind study
B. correlational study, most likely a survey, but perhaps a naturalistic observation, too; confirmation or expectancy biases can occur, though

C. correlational study, most likely a naturalistic observation, but perhaps a survey, too; all three biases can occur (issues with children often bring out strong emotions)

D. correlational study with a likelihood of survey research; all three biases can occur

E. case studies (this is a very unusual population of children); all three biases can occur

65) A. Shield participants from potentially harmful procedures, B. Information is confidential

66) A. Institutional Review Boards, B. debriefed, C. voluntary, informed, D. Informed consent

67) In some studies, if participants know what you are trying to find out, they may behave very differently from how they normally would behave. Thus, your data would not be accurate. Deception cannot include large risks to participants. And, participants must be debriefed after the study so that the deception is revealed and the true nature of the study is explained.

68) A 1985 U.S. federal law regulates animal research. In addition, the APA has a Committee on Precautions in Animal Experimentation and has recently stressed that research animals must have decent living conditions and that the value of the information gained from the research must outweigh any discomfort the animals are exposed to.

70) The text discusses harm associated with both lobotomies and the idea that positive thoughts can cure illness.

71) A. autism, B. unfounded, C. scientific, D. did not make sense

72) We need to be skeptical of extreme claims, we need to look at evidence and make sure it's scientific evidence rather than anecdotal evidence, and we need to see if biases (such as the expectancy bias or emotional bias) could be playing a role.

Practice Tests

Item Number	Practice Test 1	Practice Test 2	Practice Test 3	Comprehensive Test
1	C	C	B	C
2	B	C	A	A
3	C	A	A	D
4	D	B	C	C
5	A	B	D	C
6	C	C	A	D
7	D	B	D	D
8	A	C	A	C
9	A	B	D	C
10	C	C	C	B
11				B
12				C
13				D
14				A
15				A

Critical Thinking Essays

1. Discuss the differences between correlational studies and experiments and how only the latter design can assess causality.

2. Discuss the scientific method, the experimental design of research, and the fact that such methods are not used in pseudo-psychology. Discuss biases (confirmation bias, emotional bias, expectancy bias) that could be operating in pseudo-psychology because of the lack of scientific methodology and its controls for such biases. As for the persistence of pseudo-psychological beliefs, many issues can be discussed, such as the public's lack of understanding of the scientific method, people's poor critical thinking skills (refer to the six main critical thinking skills in the text), and people's emotional and other biases.

3. When you compare and contrast the different perspectives, you can discuss the topics that are investigated in each, the perspectives' views on nature and nurture, and the ability to perform controlled experiments to test ideas within each perspective. You also need to talk about "hybrid psychologists" (e.g., cognitive behaviorists) who combine different perspectives.

1) A. F (it weighs about three pounds), B. F (it's 100 <u>billion</u> cells), C. T
2) evolution
3) medicine, ministry, the Beagle, South America, common ancestry, variation, natural selection, On the Origin of Species
4) These help explain why phobias are more likely to involve snakes, blood, and lightning, which are things that would pose threats to our ancestors.
5) A. Chromosomes, B. genotype, C. 99.9, D. phenotype, E. gene, F. 46, G. 23, H. deoxyribonucleic acid, I. nucleotides, J. XX, XY, K. four, L. 30,000, M. 21, N. socially, O. genome
7) A. nervous system, B. endocrine system
8) the brain
9) nervous system, neuron, endocrine system, hormones
10) A. sensory neurons (afferent neurons) transmit signals from the senses to the brain and spinal cord

    B. motor neurons (efferent neurons) transmit signals from the brain and spinal cord to the muscles, glands, and organs

    C. Interneurons are "go-betweens" between the sensory and motor neurons. They also connect to other interneurons. The brain and spinal cord are made up mostly of interneurons.
11) 1. cell body (soma), 2. dendrites, 3. axon (surrounded by the myelin sheath), 4. terminal buttons of the axon
12) D, C, A, G, I, E, L, B, J, F, K, H
13) A. both options are correct, B. soma, C. cell body, D. both options are correct, E. synaptic transmission, F. resting, G. 5,000, H. positive, axon (<u>near</u> the soma)
14) A. F (neurotransmitters go across the synaptic gap), B. T, C. T, D. T, E. F (it can cause epileptic seizures), F. F (it's when they are drawn back into the vesicles of the originating neuron), G. F (dopamine does this), H. F (GABA is the most prevalent inhibitory neurotransmitter, whereas glutamate is the major excitatory neurotransmitter in the CNS)
15) Reuptake is the process whereby many of the neurotransmitters in the synapse are drawn back into the vesicles of the neuron that released them. Some drugs operate by interfering with reuptake, thus leaving the neurotransmitters in the synaptic gap longer.
16) dopamine, serotonin, norepinephrine, acetylcholine, GABA, glutamate, endorphins
17) E, F, D, D, C, B, G, A
18) A. They provide structural support for neurons, B. They help neurons form new synapses, C. They form the myelin sheath around axons, D. They protect neurons, E. They help conduct neural messages along the axon.
19) A. F (some use electrical signals and engage in synchronous firing), B. F (the text describes the brain implants in a paralyzed patient), C. T, D. F (that was originally thought, but it was found to be incorrect)
21) The nervous system is a network of neurons, also called nerve cells. Neurons are supported by glial cells, which form the myelin sheath. Neurons store their chromosomes in the cell

body, also called the soma. Vesicles are sacs in the axon's terminal buttons, which are bulblike structures at the end of the axon. The axon fires using the all-or-none principle.

22) A. The central nervous system (CNS) consists of the brain and spinal cord. The spinal cord governs basic reflexes and sends signals from the brain to the peripheral nervous system. The brain makes decisions, initiates behaviors, and coordinates functions.

B. The peripheral nervous system (PNS) connects the CNS to the rest of the body. It carries incoming signals from the senses to the CNS and carries outgoing signals from the CNS to the internal organs, sense organs, and muscles.

C. The somatic nervous system is a subset of the PNS and it links the CNS to the skeletal muscles and to the senses. (Sensory neurons carry messages from the senses and motor neurons carry messages to the muscles.)

D. The autonomic nervous system is also a subset of the PNS and links the CNS to the internal organs. This functions without conscious awareness.

E. The sympathetic division is a subset of the autonomic nervous system and is the arousing part that can activate the "flight-or-fight" response.

F. The parasympathetic nervous system is also a subset of the autonomic nervous system and it's the calming aspect, returning the body to a collected state.

23) Contralateral pathways refer to the fact that most of the motor and sensory neurons in the peripheral nervous system cross over, through the spinal cord or the brain stem, to the opposite side of the brain.

25) The peripheral nervous system communicates with the central nervous system and contains the somatic nervous system, which controls the skeletal muscles. The autonomic nervous system consists of the calming parasympathetic nervous system and the arousing sympathetic nervous system. The spinal cord governs basic reflexes.

26) D, E, A, B, C, F, A, A

27) hormones, neurotransmitters, pituitary, hypothalamus

28) Agonists are drugs that enhance or mimic neurotransmitters. Antagonists are drugs that dampen or inhibit the effects of neurotransmitters.

29) Neural pathways are bundles of nerve cells that generally follow the same route and use the same neurotransmitter. However, different pathways can use the same neurotransmitter—but for different functions. So, for example, there are many different pathways that use serotonin. Some use it for mood, some for sleep, some for appetite, and some for thinking. Therefore, if a person takes serotonin to treat depression (improve mood), the serotonin can also affect (often negatively) sleep, appetite, and thinking. These, then, are unwanted side effects.

30) In 1848, Gage was involved in an explosive accident where an iron rod was driven into his face, up through the front of his brain, and out through his skull. Although he amazingly survived and lived another twelve years, his personality was completely changed. Thus, through his experience, we got information about the functions that those damaged areas served.

31) A. Electroencephalograph (EEG) measures brain waves through electrodes on the scalp and can tell what parts of the brain are active. However, it's not very precise and can't give a detailed picture of the brain.

B. Electric probes are stuck in the brain and, by asking awake patients what they feel, one can map the functions of the brain. Certainly, a limitation is that it's brain surgery!

C. Computerized tomography (CT) scanning uses x-rays to form digital images of the brain at various angles, so one can get good 3-D images of the brain structures. However, it exposes people to radiation.

D. Positron emission tomography (PET) scanning can assess the activity, not just the structure, of the brain by sensing the amount of radioactive glucose being used by various brain areas. Once again, though, radiation is involved.

E. Magnetic resonance imaging (MRI) uses bursts of magnetic energy to get 3-D scans of the brain. It costs more than CT scanning, but doesn't expose people to radiation.

F. Functional magnetic resonance imaging (fMRI) can assess brain activity as well as structure, by monitoring blood and oxygen flow in the brain.

33) A. brain stem, B. limbic system, C. cerebrum

34) This is where many of the pathways from the left side of the brain cross over to the right side of the body, and where many from the right side of the brain cross over to the left side.

35) medulla, pons, reticular formation

36) The limbic system consists of brain structures related to emotion, memory, and motives. The hippocampus, amygdala, and hypothalamus are part of this system.

37) F, A, E, C, B, C, H, D, F, H, B, E, E, G, D, H

38) A. pituitary, B. cerebral cortex, C. corpus callosum, D. hypothalamus, E. thalamus, F. cerebellum, G. brain stem

39) The cerebral cortex is the outer gray matter layer (one-quarter inch thick) of the cerebral hemispheres (the large, symmetrical halves of the brain located on top of the brain stem) that is responsible for thinking and perceiving. The hemispheres are connected by the corpus callosum so that the two halves of the cerebrum can communicate with each other.

40) four, frontal, motor, parietal, somatosensory, touch, occipital, temporal, auditory

41) Mirror neurons are located mainly in the frontal lobes and fire when we observe actions, even if we don't actually perform those actions. These fire "empathetically" when we observe someone's emotions, too. Some researchers think that people with autism may have a deficiency in their mirror neurons.

42) A. frontal (left, Broca's area), B. temporal (left, auditory cortex special section called Wernicke's area) and/or parietal (left), C. frontal, D. temporal, E. frontal, F. frontal (right, motor cortex), G. parietal (right), H. parietal (left, somatosensory cortex), I. occipital

43) The association cortex consists of all regions of the cerebral cortex (the majority) that are not specialized for certain functions, but instead integrate information from other areas.

44) A. L, B. L, C. R, D. R, E. R, F. L, G. R, H. L, I. R

45) It is the tendency for some processes to be more under control of one hemisphere than the other. However, people often fail to realize that both hemispheres work together (except perhaps in split-brain patients whom you'll learn about later).

46) A. T, B. F, C. F, D. F (Everyone's eyes are hooked up that way, but in split-brain patients, unlike the rest of us, the information cannot immediately travel across the corpus callosum to the left visual cortex.), E. T, F. F (they would use the left hand, which is controlled by the right hemisphere, because the right hemisphere saw the object), G. T, H. F

49) The more neural pathways you use, the more memory components you will build in your brain. So, you can enhance learning by using a) visual processing to read the material, b) auditory processing to listen to lectures and to online tutorials and demonstrations, c) motor

pathways in writing notes, d) spatial processing in exploring concept maps and images, and e) decision making by employing this study guide.

50) Both hemispheres are involved in processing information, not just one or the other. Even if a person has a different "style" of thinking, he or she is still using both hemispheres of the brain.

Practice Tests

Item Number	Practice Test 1	Practice Test 2	Practice Test 3	Comprehensive Test
1	B	C	A	C
2	B	B	A	C
3	A	C	C	B
4	A	B	B	B
5	D	D	D	D
6	A	A	B	C
7	D	C	C	C
8	B	C	A	A
9	A	A	C	B
10	B	D	B	B
11				D
12				D
13				D
14				A
15				B

Critical Thinking Essays

1. Your reticular formation is keeping you awake and your attention focused. The thalamus is getting information from all the senses and routing that information to the correct parts of the brain. Your cerebellum is keeping your running and soccer skills coordinated and relatively automatic. Your amygdala kicks in with your angry, aggressive shouting. Your hypothalamus is monitoring thirst, nutrients, and body temperature. It also links to the endocrine system to help regulate your arousal and stress. In the frontal lobes of your cerebral cortex, your motor cortexes are sending messages to move your body, while the somatosensory cortexes in the parietal lobes are letting you have the sense of touch to kick the ball, feel the ground under your feet, and feel any pain. Your visual cortexes in the occipital lobes allow you to process visual information. Your auditory cortexes in the temporal lobes allow you to hear. In the left frontal lobe is Broca's area, which allows you to talk and yell "stop." In your left temporal lobe and left parietal lobe are areas allowing you to understand language. The association areas in your cerebral cortex are integrating all the information. All these brain areas are part of your central nervous system.

   In terms of your peripheral nervous system, your sympathetic division (part of your autonomic nervous system) is activated, especially while you're on the field. Off the field, the parasympathetic division (of your autonomic nervous system) helps calm your body functions down. Your somatic nervous system is responsible for all your skeletal muscle movements and the retrieval of information from your senses.

2. Your answer should first include a discussion of what we know about neurotransmitters and how they function. Then discuss psychoactive drugs, both legal and illegal, and how they affect neurotransmitters to then affect emotions, thoughts, and behaviors. You'll need to discuss how some drugs—agonists—mimic or enhance the function of neurotransmitters: whereas other drugs—antagonists—inhibit or dampen the effects of neurotransmitters. You can also mention the process of reuptake and the fact that some drugs, such as Prozac, interfere with reuptake.

3. First you need to tell them that a so-called "split-brain" person has had special surgery as a last resort for severe epilepsy and that their corpus callosum (the connection between the right and left hemispheres) has been cut. You then need to point out that these people, for the most part, function normally, and that it's usually only in the laboratory that the lack of communication between hemispheres can be observed.

You'll need to explain the contralateral sensory and motor pathways, and the fact that the medulla is where such crossing over takes place. They'll need to know that the right hemisphere controls the left side of the body and that the left hemisphere controls the right side of the body. They'll also need to know that in the majority of people, the left hemisphere is more specialized for language.

You'll then need to explain how the eyes' retinas are arranged so that if one stares straight ahead and something is quickly shown in one's left peripheral vision (i.e., the left visual field), that information, in all of us, goes to the visual cortex of the right hemisphere. It's the other way around for information flashed in one's right visual field—that information goes to the left visual cortex. Explain, then, that in you and your friends, that information would immediately zip over to the other hemisphere via the corpus callosum. But in split-brain people, only that one hemisphere gets the information.

Then talk about the experiments with split-brain patients where something is flashed in the right visual field (and thus gets to the left hemisphere, but not the right) and, because the left hemisphere is specialized for language, the patients can easily tell you what they saw. However, if something is flashed to the left visual field (and therefore only gets to their right hemisphere, which has very little language ability), the patients cannot tell and do not know what they saw. If, though, you then ask them to reach behind a screen where many different objects are sitting and pick out which object was flashed on the screen, they will be able to do this. But, only if they use their LEFT hands! This is because the left hand is controlled by the right hemisphere, which is the only side of the split-brain patient's brain that got the information.

411

1) Sensation is the process of turning the stimulation of sense receptors by the outside world into neural signals. Perception is the interpretation of sensory messages—giving them meaning.

2) This means that the stimuli in the outside world do not impact directly on the brain—instead they pass through "filters," which are the sense receptors, and that sensation is then converted into electrochemical (i.e., neural) activity.

3) A) F, B) T, C) T, D) F, E) T

4) absolute, difference, just noticeable difference (JND), Weber's Law, psychophysics

5) A) high, B) can, C) changes, D) lower, difference

6) A) characteristic of the stimulus, B) background stimulation, C) the detector

7) It shows that sensation is not a yes-or-no experience, but instead can vary depending on the factors discussed in question 6. The importance of people's biases, expectations, and assumptions are taken into account in signal detection theory.

8) Sensory adaptation is the diminished sensitive to a constant stimulus. The key here is *constant* stimulus, because if there is a detectable change in stimulation, we attend to that change. So if you're trying to study while music is playing, changes in loudness, pitch, lyrics, or melody will grab some or all of your attention (away from studying).

9) The senses are all the same in that they convert physical energy from the external world into neural impulses. However, each sense involves different pathways and brain areas.

10) retina, rods, cones, fovea, optic nerve, blind spot

11) 1. cornea, 2. pupil, 3. iris, 4. lens, 6. fovea, 7. blind spot, 8. optic nerve, 9. retina

12) G, D, E, I, F, A, G, B, C, H, F, D, I

13) A) F, B) T, C) T, D) T, E) T, F) F, G) F, H) T, I) F, J) F, K) T, L) F

14) outer ear (pinna), tympanic membrane, hammer, anvil, stirrup, middle, cochlea, inner, basilar membrane, hair, auditory nerve

15) A) Pitch is determined by the frequency of sound waves, B) Loudness is determined by the amplitude of sound waves, C) Timbre is determined by the specific mixtures of tones

16) A) F, B) F, C) F, D) T, E) T

17) A) Place theory is that different places along the basilar membrane correspond to different pitches. This explains how we hear high-pitched tones (above 1000 Hz.), B) Frequency theory is that the different firing rates of the hair cells on the basilar membrane correspond to different pitches. This explains how we hear pitches below 5000 Hz.

18) A) T, B) F (olfaction isn't), C) T, D) T

19) They are special odors, mostly found in animals. Some indicate sexual receptivity, whereas others indicate danger, territoriality, or food sources.

20) A) Vestibular sense is the sense of body position that involves the semicircular canals in the middle ear. Information is then sent to the parietal lobes, B) Kinesthetic sense is the sense of body position and movement that involves feedback from muscles, joints, and tendons. Messages are processed in the parietal lobes, C) Olfaction is the sense of smell in which chemicals are received by receptor cells in the nose and messages are sent to the olfactory bulbs in the brain. These messages, unlike all other sensory messages, bypass the thalamus, D) Gustation is the sense of taste and involves chemical receptors on the papillae of the

tongue, called taste buds. Four main qualities of taste are sweet, sour, bitter, and salty. There is also umami, which relates to protein-rich foods. Taste buds renew themselves often. Taste information is processed in the somatosensory regions of the parietal lobes. E) The skin senses include touch, pain, warmth, and cold, and this information is sent to the somatosensory cortexes in the parietal lobes. Number of skin receptors varies with body part.

21) "Supertasters" are those who have a high density of taste receptors. They tend to dislike certain foods, such as broccoli and diet drinks, that they find too bitter. They also dislike foods that they experience as too sweet or too fatty, and they weigh less than nonsupertasters.

22) Synesthesia is the mixing of sensations across sensory modalities (e.g., you might taste shapes). It is rare, but seems to be found a bit more often in creative people. It appears to involve the TPO area of the cortex, which is at the junction of the temporal, parietal, and occipital lobes. So, synesthetes may have more neural connections in this area.

23) nociceptors, gate-control, top-down, placebo, phantom limb

24) A) a placebo, B) two, C) Morphine, D) both options are correct, E) both options are correct

27) A) percept, B) the binding problem, C) the binding problem, D) both options are correct, E) conceptually-driven, F) feature detectors, G) perceptual constancy, H) Change blindness, I) Top-down, J) both options are correct, K) what, L) inattentional, change, M) both options are correct

28) They help us keep track of objects in a changing world.

30) The Hermann grid involves a black-and-white grid. When one stares at the center of the grid, fuzzy spots appear at the intersections of the white bars—but when one then tries to look at those spots, they vanish. This illusion is difficult to overcome because it involves bottom-up processing more than top-down processing, so it's more related to sensation than perception.

31) A) T, B) F, C) F, D) F

32) It involves two lines of identical length, but inward arrows are placed on both ends of one line and outward arrows are placed on both ends of the other line. When this occurs, the line with the outward arrows appears longer than the line with inward arrows. This may related to a "carpentered" world with right angles, so that the line with outward arrows appears to be an inside corner of a building and the line with inward arrows appears to be the outside corner of a building. So, the brain interprets the outside corner as more distant and therefore smaller. Support for this explanation comes from a study of the Zulu tribe that only has round buildings and no straight lines. They don't see this illusion.

34) The principle of closure makes you fill in the blanks. Gestalt laws of perceptual grouping include the Law of Proximity (which groups together close things), the Law of Similarity (which groups together things that are alike), the Law of Continuity (that refers to perceiving things as smoothly continuous), the Law of Prägnanz (which is known as the minimum principle of perception and refers to perceiving the simplest pattern possible), and the Law of Common Fate (which groups together things that move together).

36) Helmholtz meant that based on our past experiences, we make inferences (predictions or guesses) about what sensations mean. Often we're right, but sometimes we're wrong.

37) A) context, B) expectations, C) perceptual set

38) A) perceptual set, B) context, C) visual cliff, six, D) two-week

39) Americans are less likely than Chinese people to perceive things holistically. Instead, Americans are more likely to focus on "figures," whereas people from China are more likely

to focus on details of the "ground." Individuals who've lived their whole life in Guam, where there are winding roads that don't provide the cue of linear perspective, are less susceptible to the Ponzo illusion than are Americans.

40) A) relative size, smaller, B) linear perspective, C) lighter-colored objects seem closer to us and darker objects seem farther away, D) interposition, E) when you move past objects, closer objects appear to move by quickly, whereas more distant objects appear to move by very slowly, F) atmospheric perspective

42) Both are binocular depth perception cues (they depend on the use of both eyes). Binocular convergence is a cue from your eye muscles so when you look at things that are close to you, there's more muscle strain. Retinal disparity is that the images on our two retinas are more different (disparate) the closer an object is to us.

43) Gestalt psychology points out that we look for meaningful patterns. So when studying, it would be best to look for meaningful patterns, too.

44) Subliminal perception is the unconscious perception of stimuli presented below one's absolute threshold. Laboratory studies of priming show its existence. Subliminal persuasion, that unconscious perceptions can affect our complex behaviors, such as buying or voting, doesn't have scientific evidence supporting its existence.

Practice Tests

Item Number	Practice Test 1	Practice Test 2	Practice Test 3	Comprehensive Test
1	D	A	B	B
2	C	C	B	A
3	C	A	A	B
4	A	A	B	B
5	D	A	D	C
6	C	B	C	B
7	A	B	A	C
8	D	D	B	A
9	B	B	C	C
10	B	D	D	C
11				B
12				D
13				C
14				C
15				A

Critical Thinking Essays

1) Our sense organs and brains respond to change rather than constancy, so any changes in the music will grab at least some attention away from studying. Certain aspects of the music may become figures that stand out from the ground. We won't experience sensory adaptation with interesting music, because it won't be constant, but instead will always be changing. Favorite music will also grab your attention—that's partly why it's your favorite.

2) Pain is more than bottom-up processing at the level of the pain receptors (nociceptors). People with phantom limb pain, who no longer have the pain receptors for that limb (because the limb is amputated), can still experience pain that seems to come from that missing limb. Therefore, the brain gives information about pain. The gate-control theory and the placebo effect also show that top-down processing is involved.

1) learning, instincts
2) B, C, D, F, D, A, F, E
3) A) reflexes, neutral, B) acquisition, C) unconditioned, unconditioned, D) conditioned, conditioned
4) A) F (responses usually are weak at first), B) F (with taste aversions, intervals of hours or even days will still bring on classical conditioning), C) F (a neutral stimulus becomes a conditioned stimulus), D) T, E) T
5) UCS = food, UCR = salivation to the food, NS = tone/bell, CS = tone/bell, CR = salivation to the sound of the tone/bell
6) *Acquisition* occurred when Ann associates the *neutral stimulus* of the smell of rubbing alcohol with the painful injections (*unconditioned stimulus*). Those injections bring on the *unconditioned response* of a racing heart. However, after many pairings, the smell of rubbing alcohol became the *conditioned stimulus* that brought on the *conditioned response* of a racing heart. In fact, *stimulus generalization* occurred because her heart raced when she smelled other alcohol, such as wine. When her parents switched to lemon-scented alcohol wipes, *stimulus discrimination* occurred and Ann's heart did not race. Eventually *extinction* occurred so that her racing heart (CR) no longer occurred when she smelled rubbing alcohol (CS). However, two months later *spontaneous recovery* occurred when she smelled rubbing alcohol and experienced a racing heart.
7) A) weakens, B) lower, C) discrimination, D) Spontaneous recovery; extinction
8) E, D, C, B, A
9) counterconditioning, extinction, relaxation
11) A) The findings make sense from an evolutionary perspective because nausea and illness are more likely to be caused by something that one ingests than by pain on the feet. And learning to avoid substances that are toxic or cause illness is adaptive. B) Pavlov thought learning was totally due to environmental effects, but the taste aversion studies show that some learning is partially innate (i.e., unlearned).
12) Pavlov won a Nobel Prize. Dogs reflexively salivated when presented with food, and food was therefore the unconditioned stimulus. The neutral stimulus in Pavlov's study was the tone/bell. An infant named Albert was conditioned to fear a white rat because the rat was repeatedly presented with a loud noise. That loud noise caused the UCR.
13) Researchers paired nausea-inducing toxins with sheep meat (wrapped in sheep skin), so that coyotes learned to associate sickness with sheep. Thus, they avoided sheep.
14) Because chemotherapy (UCS) causes nausea (UCR), patients are conditioned to associate food with nausea and thus reduce their eating to dangerous levels. So, if an unusual food item is presented before chemotherapy, only that unusual item gets associated with nausea and is therefore avoided. That food item becomes a sort of "scapegoat" but other food items then do not get associated with nausea.
15) A) operant, B) consequences, rewards (reinforcers), punishment, C) Operant, classical, D) new (or voluntary), reflexive
16) A) both researchers, after, B) the law of effect, C) Skinner's, radical behaviorism

17) A) F (reinforcement always strengthens a behavior), B) F (it's negative reinforcement), C) T, D) F (it refers to the removal of an unpleasant *stimulus*), E) F (it's used to study operant conditioning), F) T, G) F (he hated the term "Skinner box"), H) F (Skinner felt that "reward" implied that something was pleasant, which then implies that one knows the mental processes of the organism. He felt that "reinforcer" is a term that just pertains to affecting the organism's behavior and doesn't imply anything about the mental processes of pleasure or liking.)

18) A) negative reinforcement, B) positive reinforcement, C) neither (it's punishment), D) neither (it's punishment), E) negative reinforcement

19) A) positive reinforcement, B) negative reinforcement, C) negative reinforcement, D) negative reinforcement, E) positive reinforcement

20) Continuous reinforcement refers to giving a reinforcer every time the behavior occurs. It's good to use early in the learning process and is a good way to shape complex behaviors, because it makes it clear what exact behavior is desired and which ones are not desired. Intermittent reinforcement refers to giving a reinforcer only some of the time. This is a good way to maintain a behavior once it has been learned because it's more resistant to extinction than continuous reinforcement is.

21) Shaping is reinforcing successive approximations of the desired behavior. This is done when the desired behavior is very complex and the organism is unlikely to do it spontaneously (such as a dolphin jumping through a hoop ten feet above the water). So, you reinforce little steps that get closer and closer to the final behavior.

23) G, C, J, I, E, A, F, H, D, E, B, E, F, C, E

24) A) Premack Principle, B) token economy, C) Premack Principle

25) A) P, B) R, C) R, D) P, E) R, F) P

26) A) positive punishment, B) removal, a pleasant, C) negative punishment, D) positive reinforcer (it strengthened his behavior due to the pleasant stimulus of attention), E) positive punishment, F) both options are correct, G) negative, H) positive

28) A) when the threat of punishment is removed, the behavior is often no longer suppressed, B) possible rewards can outweigh possible punishers, C) punishment triggers escape or aggression, D) punishment can produce anxiety or learned helplessness, which gets in the way of learning more desirable behaviors, E) punishment is often applied unequally

29) You should warn your friend about using positive punishment and suggest he use negative punishment (e.g., taking away privileges). The positive punishment of spanking (hitting) would be particularly problematic because it would give his daughter a mixed message ("I'm hitting you because I don't want you to hit"). The punishment must be consistent and immediate. It should "fit the crime" rather than being too harsh. It should also target the *behavior* of his daughter rather than the *character* of his daughter. It would be best if he reinforces his daughter's good interactions with her brother to strengthen those behaviors.

30) A) Positive reinforcement of desired behavior that is incompatible with undesirable behavior is a good technique. B) Because it involves an unpleasant stimulus, there can be problems with this technique in terms of anxiety and disruption of learning. However, if there's a naturally occurring unpleasant stimulus that can be removed by doing a behavior, that behavior will increase. C) Punishment has many potential problems, as discussed in item #28

and #29. D) Extinction is difficult because you need total control over any potential stimuli that could intermittently reinforce the behavior.

31) B. F. Skinner was the founder of operant conditioning. He invented a device called the operant chamber. Reinforcement can be positive reinforcement, which involves the presentation of a stimulus that is pleasant. Reinforcement can also be negative reinforcement, which involves the removal of a stimulus that is aversive or unpleasant. Negative reinforcement is NOT the same as punishment.

32) A) Stimulus occurs after the behavior in operant conditioning and before the behavior in classical conditioning, B) both pleasant & unpleasant stimuli can be used in classical conditioning, C) operant conditioning produces new behaviors, D) in classical conditioning, extinction occurs when the CS is no longer paired with the UCS, E) the learner is active in operant conditioning and passive in classical conditioning

34) Core Concept 3.3 points out that some learning takes place mentally rather than behaviorally.

35) Insight learning is an abrupt reorganization of one's perceptions and thinking about problems. Köhler first reinforced chimps to learn two separate behaviors: to obtain out-of-reach bananas by using a stick, and to obtain out-of-reach bananas by piling up boxes and standing on them. Then Köhler presented the chimps with a new problem in which the only way they could reach the bananas was to combine the two previously-learned methods. After a bit of unsuccessful trying, the chimps sat down and appeared to think about the problem. Then they suddenly jumped up, piled up boxes, climbed up with the stick in hand, and reached the bananas.

36) A cognitive map is a spatial representation in one's mind. Tolman noticed that rats in a maze would sometimes take a path that previously hadn't been reinforced in order to get to a reinforcer more quickly. It seemed that they had a mental representation of the maze.

37) Bandura showed some young children a video of adults punching and kicking a BoBo doll, while other children were not shown the film. When all children were allowed to play with the BoBo doll, those that saw the aggressive model imitated those aggressive acts on the doll.

38) Psychic numbing refers to the finding that those people who watch a lot of violent media have lower emotional arousal and distress than other people when they watch violent acts. They've become habituated to the violence, so it doesn't affect them as it does other people.

40) B, A, C, A, C, B, B, A

41) A) Long-term potentiation, B) limbic system, frontal, C) neurotransmitters, glutamate, norepinephrine, D) mirror

Practice Tests

Item Number	Practice Test 1	Practice Test 2	Practice Test 3	Comprehensive Test
1	A	D	B	B
2	A	D	C	D
3	D	C	B	C
4	B	C	D	A
5	B	A	A	A
6	B	B	B	B
7	D	B	D	A
8	C	C	A	A
9	C	B	C	C
10	A	A	C	A
11				C
12				C
13				B
14				D
15				B

Critical Thinking Essays

1) In your answer, you need to focus on classical conditioning. The unconditioned stimulus is painful pinching, which elicits anxiety and sweating. The neutral stimulus used to be the revolving door, but after it was paired with the painful pinch (the UCS), the door became the conditioned stimulus, which brought on the conditioned response of anxiety and sweat. This response has yet to be extinguished, even after two years, perhaps because the person always avoids revolving doors and thus doesn't experience this CS without the accompanying UCS.

2) You first need to tell him all about the problems with punishment. His positive punishment is not immediate and likely not consistent, so those are big problems. The fact that he uses a painful stimulus can increase fear and aggression in his dog and keep it from learning good behaviors, too. You should also point out that there is something called negative punishment he might be able to use, such as taking away a favorite toy or treat when the dog misbehaves. You should also point out that positively reinforcing good behavior that is incompatible with chewing shoes will likely work well. You should point out, though, that you'll need to find objects the dog CAN chew; otherwise, instinctive drift can occur, and the dog will revert back to chewing the shoes.

3) You'll need to acknowledge that a lot of correlational studies have been done on the topic, but you'll then explain that many experimental studies have shown a causal relationship between watching violent media and behaving aggressively. Tell her about Bandura's experiments, for example. You also need to tell her about psychic numbing.

1) encodes, stores, retrieves
2) Human memory is interpretative rather than a video recording. Like an artist, memory takes in information, discards details, and then organizes the remaining information into meaningful patterns. One constructs one's memory by using bits of information and then filling in blanks.
3) A) information that we focus on, B) information we're interested in, C) the information arouses us emotionally, D) we can connect the information with previous experience, E) when we rehearse the information
4) information processing
5) encode, select, identify, label, automatic or unconscious, elaboration, storage, retrieval
6) Eidetic memory is the technical term for photographic memory. However, it's not really like a photo in that it can't get the minute detail of photos. Instead, eidetic memory produces the most accuracy for the most interesting parts of an image. Unlike normal memory, eidetic memories are visualized "outside the head" rather than in the "mind's eye." Also, these images can last for days and can get in the way of other thinking.
7) Eidetic memory is more common in children than in adults, so it may be that it goes away once the child acquires language. Evidence also shows that the eidetic memories fade when the person starts verbally describing them. In a Nigerian tribe, there are some adults who have eidetic memories, but they are all illiterate.
8) A) sensory memory, B) working (short-term) memory, C) long-term memory
9) The capacity is twelve to sixteen items. The duration is about one-quarter of a second. The structure/function is that there is a separate sensory register for each sense (e.g., iconic for vision, echoic for hearing, tactile for touch, olfactory for smell, gustatory for taste). The biological basis is the sensory pathways.
10) Sperling presented people with the display of letters for a split second and then asked them to recall as many as they could. They could usually only remember three or four. But he then flashed letters on the screen and immediately afterwards gave a tone that signaled which row to recall. Subjects always were able to say all four letters—this means that all twelve letters were available to them, but they faded away before they could tell all twelve.
11) Sensory register is the brief memory for each sense (e.g., iconic for vision, echoic for hearing, tactile for touch, olfactory for smell, gustatory for taste).
12) The capacity is about five to nine chunks. The duration is about twenty to thirty seconds. The structure/function includes the central executive that directs attention, the phonological loop that stores sounds, and the sketchpad that stores and manipulates visual images. The biological basis is the hippocampus and frontal lobes.
13) *(first column and then second column)* B, E, A, F, D, C, H, G, D, E
14) A) chunking, B) elaborative rehearsal, C) maintenance rehearsal, D) chunking
15) levels-of-processing, working, long-term, deeper, meaningful/memorable, more connections
17) The capacity is unlimited. The duration is essentially a lifetime. The structure/function includes procedural and declarative memories and then declarative memory is divided into semantic and episodic memories. The biological basis is the cerebral cortex.

18) A) declarative, procedural, B) procedural, C) declarative, D) procedural, E) episodic, F) both options are correct, G) semantic, H) both options are correct
19) A) procedural, B) semantic (subset of declarative), C) autobiographical (a subset of episodic, which is a subset of declarative), D) declarative, E) episodic (a subset of declarative)
20) Sensory memory includes the visual iconic memory (studied by Sperling) and the auditory echoic memory. Working memory is also called short-term memory. It stores information for about 20 to 30 seconds, and it has a capacity of about 7±2 items (chunks). It also contains a component called the central executive that directs one's attention. Long-term memory appears to have an unlimited capacity. It contains procedural memory (which is often unconscious) and declarative memory. Declarative memory contains semantic memory, which stores the meanings of words and concepts. Episodic memory (another component of declarative memory) stores autobiographical memory, which is like one's internal diary.
21) Schemas are clusters of knowledge that give us a context for understanding. They occur in semantic memory.
22) Childhood amnesia is the finding that most people are unable to remember events that happened before three years of age. This, then, relates to an underdeveloped episodic memory, which is likely due to having only basic language skills at those ages. However, in cultures where children are encouraged to discuss detailed stories of their life, childhood memories can extend back a bit earlier—to age two and a half.
23) A) engram, B) anterograde, retrograde, C) consolidation
24) A) F (it was anterograde amnesia), B) T, C) F (it's the amygdala that may play a role), D) T, E) F, F) T, G) F
26) It's a very clear recollection of an important or emotion-filled event.
28) A) how they were encoded, B) how they are cued
29) Explicit memory is conscious and implicit memory is unconscious. H. M. was able to learn (and thus remember) the mirror writing task and get better at if even though he couldn't remember ever having done it before. Researchers also got H.M. to learn some new semantic material in crossword puzzles.
30) It's a "search term" to retrieve memories. It can be an odor (ginger cookies bring up memories of grandma), a sound, a sight, a taste, a touch, an emotion—or a thought.
31) A) the type of memory being sought, B) the web of associations in which it is embedded
32) A) explicit, priming, B) gist, C) recall, recognition
33) Recall is retrieving information without many retrieval cues. Recognition is identifying whether or not a stimulus has been previously experienced. Recognition is easier.
34) A) encoding specificity, B) mood-congruent memory, C) prospective memory, D) continuous monitoring
36) The tip-of-the-tongue (TOT) phenomenon is the inability to recall information while at the same time knowing that you do know the information and it's "almost there." It happens often with names of acquaintances and famous people, as well as familiar objects.
37) A) inadequate context cues, B) interference (another memory blocks access or retrieval)
38) F, G, E, A, C, B, D
39) Ebbinghaus presented people with lists of nonsense syllables to remember and then, after weeks or months, he measured how quickly those people could relearn the same lists. This "savings method" allowed him to see how much material people were forgetting. When he

plotted the information on a graph, the "forgetting curve" showed an initial steep decline in memory and then a leveling off.

40) A) the greater similarity between two sets of material to be learned, the more interference B) meaningless material is more vulnerable to interference than is meaningful material, C) Emotional material can be a powerful cause of interference

41) A) proactive, B) retroactive, C) retroactive

42) A) T, B) F, C) F , D) T, E) T, F) F (the middle items are the ones most easily forgotten), G) T

43) It's when you aren't paying attention, either during encoding or during retrieval.

44) A) access, B) TOT phenomenon, C) both options are correct

45) Misattribution, reconstructive, their own

46) Loftus and colleagues have shown that when incorrect information is given to people during their time of recall, that information can distort their memories (the misinformation effect) or can even cause them to fabricate, unintentionally, memories that never happened. So, depending on whether people were asked if a car "smashed" or "hit" another car, people reported different speeds of the car, even though all people saw the exact same video of the cars. Loftus also showed people supposedly real photos of themselves doing something and people claimed to remember those events, even though the photos were computer-altered.

47) A) leading questions, B) a long passage of time, C) repeated retrieval, D) the witness's age, E) unwarranted confidence

48) Both biases can cause faulty memories. Expectancy bias is our tendency to remember things as being in line with our expectations. Self-consistency bias is that we think we're more consistent than we actually are; thus, we tend to remember our behaviors as being consistent even if they aren't.

49) A, G, D, C, F, E, B

50) A) helps keep one's memory from being overwhelmed, B) relates to the ability to shift attention, C) allows the most relevant information to come to mind, D) & E) & F) all relate to our remembering the gist rather than details, G) relates to memory for emotional experiences

51) long-term, method of loci, verbal, visual, visual imagery, natural language mediators, acronym, meaningful

52) A) Make the material personally meaningful by tying it in with your own life and thinking of personal examples, B) spread out studying sessions over time rather than cramming, C) avoid interference, so don't study with anything potentially distracting (e.g., music, TV) and be sure to clear up any confusion before the exams

53) A) whole method, B) distributed learning

54) Elaborative rehearsal will help to create a lot of associations between concepts, so the concepts can be accessed more easily. Encoding specificity involves knowing the kinds of questions likely to be asked by the professor and therefore learning the material in that form.

Practice Tests

Item Number	Practice Test 1	Practice Test 2	Practice Test 3	Comprehensive Test
1	C	B	A	B
2	D	A	D	D
3	B	D	B	A
4	C	B	A	D
5	C	C	D	D
6	B	C	C	A
7	C	B	B	D
8	A	D	B	B
9	D	A	C	B
10	C	A	D	C
11				C
12				A
13				B
14				C
15				B

Critical Thinking Essays

1) This topic is discussed in the Critical Thinking Applied section. You need to point out that there is a large incidence of child abuse, so such claims can't just be dismissed as unlikely. However, the idea of "repression" of traumatic events isn't supported by most research. Most people who experience traumatic events remember them vividly, and the memory sin of persistence is common with such events (e.g., post-traumatic stress syndrome). This ties in with the finding that we remember things better when strong emotions (such as fear) are associated with them—but not everyone is the same, so we need to keep an open mind. We do know about the memory sin of suggestibility, though. Loftus has shown how fabrications or distortions can be created in memories. There is also the post hoc fallacy that needs to be discussed (that we sometimes look back in time aand see two things that occur together as being causally related). Certainly, emotional biases can play a role, too.

2) You should tell them about making material personally meaningful, perhaps by tying it in with their own lives or thinking of their own examples. The "whole method" is an approach whereby they should first look at the big picture (by reading the chapter outline, for example) and then fill in details once they have that larger framework. You should also tell them about elaborative rehearsal and how the more connections they can make in their memories, the more easily they will later be able to retrieve that information. They should use visual imagery whenever possible, as well. Natural language mediators will help them remember, too, so they can develop acronyms and rhymes. They should study without distractions, because those can cause absent-mindedness and interference during the encoding process. If possible, they should learn to relax during the test, because anxiety/stress can block access to memories.

1) concepts, concept hierarchies, natural concepts, fuzzy concepts, prototype, Artificial concepts
2) We sometimes think in pictures (visual images) or sounds (auditory images) or other sensory images (tastes, smells, or touches). We may have a very difficult time putting those images into words. Cognitive maps (mental representations of a physical space) will rely on imagery, especially visual, but also the sense of touch or other senses.
3) A) widely, B) the same circuitry, C) modules, D) language, E) frontal, F) both options are correct
4) A) F, B) T, C) F, D) T, E) F
5) A) schema, B) script, C) event, D) schemas (or scripts), E) scripts, F) script
6) A) identifying the problem, B) selecting a strategy to solve the problem
7) Algorithms are step-by-step, logical procedures that guarantee a correct solution if they're done correctly. Programming your cell phone is an example. Heuristics are simple, basic rules that don't guarantee a solution, but often provide one (e.g., "If it doesn't work, see if it's plugged in").
8) A) working backwards (such as retracing your steps to find something you lost), B) finding analogies so you connect a new situation to something you already know, C) breaking the problem into smaller subgoals. Common element = they all involve a different perspective.
9) A) mental set, B) functional fixedness (a form of mental set), C) self-imposed limitations
10) A) Not being able to approach a problem from a different perspective, but instead only trying the strategies that have worked in the past, B) Being unable to see that an object can be used for something other than what it was created for, C) Setting personal standards that get in the way of solving a problem
11) D, A, C, C, B, A, E
12) Tyranny of choice: when we have too many choices, we sometimes fail to make a decision (or fail to make a good decision). Such choice can cause stress and waste people's time.
13) Base rate information is the probability of a characteristic occurring in the general population. Ignoring base rate information contributes to the representativeness bias.
15) Strategies include the use of heuristics (simple strategies that don't guarantee a correct solution) and algorithms (step-by-step, logical procedures that do guarantee a solution). Mental set includes functional fixedness. Decision making can be negatively affected by hindsight bias, which is also called the "I-knew-it-all-along effect." Decision making can also be negatively affected by tyranny of choice (which involves having too many options) and representativeness bias (which relates to stereotyping).
16) A) knowledge (expertise), B) high motivation, C) certain personality characteristics
17) Aptitudes are largely inborn potentialities specific to certain domains that are then developed by intensive study and practice.
18) A) independence, B) intense interest in a problem, C) willingness to restructure a problem, D) preference for complexity, E) a need for stimulating interaction
19) Low intelligence inhibits creativity, except in special cases such as savants. So, to be creative, a person has to be at least average in intelligence. Also, just because someone is

intelligent doesn't mean that person will also be creative. Sternberg believes that creativity requires that a person go against the expectations of others.

20) A) being good at finding analogies, B) developing elaborate chunks or schemas, C) having motivation and practicing or studying a lot

21) school, France, special help, current performance, innate, categorize (or label), training, opportunity, empirically, chronological, mental

22) A) the huge rate of immigration, B) new laws requiring schooling for all children, C) the beginning of World War II required the military to find ways to assess and classify recruits

22) The U.S. public accepted the idea that intelligence tests are objective and democratic, but the reality is that the tests opened the door for racial and ethnic prejudices.

23) A) Terman, B) Intelligence Quotient, C) William Stern, D) Mental Age, Chronological Age, E) Lewis Terman, F) MA divided by CA and then multiplied by 100, G) individually

24) Critics felt the measure was inconsistent because it tested different mental abilities at different ages. Test makers responded by including items assessing multiple types of abilities at all ages.

25) It makes it seem as though adults get less intelligent (mentally retarded) as they age.

26) The Flynn Effect is the fact that the average IQ score has gradually risen, by about three points per year, ever since the test was first given. It's unlikely that people are truly getting more intelligent and that people who were alive in the 1800s would be considered mentally retarded today. Instead, the increase in scores could be due to the increased complexity of society, better test-taking skills, more schooling, better nutrition, or an increased emphasis on problem-solving skills.

27) A) both options are correct, B) normally, C) regardless of their age, D) 100, E) normal, F) giftedness, G) 70

28) These are two intelligence tests developed by David Wechsler. The WAIS is the Wechsler Adult Intelligence Scale and the WISC is the Wechsler Intelligence Scale for Children. They are individually given and consist of numerous subscales.

29) A) T, B) F (the new definition does not even mention IQ scores), C) T, D) F, E) T

31) It refers to a person, typically with autism, who is mentally slow in almost every way, but then also has an extraordinary talent at something (e.g., numbers, music).

32) Psychometrics is the field of mental measurements.

33) According to Spearman, the *g* factor is the general intelligence that underlies all other mental activity. He believed it to be innate. Neuroscience has shown that tests of *g* all activate certain brain regions, especially in the frontal lobes.

34) mathematical, crystallized, fluid, independent, Crystallized, store, retrieve, semantic, vocabulary (or arithmetic, or general information), fluid, complex relationships, problems, spatial visualization (or block design).

36) Analytical intelligence includes problem-solving and logic. Creative intelligence is original thinking and innovation. Practical intelligence is everyday, real-world intelligence, including "people smarts."

37) A) analytical, B) practical, C) creative, D) practical

38) D, G, E, A, C, F, B, H

39) A) interpersonal, B) intrapersonal

40) The major contribution is that they are culturally inclusive. The main challenge is developing assessment measures.

42) You can discuss the Buganda people in Uganda, who believe intelligent people are slow and thoughtful, or the Djerman-Sonhai in Niger, who think of intelligence as a good memory combined with good social skills. In Kenya, practical skills are valued more than academic skills because they are needed to support a family. The Chinese view intelligence as having extensive knowledge, determination, social responsibility, and ability for imitation. The Cree, a Native American tribe, view intelligence as being respectful and accepting of others and listening to elders. They see this "good thinking" as very different from "school" intelligence.

43) A) F, B) T, C) F (Allen and Beatrix Gardner did), D) F, E) F, F) T

44) It's we when live up to expectations, either our own or other people's. The researchers told elementary school teachers that a few of their students were extra bright and capable (although students were actually randomly assigned to that label). At the end of the school year, those kids were rated by the teachers more highly than the other kids. In addition, those kids gained more IQ points than did the other kids.

45) Although there is agreement that each individual's intelligence is determined by both nature and nurture, there are differing views as to whether nature or nurture plays a bigger role in group differences in IQ scores. To assess individual differences in IQ, adoption studies are used to compare adopted children's IQ scores to their adoptive parents' scores and to their biological parents' scores to see if scores are more strongly correlated with adoptive or biological parents' scores. There is a stronger correlation with biological parents' scores than with adoptive parents' scores, which indicates that genes play a bigger role than environment. However, there is also evidence that people raised in the same environment are more similar to each other in terms of IQ than are people who are raised in different environments, so that shows that environment plays a role in IQ. In terms of *groups*, heritability estimates can only tell us about variations *within* groups, but not *between* groups. Because environments are so different for different groups (such as racial or ethnic groups), any differences in IQ we observe between groups cannot be attributed to genes. In addition, in terms of race, there are no biological boundaries defining different races.

46) He was an influential psychologist who believed that intelligence was a genetic trait, so he convinced the government to require mental testing of all immigrants (the 1924 Act) to keep "mentally defective" people out of the U.S. All tests were given in English—even though most immigrants didn't speak English!

47) A) biological, adoptive, B) both options are correct, C) fraternal

48) A) longitudinal, B) language, C) memory, D) companionship with other monkeys, E) narrowing

49) Heritability, within a group, environment, differences

50) A) F (there are none), B) T, C) F (traditional IQ tests do a better job), D) T, E) F (scores were higher than biological parents' scores but not as high as adoptive parents' scores), F) F (parents are involved), G) T, H) F (it's actually the opposite), I) F

51) Many different effects can be listed, such as A) environmental toxins, B) poor schooling, C) poor nutrition, D) poor health care, E) poor prenatal care by mothers, F) discrimination/bias

52) Stereotype threat: a person who belongs to a group about which there are stereotypes worries about living up to those stereotypes and thus performs poorly. In a way, it's similar to a self-fulfilling prophecy, but it always has to do with being part of a stereotyped group. It's not really similar to expectancy bias, because with stereotype threat, the person isn't "expecting" to perform poorly—instead, the person is worried about performing poorly.

Practice Tests

Item Number	Practice Test 1	Practice Test 2	Practice Test 3	Comprehensive Test
1	B	D	B	B
2	A	B	C	C
3	C	C	D	A
4	B	A	D	C
5	C	A	A	B
6	B	C	C	D
7	C	C	A	A
8	D	D	D	D
9	D	B	C	B
10	A	A	D	B
11				A
12				C
13				C
14				D
15				A

Critical Thinking Essays

1) The representativeness bias completely ties in with prejudice and stereotyping, because one judges the likelihood of something based on how well a person fits the prototype of a group. Prototypes tie in with stereotypes. The availability bias also ties in with prejudice and stereotyping because often the instances most available to memory are ones that involve our biases and stereotypes. Confirmation bias allows us to focus only on information that confirms our prejudices and stereotypes, while we ignore information that is contrary to those biases. Mental set can also relate to bias, when we are trying to solve problems involving people. We may stick with our preconceptions and fail to see things from a different perspective.

2) On the side of heredity, research shows that adopted children's IQ scores are usually more highly correlated with their biological parents' IQs than with their adoptive parents' IQs. In addition, the closer the genetic relationship between family members, the more similar their IQ scores. When looking at fraternal twins and identical twins, identical twins (who have the same genes) are more similar to each other in intelligence than are fraternal twins—and even when identical twins are raised apart from each other, their IQ scores are more highly correlated than are the scores of fraternal twins raised together!

On the side of environment, research shows that early educational intervention (such as Head Start) causes increases in children's IQ scores. Also, the Flynn effect shows that there are environmental effects on intelligence. Animal studies show the importance of stimulating environments and companionship with others on intelligence. With humans, studies of impoverished children have shown that the more stimulating their environment, the better the children's language skills. Also, the more nurturant the parents, the higher the children's memory skills.

1) A) Developmental, B) Nature, nurture, C) identical, fraternal, D) biological, adoptive
2) A) find nourishment, B) avoid harm, C) interact with others
3) A) division, implants, uterus, placenta, B) Embryonic, Embryo, differentiation, heart beat, drugs or other teratogens, C) reflexes, brain, hear sounds outside the womb
5) They are any substance that can harm the developing organism while it's in the uterus. They include alcohol, nicotine, viruses, chemicals, some drugs, and some herbs.
6) A) both options are correct, B) mental retardation, C) both options are correct, D) placenta
7) neonatal, sweet, 12, banana essence, human faces, contrast, 12, female, male
8) They wanted to find out if newborns' auditory preferences are innate or learned. They found that after babies were born, the babies showed a preference for the audiotape of their mothers reading *The Cat in the Hat* rather than a different story: learning caused the preference.
9) A) mimicry, B) synchronicity
10) A) postural reflex allows them to sit up with help, B) grasping reflex lets them cling to the caregiver, C) rooting reflex is when something strokes their cheek, they turn and try to suck on it, D) stepping reflex is if you hold babies upright above a solid surface, they lift their legs up as though marching (stepping)
11) A) T, B) F (they're called sensitive periods), C) F (it's the destruction of connections between neurons, not the neurons themselves), D) T, E) T, F) T, G) T, H) F, I) T, J) F
12) A) genetic leash, B) monkeys, C) contact comfort, D) attachment, E) imprinting, F) attachment, G) Strange Situation, H) psychosocial, trust versus mistrust I) lifespan
13) D, A, B, C, B
15) A) self-control, self-control, B) Improvisational (i.e., Unstructured), structured, C) self-control, D) Executive function
16) Noam Chomsky, Language Acquisition Device (LAD), Human Genome Project
17) A) four months, repeated syllables of any language sounds until about six months of age when they produce only language sounds in the language heard around them, B) age one, full words and then "naming explosion" at eighteen months, C) age 2, have about 1000 words
18) A) 25, 1000, B) daughters, sons, C) morphemes, D) telegraphic, E) overregularization, F) Grammar, G) all, 40,000
19) They need to learn the social rules of conversation, such as how to take turns, how to join a discussion, and how to make relevant contributions. They also need to understand facial expressions, intonations, and body language. They need to be able to get feedback from the listener and must be able to take the other person's perspective.
20) A) schemas, B) Assimilation, C) accommodation, D) assimilation, accommodation, E) mental operations
21) A) irreversibility, B) conservation, C) animistic thinking, D) object permanence, E) egocentrism, F) centration
22) F, C, B, A, B, D, E, C, F, both E and F
23) Piaget's theory is about cognitive development. The sensorimotor stage includes the development of object permanence, which begins at about eight months of age. The

sensorimotor stage leads to the preoperational stage, which includes the child's egocentrism (assessed by using the Three-Mountain Task) and centration (which involves a narrow focus). The concrete operational stage involves the child's mastery of conservation. The formal operational stage involves the development of abstract thought.

24) A) Object permanence has been found to occur as early as four months of age, B) By age three or four years, children do not show centration about what the inside of objects might look like, C) Three- to five-year-old children can tell the difference between real and imaginary things, which calls into question animistic thinking, D) Children at age four do not show egocentrism when talking to two-year-olds, because they shorten their words and use simple language, E) Children as young as six months of age demonstrate a "theory of mind" which leads to empathy, and deception, among other things.

26) It's the idea that development does not occur in abrupt transitions to new stages (as Piaget supposed), but that instead development is more like overlapping waves that ebb and flow as the child explores new cognitive strategies.

27) Temperament is one's inborn disposition. Socialization can enhance/strengthen it, or can change it.

28) A) F (it's 20 percent), B) F (it's just the opposite), C) T, D) T

29) A) permissive, B) authoritative, C) uninvolved, D) authoritarian

30) A) authoritative, B) both options are correct, C) stricter, D) 60 percent, E) as well as, F) paid providers, relatives, G) both options are correct

31) A) T, B) F (it's seven hours per day), C) F (it decreases), D) F (it's just the opposite), E) T, F) F (it's just the opposite), G) T, H) F (they spend less time)

32) Boys play more aggressively, competitively, and in larger groups than do girls. Girls play more cooperatively and in small groups.

34) A) Industry, ages six to twelve, children need to be allowed to try to achieve success at things so that they can feel a sense of competence (or else they will develop a sense of inferiority), B) Autonomy, eighteen months to three years, toddlers need to be allowed to develop a sense of independence—that they can do things on their own (or else they will develop shame or self-doubt), C) Guilt, preschool years (three to six), they need to be allowed to try to initiate activities themselves (or else they'll develop guilt)

35) A) F (it's 3 to 5 percent), B) T, C) F (20 percent are girls), D) T, E) T, F) F (it's 50 percent of cases), G) F (that's a myth), H) T, I) T, J) T, K) F (it's dopamine, not serotonin), L) F

36) puberty

37) They are social rituals that mark the passage between developmental periods, such as between childhood and adolescence. In the U.S., getting a driver's license and graduating from high school are rites of passage. So, too, are bar mitzvahs, bat mitzvahs, and quinceaneras. In other cultures, the rites can be very painful (such as scarring or circumcision), can involve seclusion or survival rituals, or can involve instruction in sexual or cultural practices.

38) A) menarche, B) eleven, fourteen, C) body image, D) puberty

39) Girls tend to have a more negative body image than boys do. This is especially true for early-maturing girls. Early-maturing boys tend to have a positive body image. Girls' self-esteem is tied to physical attractiveness, whereas boys' self-esteem is tied to athletic ability and achievement of goals. (This mirrors many cultures' ideals of female beauty and male

strength.) Girls are more likely to be unhappy about their weight and shape. Self-esteem for white adolescents is more tied to physical attractiveness than it is for black adolescents. In Hong Kong, body fat is not related to self-esteem as it is in the U.S.

40) A) 17, B) 75 percent, C) 90 percent, 60 percent, D) females, E) 8 to 12 percent, F) early

41) The frontal lobes are the last to develop in adolescents, and those lobes are responsible for rational thought and good decision making. Also, the amygdala's signals (related to emotion) may not be able to be processed effectively by the frontal lobes.

42) Pruning increases, so that unused neural pathways are trimmed away.

43) It's the formal operational stage. This stage involves abstract, introspective, systematic, and hypothetical thinking. Research doesn't support his idea that adolescents necessarily develop this type of thinking. Many adults do not, and it seems linked to education and experience.

44) moral dilemmas, Heinz, six, reward, punishment, perspectives, social approval, maintaining social order, social contract, universal principles of conscience.

45) Gilligan believes females are more oriented toward social relationships and personal caring. Most research, though, shows no gender differences in moral reasoning.

46) D, A, C, A, F, E, A, B

47) A) Moral reasoning often doesn't relate to moral behavior, B) Reasoning may come after people have already made emotional decisions, so reasoning is really just a rational justification for an emotional decision, C) The higher stages are not always found in other cultures, and often not even in the U.S. Education and verbal ability seem to play a big role.

48) A) identity vs. role confusion, B) peers, adults, C) shaming or humiliating, D) are not, E) authoritative

50) Perry found that first students viewed college as a place to get the Right Answers. Then they unexpectedly found diversity of opinion. They attributed this to confused and poorly qualified experts (such as their professors). Eventually students decided that differing views were legitimate in "fuzzy" areas of study such as the humanities and social sciences, because the Right Answers hadn't yet been found. But they still felt that in the "hard" sciences, there are Right Answers only. Later, some students (not all) decided that in some areas of study there are no right answers. However, they believed that math and science are areas where Right Answers are the norm. Finally, the most mature students realized that all areas of study are changing and have multiple perspectives.

51) It's a new view of aging in industrialized countries, due to better health care, greater longevity, and more lifestyle choices that are available.

52) A) love, work, B) love, belonging, esteem, fulfillment, C) affiliation/social acceptance, achievement/competence, power, D) intimacy, generativity

53) A) F, B) T, C) F (emerging adulthood is), D) F (1/2 do this), E) F (intimacy or personal relationships), F) T, G) F

54) A) generativity, B) do not, transition, C) dialectical thinking, D) both options are correct, E) a midlife crisis

55) A) Activity, B) ego-integrity vs. despair, wholeness, C) Alzheimer's disease, D) differently (bringing more regions into play), E) relationships with others, F) Selective social interaction

57) One criticism is that the effects of environment also show up in each pair of twins. Another is that because identical twins usually look alike, they are likely also treated alike, thus they

get very similar environmental experiences. Another criticism is that the researchers' expectancy bias could have played a role.

58) The Mozart effect refers to an empirical study that showed that college students who listened to Mozart got higher IQ scores after the listening session. The media jumped at this finding and then people capitalized on it by selling Mozart audiotapes for babies, telling pregnant women to put headphones on their bellies so the fetus could listen to Mozart, etc. . . . Even though the study was on undergrads, people generalized to babies and fetuses, which is bad science. Also, the IQ findings in the original study were only temporary, and the IQ measure was one of visual-spatial reasoning—only one element of IQ tests. Recent research shows that positive mood, induced by the music, is more likely what affects performance.

Practice Tests

Item Number	Practice Test 1	Practice Test 2	Practice Test 3	Comprehensive Test
1	A	B	D	D
2	B	A	B	A
3	B	C	B	C
4	D	D	B	B
5	C	A	A	C
6	C	D	B	C
7	A	C	D	D
8	C	C	C	A
9	C	B	D	D
10	A	D	C	C
11				C
12				B
13				C
14				A
15				D

Critical Thinking Essays

1) Piaget's sensorimotor stage generally has no relation to Kohlberg's stages of moral reasoning, until maybe at the very end, when children acquire language. At that point, their toddler reasoning would be Stage 1 of Kohlberg's theory. Piaget's preoperational stage ties nicely with Kohlberg's Stages 1 and 2, because preschoolers are egocentric (Piaget's term) and therefore would think about moral issues in terms of how things would affect themselves. By the concrete operational stage, when kids are no longer bound by centration, egocentrism, and irreversibility, they are better able to understand how issues affect others. This can move their moral reasoning up to Stages 2 and 3, and maybe even 4. By the formal operational stage, adolescents and adults should ideally be able to reason at Kohlberg's highest levels because of the need for abstract, hypothetically thinking at those stages. This rarely happens, however.

2) A stereotype about midlife is the midlife crisis, but research shows that most adults do not experience a crisis. Instead, midlife is more a time of transitions, both positive and negative. Another stereotype is the empty-nest syndrome, where middle-aged parents get depressed when their kids leave home. Most people do not experience this, though.

   In terms of late adulthood, a stereotype is that everyone gets Alzheimer's disease or loses their memory. Some types of memory do indeed decline, but others do not. Also, only about 10 percent of people over 65 have Alzheimer's, although that increases to more than 50 percent of people over age 85. Other stereotypes, about sex, sensory abilities, cognition, and social relationships, can also be discussed.

1) A) Structuralists, B) John Watson, C) Cognitive, D) serially, E) Nonconscious
2) Consciousness, attention, selective attention, cocktail party phenomenon, working memory, working memory
3) They showed that we consciously manipulate our mental images (such as by mentally rotating them or mentally zooming in to see details).
4) James saw consciousness as a stream that flows by with ever-changing sensations, perceptions, thoughts, emotions, and memories. Freud saw it as the tip of an iceberg, believing that the majority of mental processing was below awareness. Modern cognitive psychologists use a computer metaphor, so that what appears on the screen is consciousness while nonconscious activity is deep in the machine.
5) A) T, B) F, C) T, D) F, E) F
6) A) Restriction: restricts attention so the brain isn't overwhelmed, B) Combination: provides a place where sensations, emotions, memories, motives, and other psychological processes can combine into perceptions, C) Manipulation: allows us to create a mental model of the world that we can manipulate, so that we don't have to live in the present.
7) A) F, B) F, C) T
8) A minimally conscious state is when a person is gradually on his or her way out of a coma, and shows some reactions to outside stimuli. A persistent vegetative state is when a person shows no reactions to outside stimuli. There is very little brain activity and are just basic reflexes. It's extremely unlikely that a person will awaken from this state.
10) A) study the gist (the meaning) rather than just memorizing, by using examples from your life and y putting things in your own words, B) make connections between concepts, C) anticipate the most likely cues
11) A) every day, B) thirty, C) decline, D) interfere with, E) both options are correct
12) Daydreams are not as vivid as night dreams; they do not vary with biological cycles, and they are more under one's control.
13) E, H, I, A, D, J, B, A, F, B, G, C, A
14) A) the ninety-minute cycles, B) the occurrence of deepest sleep near the beginning of the night, C) the increased duration in REM sleep as the night progresses
15) It is what happens after you are deprived of REM sleep. Once you get a chance to sleep without being disturbed, you spend much more time in REM sleep than usual. This indicates that we have a biological need for REM sleep.
16) A) According to evolutionary psychologists, it may have evolved to conserve energy and to keep animals out of harm's way, B) Some experiments show that it may help memory and problem solving, C) It has a restorative function, D) It may help the brain clean out the day's accumulation of unwanted and useless information.
17) A) longer, B) increases, Stage 4, C) sixteen, REM, D) nine, seven and a half, E) fifteen, F) loss, gain, G) restlessness, H) both options are correct, I) the same as
18) C, E, B, D, A, A
19) According to Freud, dreaming guards sleep by keeping out intrusive thoughts (by turning them into symbols) and serves as a source of harmless wish fulfillment. Freud said the

manifest content of dreams (their story line) actually contains symbolic meaning (the latent content). Thus, a psychoanalytic therapist would look for the symbols in the dream in order to understand the person's unconscious motives and conflicts. Little solid scientific evidence supports this theory.

20) Dreams tend to reflect life events, often the most recent ones, so those life events will vary by culture.

21) A) T, B) T, C) F, D) T, E) F

22) A) immerse yourself in the problem you're interested in, B) don't push for a solution, but instead distract yourself so your creative ideas can develop, C) allow yourself plenty of time

24) activation-synthesis, sleeping, sleeping brain stem, cerebral cortex, random, making sense, nonsense

25) B, A, A, C, D, C, B, C, A, B, B, C, D, C

27) A) deep relaxation, B) heightened suggestibility, C) focused attention

28) A) F, B) F, C) T

29) A) it's a distinct state of consciousness, different from all others, B) it is simply suggestibility, C) it is a social process involving role playing of a "hypnotized" person, D) it is a dissociated state where there is a "hidden observer" in a person's mind that is operating along with normal consciousness, E) it is a shift in top-down processing so that one is driven by thoughts, imagery, and expectations, rather than external stimuli.

30) It can help as a research tool for studying mind-body connections; it can help reduce pain; and it can be used in psychological treatments for stress, phobias, or eliminating unwanted behaviors.

32) concentrating, repetitive, external stimulation, an altered, captures reality, frontal, increased, amygdala, relaxation

33) Psychoactive drugs affect mental processes and behavior by affecting the brain. Many negatively affect brain processes that help us make decisions. Many stimulate the brain's "reward circuits" so they produce pleasure and make our bodies "think" that the drugs are good for us.

34) Psychoactive drugs induce hallucinogens, which alter perceptions and create hallucinations. Cannabis contains the active ingredient THC, which is chemically similar to the brain chemicals called endocannabinoids. Psilocybin is made from a mushroom. Opiates are like brain chemicals called endorphins. Opiates include heroin, which is derived from morphine. MDMA is also called Ecstasy. Stimulants include methamphetamine, which causes widespread brain damage. Depressants (and antianxiety drugs) slow down the central nervous system. Depressants include barbiturates, which are prescribed for sedation. Benzodiazepines are prescribed to treat anxiety.

35) A) both options, longer, B) chemotherapy, C) dopamine, many, D) both options, diarrhea, E) sleeping pills, F) opiates, are not, G) both options, H) Benzodiazepines, barbiturates, I) has, slowly, J) decrease, K) alcohol, L) smoking, M) MDMA, N) methamphetamine

36) A) sedation, B) unconsciousness, C) immobility, D) amnesia

37) tolerance, physical dependence, withdrawal, addiction, psychological dependence

38) A) F, B) F, C) T

39) A good thing about the disease model of addiction is that when people are viewed as having an illness, they are more likely to be placed in a treatment facility. If, instead, they are

viewed as having character defects, they are sent to prison, which does little to break the cycle of drug abuse (and the crimes that often go along with it). However, viewing addiction as a biological disease may ignore the powerful environmental (e.g., social, economic) influences that contribute to addiction. Alcoholism treatments that see it as a behavioral problem are more successful than those that view it as a medical problem. Heroin addicts who picked up their addiction in the Vietnam War were more likely to get rid of the addiction than heroin addicts who got their addiction on the streets of the U.S.; this is most likely because the Vietnam vets returned home to an environment that didn't include heroin, whereas the other addicts, after treatment, returned to the same environment in which they had developed their addition.

38) Freud paid attention to information that confirmed his beliefs, he assumed the existence of the very thing he was trying to prove, and he claimed that resisting his ideas about the unconscious were evidence of unconscious conflicts at work.

Practice Tests

Item Number	Practice Test 1	Practice Test 2	Practice Test 3	Comprehensive Test
1	C	D	B	C
2	C	B	D	B
3	D	A	B	A
4	B	D	C	B
5	A	A	B	A
6	B	B	A	A
7	C	D	A	D
8	C	A	C	A
9	D	C	C	D
10	D	B	A	B
11				D
12				C
13				A
14				C
15				A

Critical Thinking Essays

1) You need to discuss issues such as sleep debt and the fact that individuals don't realize their tiredness is due to it, how sleep debt can have the same cognitive and motor coordination effects as intoxication, and the ways in which some major disasters (e.g., Exxon Valdez oil spill) have been related to sleep debt. Discuss how cutting one's night sleep short is likely to affect REM sleep, because REM sleep occurs more during the later part of the night's sleep. As REM rebound shows, there's a biological need for REM sleep. Stage 4 sleep is also important, due to its restorative effects.

2) They both involve extreme relaxation and focused attention, some people consider them altered states of consciousness, they both can reduce stress, and they both have multiple explanations.

1) It's all the processes that help in initiating, directing, and maintaining activities (physical and psychological).
2) A) *n Ach*, B) Internal, C) need for achievement, D) both options are correct, E) individualism, individualism, F) Collectivist, individualist G) both options are correct
3) A) need for achievement, B) need for power, C) need for affiliation
4) It is when external rewards diminish a person's internal motivation. This occurs only when rewards are given without regard for the quality of one's performance.
5) A) they can help motivate people to do things that they wouldn't ordinarily do, B) they can help increase intrinsic motivation when contingent on good performance, C) they can reduce intrinsic motivation when given without regard for the quality of the work
6) flow
7) Instinct, fixed-action patterns, biological drive, need, biological drive, biological drive, homeostasis, increase
8) C, A, B, C, D, B, D
9) A) self-actualization (personal fulfillment by reaching one's potential), B) esteem needs (viewing self as competent, liked, and respected), C) attachment and affiliation needs (need to feel loved and a sense of belonging), D) safety needs (motivated to avoid danger), E) biological needs of survival (hunger and thirst)
10) He added self-transcendence, which is like generativity in that the person needs to further a cause beyond himself or herself.
11) Instincts are also called fixed-action patterns. Drive theory proposes that we possess biological needs, which produce aroused states called drives. Drives must be reduced to return the body to a balanced state called homeostasis. Freud's theory asserts that motivation mainly comes from the id, which contains the basic desires of eros (erotic desire) and thanatos (the destructive impulse). Maslow's theory proposes a hierarchy of needs. Biological needs, when satisfied, lead to safety needs. Attachment and affiliation needs, when satisfied, lead to esteem needs. Esteem needs, when satisfied, lead to self-actualization.
13) A) doesn't explain complex human behaviors; B) often people do things to increase arousal and not be in homeostasis, and it doesn't explain psychological drives; C) the focus on self is more common in individualistic cultures than collectivistic cultures, and it doesn't explain why people are motivated to do risky activities that override their safety needs.
14) A) Proximal, B) Developmental, C) Functional
15) A) T, B) T, C) T, D) F
16) Adler was referring to a person's need for cooperation and acceptance by others.
17) This is the idea that biology is not all there is to hunger, and instead we must look at various systems, such as: a) the body's biological systems and food preferences, b) emotions, c) learning, d) cognitions, e) media, and f) culture.
19) A) T, B) F, C) T, D) F, E) F, F) F, G) T, H) T, I) T, J) T, K) T, L) F, M) T
21) A) F, B) F, C) T, D) F

22) A) In the excitement phase, blood vessel changes occur in the pelvic region and cause the clitoris to swell and the penis to become erect. B) In the plateau phase, the maximum level of arousal is reached and there are rapid increased in heartbeat, breathing, muscle tension, and glandular secretions. C) In the orgasm phase, both genders experience an intense, pleasurable release of sexual tension that is characterized by rhythmic genital contractions. Men experience ejaculation and women experience clitoral and vaginal sensations. D) In the resolution phase, the body gradually returns to its preexcitement phase.

23) A) Kinsey, B) interviews, C) interviews, 79, D) physiology, E) Masters and Johnson, similar, biological, F) women, G) women, men, H) evolutionary, both options are correct

24) A) on average, men show more interest in sex than do women, B) women are more likely than men to view sex as part of an emotionally committed relationship, C) sex is more often linked with aggression for males than for females, D) women's sexually is more likely than men's sexuality to vary with cultural and social factors.

26) They put the motive of sex NOT with hunger, thirst and other biological needs. Instead, the sexual motive is associated with needs for attachment, affiliation, belongingness, and parenting.

27) A) half, B) Transvestism, C) both options are correct, D) aren't, E) more, F) is not, G) 1970s, H) bonobos, I) no differences, J) correlational

29) A) they help us attend to and respond to important situations, B) they help us convey our intentions to others

30) A) physiological arousal, B) cognitive interpretation, C) subjective feelings, D) behavioral expression

31) It's a sort of emotional "body image," and is associated with the subjective feeling component.

32) Mirror neurons tie in with the subjective feeling component, in that they produce the somatic markers of emotion.

33) Approach emotions tend to be positive ones, such as happiness and love. They make things attractive and therefore something we want to approach. They involve the dopamine reward systems in the brain. Avoidance emotions tend to be negative ones, such as fear and disgust. They involve the amygdala.

34) Emotions attach *values* to different alternatives in a decision.

35) Ekman's circled ones are anger, disgust, fear, happiness, sadness, contempt, and surprise. Plutchik's underlined ones are joy, acceptance, fear, surprise, sadness, disgust, anger, and anticipation. Izard's X'd out ones are interest, happiness/joy, sadness, anger, disgust, & fear.

36) A) Some animals show similar facial expressions to humans' expressions for the same emotion (such as fear or anger). B) Babies express emotions almost at birth.

37) These are the permissible ways for people to show emotions in a culture/society. For example, it's permissible in the U.S. to show negative emotions, but in many Asian cultures this is very much discouraged. There are different display rules for males and females, too.

38) Display rules, gender, Cultures, Israel, Italy, Britain, Spain, Switzerland, Germany, collectivist

39) A) F, B) T, C) F, D) F

40) A) Autonomic nervous system, parasympathetic, sympathetic, B) ventromedial prefrontal cortex, amygdala, hippocampus, lateralization, right, left, C) norepinephrine, epinephrine, D) Limbic System, amygdala

41) It refers to the graph of the relation between level of arousal and level of performance that resembles an upside-down letter U. It indicates that performance is generally low when arousal is either too low or much too high, but optimal performance generally occurs with some intermediate amount of arousal. However, it depends on the task! Very rehearsed, more automatic behaviors (e.g., sports) require more arousal than tasks that involve a lot of thinking and planning (e.g., brain surgery). Also, there are individual differences. Some people are sensation seekers who seem biologically to need more arousal than most people.

42) B, A, C, A

43) A) perceiving emotions in oneself and others, B) use one's emotions for thinking and solving problems, C) understand the complex interactions between emotions in oneself and in others, D) regulating one's own emotions and influencing other people's emotions

44) In this experiment, four-year-old children were told that they could either have one marshmallow immediately—or, if they waited, they could have two marshmallows. Some kids couldn't wait and immediately ate one, whereas others were able to control themselves (while the marshmallows sat in front of them) and waited the required amount of time to get both marshmallows. When these kids were then tracked down during adolescence, those who were able to control themselves and delay gratification at age four were, as adolescents, more self-reliant, better students, higher in self-esteem, better at handling interpersonal relationships, higher scorers on the SAT, and better able to handle stress and frustration than were those who, at age four, chose to take only one marshmallow immediately.

45) learned, relationships, self-respect, academic achievement, extraversion

47) It's a myth that venting one's anger is a good thing to do. It's also a myth that "bottling up" one's anger is bad because it causes the person to "explode" with anger. Research shows that venting anger increases anger rather than decreases it in future, similar situations. The best anger management appears to be calming down so that you can make more rational choices.

48) A) more, B) dilation, more, C) face, body, D) tell the truth, E) more

49) A polygraph is often called a lie detector. However, what it measures is a person's heart rate, breathing rate, perspiration, and blood pressure (and sometimes voice). The theory is that lying produces physiological arousal and can therefore be detected by the polygraph.

50) One problem with the polygraph is that other things can increase people's arousal, such as just knowing they're a suspect in a crime, or knowing that the polygraph can sometimes be wrong and produce a false positive. Another problem is that some people can learn to control their physiological responses (or take drugs that do so), so even if they're lying, the polygraph won't show anything (a false negative). As stated previously, false positives are a definite problem, so that innocent people will be accused of lying. Another problem is that there are no standard procedures for administering a polygraph test or for interpreting its results. Some polygraph testers employ tricks during the test, too.

Practice Tests

Item Number	Practice Test 1	Practice Test 2	Practice Test 3	Comprehensive Test
1	A	D	C	D
2	D	D	B	B
3	A	D	A	B
4	B	B	A	C
5	A	C	C	D
6	B	B	A	B
7	D	C	D	B
8	C	C	A	C
9	D	B	C	A
10	D	C	C	B
11				A
12				C
13				D
14				B
15				A

Critical Thinking Essays

1) Incentives (e.g., bonuses, gifts) work well when they are contingent on performance; therefore, rewarding people for a job well done can help sustain or increase performance. However, if incentives are not contingent on performance, then they can decrease performance and cause overjustification.

2) There are actually very few strengths of polygraphs, overall. One strength is that some people, when faced with an upcoming polygraph test, may indeed truthfully confess to a crime. But there are many more potential problems with these "lie detector" tests. The assumption is that there are physiological changes when people lie that can be picked up by the polygraph, which measures heart rate, breathing rate, blood pressure, and perspiration. However, those physiological changes can be caused just by the stress of being suspected of a crime and questioned (thus producing false positives). In addition, some people are able to control their responses even when they're lying (thus producing false negatives). Taking certain drugs can subdue those responses, too. There are no standard procedures for administering and interpreting the test, so it's open to bias. The National Academy of Science has issued a report saying that the polygraph is not useful for trying to identify possible terrorists or other security risks.

1) Personality is all the psychological characteristics that bring continuity to a person's behavior at different times and in different situations. It is the qualities that make us who we are.
2) displacement, scapegoating, biology
3) A) half, B) early childhood, C) have a career that requires intellect, D) environmental, inborn
4) Dispositional theories describe relatively stable personality characteristics (i.e., dispositions), whereas process theories go beyond description to discuss internal processes of personality, such as motivation, perceptions, learning, and development.
5) Individualism is a focus on the individual and his or her needs and goals. Collectivism is a focus on the group and their needs and goals, as well as social harmony. Western cultures tend to emphasize individualism, whereas Asian, African, Latin American, and Middle Eastern cultures tend to emphasize collectivism.
6) More Asian Americans than Jewish Americans describe themselves as shy. This may be due to the different ways in which Asian and Jewish cultures explain success and failure. Asians' success is credited to external causes and failure is blamed on internal causes, but the opposite is true for Jews.
7) A) The emphasis is on motives and emotions, many of which are unconscious. B) The emphasis is on a person's potential and his or her unmet needs. C) The emphasis is on perceptions, cognitions, and learning.
8) Traits are multiple dimensions of personality. Types are personality categories, rather than dimensions. Temperament refers to the global disposition of personality that has a strong biological basis. All fall under the general heading of "dispositional theories."
9) humors, choleric, melancholic, sanguine, phlegmatic
10) A) F, B) F, C) T, D) F (it's neurotransmitters), E) F, F) T, G) T
11) A) openness closed-mindedness, B) conscientiousness irresponsibility, C) extraversion introversion, D) agreeableness coldness, E) neuroticism emotional stability
12) A) openness, B) introversion, C) conscientiousness, D) neuroticism, E) agreeableness
13) A) factor, B) isn't, C) has, D) both options are correct, E) NEO-PI, F) serious mental problems, G) describe, H) predict, both options are correct, I) validity
14) A) F, B) T, C) T, D) F, E) T, F) F
16) process, psychodynamic, social-cognitive, Humanistic
17) A) Eros, B) unconscious death instinct that results in aggressive and destructive behaviors committed against others or against oneself; smoking, compulsive gambling, reckless driving, drug abuse, C) unconscious sexual energy produced by Eros
18) A) both options, id, B) id, ego, C) superego, both options are correct, D) oral, genital, E) a fixation, anal, F) Oedipus, G) phallic, H) fixation, I) reject, J) identification, K) defense mechanisms, preconscious, L) psychoanalytic, psychoanalysis
19) G, C, F, E, A, D, E, B
21) Projective tests supposedly allow one to project unconscious motives or drives onto interpretations of ambiguous stimuli. The Rorschach is a projective test that shows people symmetrical inkblots and asks them to say what they see. However, this test doesn't have very good accuracy or consistency. The TAT shows ambiguous pictures and then people

have to tell what they think is going on in the picture, as well as what happened before it and what will happen after it. In both tests, the examiner looks for themes in people's answers.

23) This is the psychoanalytic idea that all our behaviors are caused by unconscious memories, conflicts, motives, and desires. Therefore, the way one feels unconsciously will always somehow appear in one's actions (e.g., through Freudian slips, mental illness, or dreams).

24) A) His theory is not scientific, B) His theory explains past behavior (maybe due to the hindsight bias) but is a poor predictor of future behavior, C) He is sexist in terms of his attitudes toward women, D) Newer research shows that the unconscious is not as smart or purposeful as Freud thought.

25) They are "new Freudians"—theorists who retain the psychodynamic emphasis, but who disagree with Freud about specific motives that create personality.

26) A) Jung thought Freud overemphasized the motive of sexuality and didn't pay attention to an equally important unconscious motive—spirituality. B) Jung disagreed about the structure of the unconscious mind (i.e., the id, ego, and superego).

28) The personal unconscious is essentially the same as the id. The collective unconscious includes ancient images called archetypes. Animus is the masculine side of our personality. Anima is the feminine side of our personality. The shadow represents tendencies that are destructive and aggressive, and is similar to Freud's idea of thanatos. The principle of opposites creates an overall stable, enduring pattern called a personality type. Opposing pairs of dispositions include introversion-extraversion.

29) A) F, B) F, C) T, D) F, E) T, F) F, G) F

30) A) need for affection/approval, B) need for a partner and dread of being alone, C) need to restrict one's life and remain inconspicuous, D) need for power and control over others, E) need to exploit others, F) need for recognition or prestige, G) need for personal admiration, H) need for personal achievement, I) need for self-sufficiency and independence, J) need for perfection and unassailability

31) A) move toward others (for love and approval), B) move against others (competing with or attacking others), C) move away from others (close self off from intimacy or support)

33) third force, maladjustment, self-actualizing personalities, fully functioning person, positive, congruent with reality, phenomenal field, personality, unconditional positive regard

34) creativity, good humor, spontaneity, accepting of one's own and others' limitations, feeling free to fulfill their potentialities

35) A) they contain "fuzzy concepts," B) they don't explain whether things are inborn or learned, C) they don't recognize the power of the unconscious, D) they emphasize the "self" too much, which may represent an individualistic culture perspective

36) It is similar to humanistic psychology in that it focuses on positive mental health rather than mental disorder. However, it differs in that it is trying to be more scientific.

37) expectations, observing, role models, behavior, cognition, environment, reciprocal determinism, power, locus of control, trait, process, emotions, behaviors, internals, externals

39) A) The interactions between people are being looked at. For example, family systems theory looks at how the individuals in a family influence each other. B) The role of culture is being taken into account more. C) The role of gender is being taken into account more.

41) external

42) implicit personality theories

442

43) A) They don't work very well outside one's own culture, B) they are often stereotyped, C) they can be influenced by people's current motives and feelings, D) our mindset may contain the idea that personality is fixed and unchangeable, which can then affect one's attitudes and behaviors toward others, E) we may wrongly assume that certain traits go together

44) self-narrative, self-concept, redemptive, generativity

45) It is when we attribute someone's behavior to something internal to them and discount the effects of the environment. It's more common in individualistic cultures.

47) A) five, B) future, C) Conscientiousness, D) both options are correct

48) It is the issue about which plays a bigger role in one's behavior—his or her personality (i.e., person) or the environment (i.e., situation). Mischel asserted that knowledge of the situation is more important in predicting a person's behavior than is knowledge of that person's personality traits. Research shows that people are most consistent in their behavior when someone is watching and when the situation is familiar. Also, personality traits have more influence on a person's behavior in individualistic cultures than in collectivistic cultures. Mischel felt that behavior is a function of the situation, the person's interpretations of that situation, and the person's personality.

Practice Tests

Item Number	Practice Test 1	Practice Test 2	Practice Test 3	Comprehensive Test
1	B	D	B	C
2	D	D	D	D
3	C	B	D	C
4	B	A	D	A
5	D	C	D	D
6	C	C	C	C
7	A	A	A	B
8	A	C	C	C
9	D	B	C	C
10	C	A	A	A
11				A
12				C
13				B
14				D
15				C

Critical Thinking Essays

1) The person-situation controversy concerns people's behavior and whether it is more influenced by their relatively stable personality or by the situation they are in. Mischel believed that the situation plays a bigger role. Most psychologists believe that behavior is an interaction of the person and the situation. However, in individualistic cultures, people tend to think that the dispositions of the person play a bigger role than the situation. That's why

the fundamental attribution error is more common in individualistic cultures. Bandura also points out that the environment plays a large role in people's behavior.

2) Maslow and Rogers both focus on positive growth, with Maslow's highest needs being self-actualization and self-fulfillment and Rogers' positive development producing a fully functioning person. Maslow's theory is hierarchical, but Rogers' is not. Positive psychology researchers would empirically test these theories using scientific methodology.

1) A) the power of social situations to control people's behaviors, B) the personal construction of a subjective social reality, C) who or what creates situations and maintains them

3) Situationism is the idea that the environment/setting has a bigger effect on a person's behavior than do internal characteristics of a person, such as their genes, personality, and abilities. Dispositionism is just the opposite. Situationism ascribes to the power of the situation.

4) C, B, A, D, A, C

5) A) they first notice the uniformities and regularities in behaviors, B) they observe the negative consequences when someone violates a social norm

6) A) when a judgment task is difficult or ambiguous, B) when group members are perceived as especially competent, C) when responses are given publicly rather than privately, D) the group majority is unanimous.

7) Conformity includes the Asch effect, which is the influence of a majority group on the judgments of an individual. The Asch effect is influenced by the size of the majority and by the presence of a partner who also dissents from the majority. Conformity also includes the chameleon effect, which is the tendency to mimic other people. Conformity also includes groupthink, which is most likely to occur when there is a dominant leader, when there's high group cohesiveness, and when there's homogeneity of members' background and ideology.

9) All have been shown to promote groupthink except A, E, G, and L

10) A) one-third, two-thirds, B) emotions, were independent and against, social neuroscience, C) autokinetic, Sherif, norm, D) both options are correct, E) groupthink, F) perceptual illusion, G) both options are correct, H) Japanese, American

11) A) F, B) T, C) T, D) F, E) T, F) F, G) F, H) T, I) F, J) T

13) According to a newspaper report in 1964 in Queens, NY, thirty-eight people in an apartment complex watched and listened as a man with a knife attacked Kitty Genovese three separate times. Nobody tried to help her or call the police until after she was raped and killed (and then only one person called the police). Some of the details were later disproved (e.g., many phone calls to police were made), but the tragedy illustrates the bystander intervention problem.

14) bystander intervention, number of other people (bystanders), more, diffusion, responsibility, conformity

15) the number of other people present (i.e., group size)

16) Yes, training can reduce the problem. In the case of medical emergencies, if people know first aid or CPR, they are more likely to help. Also, just learning about the bystander intervention problem in a psychology class made people more likely to help someone.

17) A) ask for help instead of assuming people know you need it, B) reduce ambiguity by explaining to them what the problem is and what they need to do, C) identify specific individuals to help, so that people don't diffuse the responsibility to others

18) conformity so as to be part of the "in-group" (the group one identifies with) rather than the "out-group" (i.e., "them," "other people")

19) it's our subjective interpretations of other people and of our relationships with them

20) A) similarity, B) proximity, C) physical attractiveness, D) self-disclosure

21) The reward theory states that we want to be with people who somehow give us maximum rewards at minimum costs; we tend to be attracted to people who are nearby rather than far away, because there is less of a cost in terms of effort. We tend to like similar people because that is, in effect, rewarding one's self. We tend to like physically attractive people because that reflects well on us and is therefore rewarding. We tend to find it rewarding when we can safely self-disclose to others. Much research supports this theory, but it doesn't explain abusive relationships. Cognitive dissonance theory explains those sorts of relationships better.

22) cognitive dissonance

23) A) physical attractiveness, B) Men, women, C) social learning, D) both options are correct, E) male, F) matching hypothesis, attractiveness, G) both options are correct, H) poorly, I) Expectancy-value, J) both options are correct, K) the U.S., Japan

24) cognitive dissonance, reduce, inconsistent, foolish, justify, disown (not take)

25) A) triangular, B) passion, intimacy, commitment, C) commitment, D) complete (consummate)

26) A) liking, B) infatuation, C) romantic love, D) companionate love

27) A) it must be rewarding, B) it needs to be equitable, C) communication needs to be open, ongoing, and mutually validating, D) each partner needs to take responsibility for his or her own identity, self-esteem, and commitment to the relationship

28) Both have to do with attributions. The FAE is when we attribute another person's behavior to dispositional (internal) factors. The self-serving bias is when we attribute our own failures to something external (situational), but our own successes to something internal (dispositional). These attributions then make us feel better about ourselves.

29) A) perceived warmth, B) perceived competence

30) Those with both high warmth and high competence are people we look up to and with whom we want to associate. Those with high warmth but low competence are people we tend to pity or want to help. Those with both low warmth and low competence we feel disdain for and want to avoid. Those who have high competence but low warmth we tend to envy or be angry at.

31) It is more common is the U.S. than in Japan, likely due to the larger focus on the self in the U.S. (and individualistic culture). In Japan, people are encouraged to develop a self-critical focus, but in the U.S., people are encouraged to develop a sense of uniqueness and entitlement.

33) Prejudice refers to negative attitudes toward individuals who belong to a certain group, whereas discrimination refers to negative behaviors toward those individuals. Prejudice can lead to discrimination.

34) A) dissimilarity and social distance, B) economic competition, C) scapegoating, D) conformity to social norms, E) media stereotyping, F) dehumanization

35) A) F, B) T, C) F, D) T, E) T, F) F, G) T, H) F (ONLY if they have equal social status)

36) A) new role models (the least effective because it is better for preventing than eradicating), B) equal status contact, C) jigsaw classroom, D) legislation

37) When people are aware of negative stereotypes about the group to which they belong and they anxiously don't want to live up to those stereotypes, their performance suffers. So, if

women take a math test and have to check the gender box (Female), they perform worse than if they didn't have to indicate their gender before the exam.

38) stereotype lift

39) Values affirmations are when people write or think about their strong, positive qualities before performing a task. These affirmations tend to improve performance on the task.

40) It's the sources of influence that come top-down from institutions and organizations to maintain or create situations that in turn impact the actions of individuals.

41) Both looked at the effects of obedience, authority, conformity, and the power of the situation. The prison experiment, however, also looked at the effects of *system* power on people's behavior, whereas Milgram's study looked at the effects of *individual* power.

43) Systems create situations that then affect people. So, we must look at not only situational and dispositional factors, but also systemic factors, if we wish to understand people's behaviors. Systems can authorize or disapprove of certain behaviors, often through ideologies and the programs and structures developed to support those ideologies. Systems create situations.

44) A) Situations, systems, B) public health, C) individual, system

45) A) deindividuation, B) dehumanization, C) enemy image, D) groupthink, E) moral disengagement, F) social facilitation

46) A) T, B) F, C) T, D) T, E) T, F) F

47) A) This is when an opposing idea or person is linked with some sort of negative (most often false or misleading) information (i.e., a "parasite") that sticks in people's memories and then affects their attitudes. B) Authority is a type of pressure, so we are more likely to unquestioningly believe and follow an authority figure. C) This is the fact that we often go along with the crowd.

48) This statement is simplistic and doesn't look at the bigger picture or other perspectives (such as the perspectives of the terrorists themselves). It focuses on dispositional causes, even though there is a lot of empirical evidence showing that situational and systemic forces strongly affect people's behaviors.

Practice Tests

Item Number	Practice Test 1	Practice Test 2	Practice Test 3	Comprehensive Test
1	B	A	B	A
2	B	C	B	B
3	D	B	D	C
4	C	C	C	B
5	A	B	C	A
6	D	A	A	C
7	C	D	D	C
8	A	D	A	D
9	B	D	D	C
10	C	A	B	B
11				A
12				D
13				A

14				D
15				C

Critical Thinking Essays

1) They both showed the power of the situation. Asch studied conformity and showed that the larger the majority group, the more likely participants were to conform. Also, if there was at least one dissenter, then participants were less likely to conform. However, some of participants were independents and did not conform at all. Thus, there is a dispositional factor that plays a role. Darley and Latané studied bystander intervention and found that the more other people there were, the less likely people were to intervene or help. This may be due to the diffusion of responsibility felt when there are more people around. It could also be due to conforming to others who are doing nothing. However, training can help reduce the bystander intervention problem, which shows that dispositional factors play a role.

2) Factors contributing to it are economic competition, blaming others for one's own misfortunes (scapegoating), viewing others as dissimilar and thus increasing social distance, unthinking conformity to the status quo (social norms), media stereotypes, and dehumanization. The least effective strategy for reducing it is education, because the people who need the education dismiss it. Role models that combat stereotypes help prevent prejudice, but don't cure it. Equal status contact reduces social distance and economic competition. The jigsaw classroom works very well. Legislation works well in reducing prejudice, too.

1) Rosenhan's accomplices complained of hearing voices and were therefore admitted to a mental hospital. Once admitted, they never complained of hearing voices again and instead behaved in their typical fashion. They took notes on what they observed and this note taking was seen as a symptom of their illness (supposedly schizophrenia). This study showed how subjective the diagnosis of psychopathology is.

2) A) both options are correct, B) 450, C) depression, D) medical, E) psychological, both options are correct, F) normal, G) part of a continuum

3) A) Hallucinations are false sensory experiences, B) Delusions are extreme disorders of thinking that involve persistent false beliefs, C) Extreme affective (emotional) disturbance is when someone is constantly fearful, depressed, manic, worried, or shows no emotion at all

4) A) physical, B) both options are correct, demons and spirits, C) medical, eighteenth, D) fungus

5) A) It leads to a "doctor-knows-best" approach, so that the patient becomes a passive recipient of medication and advice, rather than an active participant, B) it encourages unnecessary drug therapy and doesn't do much to help the patient develop coping skills, C) it assigns psychologists to second-class professional status, beneath that of psychiatrists

6) psychological, medical, reciprocal determinism, cognition, biology, Genome, behavioral, multiple, environment

7) The medical model is more biological, and its treatments usually consist of medications. The psychological model looks at how disorders are created and maintained by socio-cultural, behavioral, developmental, and/or cognitive factors.

8) A) distress, B) maladaptiveness, C) irrationality, D) unpredictability, E) unconventionality and undesirable behavior

9) B, E, C, D, A

10) A) F, B) T, C) F

11) The caution is not to read about the disorders and then think that you have an abnormality. A trained professional is needed to diagnose mental disorders, not someone who read a textbook. Also, the reader needs to remember that all psychological disorders include normal tendencies—it's just that those tendencies are exaggerated.

12) A) legal, B) both options are correct, C) one, D) both options are correct

13) It requires an illegal act and the intent to commit it. The issue of intent is where the insanity plea comes into play, because if someone is so mentally ill that he/she did not have the rational intent to commit the crime, then he/she shouldn't be held totally responsible.

14) *Diagnostic and Statistical Manual* (4th edition)

15) A) mental, B) behavioral

16) Neurosis used to mean any relatively common pattern of distress. This term has been replaced with the term "disorder." Psychosis used to mean any mental disorder that was an extreme form of neurosis. In the *DSM-IV*, it refers to a very distinct condition—a loss of contact with reality.

17) A) 1994, Psychiatric, 2000, B) health insurance, pay for, C) neurosis, D) psychosis, E) medical, F) normal, G) V (five)

18) Diagnosis relies on subjectivity rather than objectivity. Some clinicians don't like that diagnosis in "all-or-none," and instead believe that many disorders fall onto a continuum. Some clinicians don't like the idea that disorders are viewed as "diseases."

19) A) both options are correct, B) manic-depressive disorder, C) depression, D) fifty, E) learned helplessness, F) high, G) left, frontal, H) cerebral cortex, 25, depressed, I) mild

20) It is thinking about one's mood or other negative things over and over again. Thus, it seems to perpetuate or even worsen depression. Women tend to do this more than men do.

21) It is depression that occurs during winter months. It involves the hormone melatonin and the best treatment is exposure of special light-sensitive cells in the retina to light.

22) A) They may ruminate more than men do, whereas men are more likely to distract themselves when they have unpleasant emotions or else do something physical to take their minds off their mood, B) Women may be more willing to report depressive symptoms

23) Drugs used to treat unipolar depression don't work on bipolar depression, and may make things even worse

25) A) social phobia, B) fear of public places and open spaces, C) claustrophobia, D) fear of snakes, E) acrophobia

26) A) target, B) duration

27) A, B, B, C, D, C, D

29) They are psychological disorders appearing as bodily complaints or physical symptoms, or as excessive worry about disease. They are different from psychosomatic disorders in which stress or other mental conditions cause actual physical illnesses.

30) A) conversion disorder, B) hypochondriasis

31) A) F, B) T, C) F, D) F, E) F, F) T, G) T

32) C, B, A, D, D

33) fragmentation of the personality—the sense that the parts of the personality have detached from each other (i.e., dissociated)

34) A) Psychodynamic theories explain it as the ego breaking apart due to defense mechanisms not allowing conflicts and traumas to escape from one's unconscious, B) Cognitive theories see it as a form of role-playing or a form of memory bias in which events experienced during a certain mood are recalled better when one is again in that mood, C) Some see it as totally fake

35) Dissociative identity disorder used to be called "multiple personality" in previous editions of the *DSM*. Some people mistakenly use the term "split personality" and "multiple personality" interchangeably, too. But "split personality" is actually an outdated term for schizophrenia. However, schizophrenia is NOT a dissociative disorder. Instead the term "schizophrenia," which literally means, "split mind," refers to the person's split from reality.

37) A) Residual, B) Disorganized, C) Paranoid, D) Undifferentiated, E) Catatonic

38) Positive symptoms are "active" processes like hallucinations and delusions. Negative symptoms are deficiencies and passive processes, such as the lack of affect, lack of pleasure, social isolation, and lack of thought. Drugs that help positive symptoms don't help negative symptoms, so that supports this distinction. However, both types can occur in one person. And the negative form of schizophrenia looks a lot like major depression.

39) This means that biological factors may place a person at risk for schizophrenia, but that person then must experience environmental stressors that turn this potential into the disorder.

40) A) antipsychotic drugs that interfere with dopamine receptors can get rid of the symptoms of positive schizophrenia, whereas drugs that stimulate dopamine bring on symptoms. Deficiencies in glutamate appear to play a role, too. B) Brain scans show brain abnormalities and also that the brain doesn't synchronize neural activation across the cortex. C) Schizophrenia is more likely the more closely genetically related one is to a person with the disorder.

42) A) Autism, language, B) autism, both options are correct, C) 500, 5, 5 percent, D) English, Italian, E) autism

45) C, B, A, B

47) They are relatively mild problems, such as marital problems, school problems, mild depression, and bereavement. They are very prevalent.

49) Mood disorders include bipolar disorder, which involves swings of mood, as well as seasonal affective disorder, which is related to the hormone called melatonin. *DSM-IV* categories include somatoform disorders, which involve the body. Conversion disorder involves physical problems with no discernable cause. Hypochondriasis involves a preoccupation with health and illness. Anxiety disorders include panic disorder, which involves sudden anxiety. In addition, there is obsessive-compulsive disorder, which involves persistent, unwanted thoughts and behaviors. Dissociative disorders are characterized by fragmentation of the personality.

50) Depression and anxiety disorders are more common in women. So are eating disorders. Men are more likely to develop antisocial personality disorder, schizophrenia, autism, dyslexia, ADHD, violence, and substance abuse. Social norms may encourage women to talk about their depression and anxiety more than men do. Social norms also encourage men to act out in physical ways.

51) Men's brains tend to be more lateralized than women's brains. This means that each side has specialized regions that are not found on the other side.

52) Shyness itself is not in the *DSM-IV*, but extreme shyness can become social phobia or avoidant personality disorder.

53) A) there can be a stigma that follows them forever, B) they may be viewed as having inferior status and may thus be neglected, C) they may suffer depersonalization in which they are viewed as objects rather than individuals

54) It is the idea that abnormality is an interaction between individuals and the sociocultural context; disorder occurs when there is a mismatch between a person's behavior and what the situation calls for. Evidence in support of this is that the incidence of certain disorders varies from culture to culture, and that there are within-culture generational differences in the incidence of certain disorders.

55) A) the myth that all cultures have similar rates of mental disorders, B) the myth that mental disorders are caused by biology and culture only shapes the way the disorder is expressed, C) the myth that only exotic places have culture-specific disorders

56) A) Critics pointed out that "insanity" is a legal term. However, Rosenhan meant "psychosis" when he used the term "insanity." B) Critics stated that people don't usually lie about symptoms, therefore the pseudopatients set up a false situation. Plus, doctors should err on the side of caution. Rosenhan's response was that doctors should have eventually noticed the lack of disorder in the pseudopatients because they never lied about symptoms again. C)

Critics state that Rosenhan's study doesn't have data, but instead is a story (his impressions) about what happened. A response to this criticism is that diagnosis is also an impression. D) Critics also pointed out that Rosenhan's study of fake patients doesn't tell us anything about how well doctors diagnose real patients. Rosenhan pointed out that his study is just one of many that call into question the reliability of diagnoses.

57) He believed that attitudes about mental illness contain fear, mistrust, and misunderstanding. He also saw the situation of the hospital as creating depersonalization.

Practice Tests

Item Number	Practice Test 1	Practice Test 2	Practice Test 3	Comprehensive Test
1	C	C	C	A
2	D	B	D	A
3	B	C	B	B
4	A	A	D	D
5	A	C	B	D
6	B	D	D	C
7	C	C	D	B
8	B	A	C	B
9	A	B	A	D
10	A	A	C	C
11				B
12				B
13				A
14				C
15				B

Critical Thinking Essays

1) Males are more likely to have antisocial personality disorder, violence problems, and drug and alcohol abuse. Females are more likely to have depression, phobias, and anxiety. These differences may be tied to social norms that encourage males to be physically aggressive and encourage females to express negative emotions that make them vulnerable. Also, females tend to ruminate more than males do, and rumination is tied to depression. Males are also more likely to develop schizophrenia, autism, dyslexia, and ADHD. Some researchers believe that these disorders are related to the fact that males' brains are more lateralized (specialized in different hemispheres) than are females' brains.

2) The myths are that a) psychologists and psychiatrists are contributing to this by diagnosing criminals as insane, and b) many criminals don't get punished due to the insanity plea. However, the term "insanity" is a legal term, not a diagnostic label. It has to do with whether there was true intent to commit the crime. If there's lack of intent, one can plead insanity, so mental retardation and a jealous rage are also included as "insane." Less than 1 percent of criminal cases use the insanity defense, and only a small proportion of these are successful.

1) A) patient, mental illnesses, B) both options are correct, C) unable to resolve a problem by themselves

2) A) friends and family are not trained, B) friends/family may have their own agendas and be part of the problem, C) with a therapist you will have confidentiality

3) It is the relationship between therapist and client whereby they work together as allies to achieve the same goals.

4) A) identifying the problem, B) identifying the cause of the problem or the conditions that maintain the problem, C) deciding on and implementing some form of treatment

6) A) Training is usually a PhD, PsyD, or EdD. Areas of expertise usually are less severe "problems of living." They cannot prescribe drugs. B) Training is usually a PhD or PsyD. Areas of expertise are usually more severe problems, but they can also work with clients with less severe problems. They usually cannot prescribe drugs, although with extra training is the state of New Mexico, they can. C) Psychiatrists are medical doctors (MDs). They usually deal with those with severe problems and they can prescribe drugs. D) Some have PhDs, but others are psychiatrists with extra training in Freudian analysis. If they are an MD, they can prescribe drugs. E) They are registered nurses with extra training about mental disorders. They can prescribe drugs. F) They have a master's of social work degree and deal with mental disorders from the viewpoint of the social context. They cannot prescribe drugs. G) They are religious leaders who specialize in treating psychological problems through spiritual guidance and practical counseling. They cannot prescribe drugs.

7) Many military psychologists can prescribe drugs already. In New Mexico, psychologists with many years of extra training can prescribe drugs. The controversy is that some psychologists feel they should be granted the privilege of prescribing drugs in order to treat the whole person, but many psychiatrists are opposed to this and feel that drug therapy is the medical field's domain. Some psychologists are also opposed to prescription privileges because they feel that the drug companies have duped the public into believing drugs are the best way to treat mental illnesses.

8) A) Intent: to shield patients from stressors and from brutal "therapies" B) Reality: they were neglected, received only custodial care at most, and continued to receive brutal "therapies"

9) A) insight, B) behavioral, C) cognitive-behavioral

10) They receive on-the-job training rather than graduate training and certification. Studies show that they are just as effective as professionals when insight therapies are used, but such equivalence has not yet been shown for behavioral therapies.

11) A) T, B) F, C) F, D) T, E) F, F) F, G) T, H) T, I) T, J) T

12) A) the importance of the ego rather than the id, B) the importance of later-life experiences rather than just early-childhood experiences, C) The importance of social needs and interpersonal relationships

13) They believe people are motivated by healthy needs for growth and psychological well-being.

14) The therapist would try to increase the client's self-esteem, have the client recognize his or her freedom, and help the client reach his or her full potential

15) client-centered, self-image, criticism, reflection of feeling, reflective listening

17) A) empathy, B) positive regard, C) genuineness, D) feedback

18) A) rational thinking, B) self-talk, C) humanistic, D) trial-and-error experiences of early support-group members, E) both options are correct

19) A) Participant modeling is a social learning therapy wherein the therapist performs a behavior and the client then models it, B) Systematic desensitization is when Jim imagines getting near spiders while using relaxation techniques at the same time, C) Dalia is using exposure therapy to have direct contact with her feared object, D) The teacher is using contingency management, giving out reinforcers (attention and responses) only when polite behavior occurs, E) A token economy is being used so that they are reinforced with points that they can then trade for food or privileges.

20) C, C, B, B, A, C

21) Albert Ellis developed REBT, which is a therapy to try to get rid of clients' unrealistic expectations and "neurotic goals." They replace "shoulds" and "oughts" with rational, obtainable goals.

22) Seligman's positive psychotherapy is similar to humanistic therapies in that it focuses on positive human growth, health, and happiness. Clients are helped to focus on the positives in their lives. It differs from humanistic therapies, because it is largely cognitive-behavioral and there is an emphasis on research, too.

23) Insight therapies include psychoanalysis, which was created by Freud. They also include humanistic therapies, such as Rogers's client-centered therapy. In Rogerian therapy, the technique of reflection of feeling (reflective listening) is used, so that therapists paraphrase client's words. Cognitive therapies are another type of insight therapy, and focus on clients' thoughts and feelings. Classical conditioning therapies include exposure therapy, which is used to treat phobias. Operant conditioning therapies include token economies, which are a behavioral version of group therapy.

25) Experimental designs with a control group need to be done. Testimonials are not scientific and can be biased.

26) He looked at clients involved in insight therapies compared to individuals on the waiting list for insight therapies to see which group did better. He found that both groups ended up getting better. This indicated that therapy was essentially useless, so this created a lot of controversy.

27) A) T, B) F, C) T, D) F

28) A) active listening, B) being nonjudgmental and accepting, C) helping the person explore alternatives

30) A) T, B) F, C) F, D) F, E) T

31) A) new neurons, hippocampus, B) MAO, norepinephrine, C) one, D) antidepressants, depressed, E) reuptake, F) lithium, bipolar disorder, G) Stimulants, H) both options are correct, I) Benzodiazepines, J) central nervous system, both options are correct

32) A) Tricyclics reduce the neuron's reuptake of neurotransmitters, B) SSRIs interfere with the reuptake of serotonin in the synapse so that more serotonin is available, C) MAO inhibitors reduce the activity of the enzyme MAO, which is a chemical that breaks down norepinephrine. Thus, there is more norepinephrine available.

33) Arguments in favor of drug therapies are that they work relatively quickly and they help reduce unpleasant symptoms. They supposedly are relatively low cost, as well (compared to therapy sessions). Arguments against drug therapies are that they are being pushed by drug companies through marketing and that there are side effects of drugs. In addition, research shows that in the long run, drug therapy may not be less costly than psychological therapy.

35) It is a psychosurgery wherein the connections of the frontal lobes to the deeper brain structures are severed. It was done to treat agitated schizophrenia patients, as well as compulsive and anxious patients, and it did indeed reduce agitation and anxiety. However, there were awful side effects, too. Patients often lost their sense of self and their ability to plan ahead, and they often became childlike and indifferent to the opinions of others.

36) ECT applies a brief electrical current to the patient's temples, which induces a short convulsion. After a three- or four-day course of treatment, severely depressed individuals become much less depressed. It's most appropriate for severely depressed people who haven't responded to drugs or to psychotherapy. TMS involve high-powered magnetic stimulation to specific parts of the brain and does not cause a seizure. It also doesn't cause the memory loss associated with ECT.

37) deep brain stimulation

38) Deinstitutionalization is the attempt to get mentally ill people out of mental hospitals (and then close those hospitals) and back into the community and their families, which are more familiar and supposedly more supportive. The community mental health movement attempted to treat individuals on an outpatient basis and have them live with families or in group homes. However, these resources have not received enough funding—plus families are not equipped to cope. So people with mental disorders are likely to get admitted to psychiatric wards in hospitals, or are shuttled from agency to agency. Many have become homeless and drug addicted, too. When there is enough funding, though, community treatment programs can work well. Also, more recently, individuals in rural areas can receive help over the phone or through the Internet—the telehealth approach.

40) A) Is medical treatment needed? B) Is there a specific behavior problem that would be best served by behavioral therapy? C) Would group therapy be helpful? D) Is the problem stress, confusion, or choice (i.e., "problems of living") that are best served by insight therapies?

41) A) antianxiety drugs for more than a brief period, B) the idea of venting aggression and anger

42) Because psychiatrists and drug companies are trying to show that medication is more effective than psychotherapy, whereas psychologists are trying to show that psychotherapy is more effective than medication. It's a battle over "turf" and money.

43) A) F, B) T, C) T, D) F, E) F, F) T, G) T, H) F, I) F, J) F, K) T

44) Empirically supported treatments are those that have been validated by research to be effective. The use of such treatments would constitute evidence-based practice. The question is whether therapists should be *limited* to the use of specific therapies. Arguments in favor include: a) there is a history of harmful "therapies" and there are currently many unsupported therapies/treatments that can harm or take advantage of people in need; b) psychology is a science and therefore should follow scientific research principles; and c) research is needed to see which therapeutic approaches are most effective for treating different disorders/problems. Arguments opposed include: a) a one-size-fits-all approach that takes

away the therapist's judgment and expertise; b) many clients have multiple problems and research tends to be done on people who only have one problem; c) a specific technique is less important than the quality of the client-therapist relationship; and d) nonmedical treatments may be discarded in favor of medical treatments, because the latter are less time-consuming.

Practice Tests

Item Number	Practice Test 1	Practice Test 2	Practice Test 3	Comprehensive Test
1	B	A	C	B
2	A	A	B	B
3	D	B	B	C
4	B	D	D	C
5	C	B	B	B
6	C	A	A	D
7	B	A	C	B
8	A	C	C	D
9	D	C	A	A
10	C	A	A	B
11				A
12				B
13				C
14				C
15				B

Critical Thinking Essays

1) A behavior therapist would likely use systematic desensitization, exposure therapy, or participant modeling. With desensitization, the therapist will have Theresa imagine an elevator while she practices relaxation techniques. Then she'll have to imagine getting closer and closer to the elevator. Then she'll imagine stepping into it without the door closing, then with the door closing, and then with it actually moving. All the while, she'll be doing relaxation techniques.

   With exposure therapy, the therapist will have Theresa deal with a real elevator instead of just imagining it. She'll work her way slowly toward getting on it, as with systematic desensitization, and she'll do relaxation techniques.

   With participant modeling, the therapist will do the systematic behaviors him- or herself, and will encourage Theresa to model his or her behaviors.

   A cognitive therapist will address Theresa's irrational thoughts about the likelihood of the cable snapping, and will have her replace those thoughts with rational, positive self-talk.

2) Some of the good things about drug therapies are that they can help to reduce symptoms of many disorders, such as schizophrenia, bipolar disorder, depression, anxiety disorders, and ADHD. They are also relatively quick-acting and perhaps lower in cost than psychological therapies. However, they often have negative side effects, and the long-term effects are generally unknown. They may often be over-prescribed, especially when the psychological problems are "problems of living," which respond better to insight therapies.

1) Stressors are external events or situations that cause psychological distress, according to psychologists. Distress is the physical and psychological changes that happen in response to the stressor. Everyday people use the term "stress" when they mean "distress."

2) Cognitive appraisal is each person's interpretation of a situation or event. It is this interpretation that relates to distress/stress more than the actual stressor itself.

3) A) T, B) F, C) T, D) T, E) F

4) psychic numbness, comprehend, automatic action, communal effort, letdown, recovery

6) It's experiencing severe stress just by being exposed to other people's trauma (such as natural disasters or wars). By limiting exposure to the news, you can reduce this.

7) A) integration, B) Integration, C) rejects them, dies, D) disenfranchised, E) both options are correct, F) twelve, G) Women, men, H) Hispanic, I) more, J) cognitive

8) distraction, disorganization, memory problems, emotional numbness, guilt about surviving, trouble sleeping, disturbing dreams, trouble concentrating, lack of pleasure from positive events, alienation from others, exaggerated startle response

10). A chronic stressor has a gradual onset and lower intensity than a traumatic stressor, and chronic stressors last longer.

11) A) societal stressors, B) burnout, C) compassion fatigue, D) major life events, E) daily hassles

12) E, D, A, C, C, B, C, D

13) Burnout is emotional, physical, and cognitive exhaustion that leads to avoiding or escaping the work. A major contributor is a problem with the organization (for example, poor working conditions), rather than with the person. Compassion fatigue is something found in caregivers, therapists, and physicians who are overexposed to trauma and its victims and thus experience exhaustion and emotional numbness. This leads to the avoidance of or escape from work. Contributors to this are emotional over-involvement with clients and overextending themselves in their work.

14) job engagement

15) A) workload, B) control, C) reward, D) community, E) fairness, F) values

16) A) focus more on compassion satisfaction, B) avoid becoming over-involved with clients, C) learn better coping strategies, D) resist over-volunteering, E) use humor judiciously

17) A) F, B) T, C) F, D) T, E) F (correlation does not mean causation), F) F

18) A) resilience, B) hardiness

20) Under stress, our bodies become physiologically prepared to either fight or escape the threat. This likely helped humans survive and pass on their genes.

21) The pros are that it can produce quick action to deal with the situation. However, if the stress reaction is extreme or prolonged, it can cause physical and mental health problems.

22) acute, autonomic, endocrine, chronic

23) It is Selye's term for our body's general reaction to all kinds of stressors. Its value is that it allows the body to combat a stressor. The first stage is the alarm phase, when the body is activated for fight or flight. The second stage is the resistance phase, when the body is still attempting to fight off the effects of the stressor. The third stage is the exhaustion phase,

when the body gives a last-ditch effort to fight the stressor. The body needs to recuperate at this point, and if it isn't able to, then there will be physical and mental deterioration.

24) A) exhaustion phase, B) resistance phase, C) alarm phase

25) A) hypothalamus, both options are correct, B) endorphins, pain, C) white, D) the original stressor, E) both options are correct, F) cortisol

26) It's the idea that under stress, females are biologically predisposed to respond to threats by tending to offspring and befriending others for social support. Hormone research shows that males under stress are more likely than females to release cortisol, which is an important steroid in the fight-or-flight response. Research also shows that another stress hormone, named oxytocin, may combine with estrogen in females to promote social support behavior. Higher levels of oxytocin are associated with calmness and decreased anxiety.

27) A) immunosuppression, B) Psycho-neuroimmunology, C) Cytokines D) telomeres E) Telomeres, DNA, F) perception (cognitive appraisal), G) cortisol, H) Cytokines

29) A) T, B) F, C) T

30) stressors, illness, moderators, cognitive appraisal

31) The checked ones should be perfectionism, competitiveness, impatience, anger, hostility, and time urgency. Anger and hostility are the only two that are predictive of heart disease.

32) A) both options are correct, B) both options are correct, C) cytokines, D) threat, E) stress-management training

33) Internals (those with an internal locus of control) generally think that if they take action, they can achieve their goal. Externals (those with an external locus of control) generally think that factors outside of their control are what cause things to occur. Internals are able to manage stress better than externals can. Internals get sick less often and recover more quickly.

35) Residents in a nursing home on one floor were allowed to make their own decisions about furniture arrangements, movie schedule, and having a plant in their room. Residents on a different floor, who were similar to those on the other floor, were not given the chance to make these decisions; instead, the staff made these decisions. After eighteen months, those who made their own decisions (had control) were happier, more active, and more alert. Plus, they lived longer!

36) A) Primary control is taking action to try to gain control over the situation or other external events. It is encouraged in individualistic cultures and, as the nursing home studies showed, it is related to beneficial health outcomes. B) Secondary control is gaining control over one's own reactions to the situation or other external events. It is encouraged in collectivistic cultures and is related to positive health in those cultures. It's also related to positive health in individualistic cultures, as can be seen by the role of cognitive appraisal.

37) Learned helplessness, dogs, Martin Seligman, gave up

38) Hardiness is when someone not only suffers no ill effects of stressful situation, but also appears to thrive under those conditions. A) Hardy people see change as a challenge, rather than as a threat. B) Hardy people are highly engaged in their lives, showing focused commitment to their involvement in a purposeful activity. C) Hardy people have an internal locus of control, and are good at solving problems. They don't develop learned helplessness.

39) Optimistic people experience more positive emotions, and those emotions boost their immune systems to fight off illness. Compared to pessimistic people, optimists tend to have

fewer symptoms, tend to recover faster, are healthier, and live longer. They also use more active coping strategies, such as positive self-talk, which help them cope with stress better.

40) A) Optimists believe that negative events are due to specific causes rather than global causes. B) Optimists believe that negative events are due to situational factors, rather than dispositional factors. C) Optimists believe that negative events are temporary rather than permanent.

41) It is the ability to adapt and achieve well-being in spite of serious threats to development. It is related to hardiness, but is broader than the three Cs. It's also related to optimism.

42) Masten is referring to the fact that it isn't just in amazing cases like Lance Armstrong's that we can see resilience. She points out that many ordinary people show this psychological strength and are capable of greater outcomes than we might expect.

44) Writing allows you to express your thoughts and feelings only to yourself, so you don't have to worry about what others will think or do, and you don't have to "explain" yourself to that other person. You can use frank language and not worry about any lack of confidentiality.

46) Defending isn't coping. Instead, it is an attempt to reduce the symptoms of stress or one's awareness of them, which can actually makes things worse because the problem hasn't been addressed. Coping involves taking action to reduce or eliminate the cause of stress, either by solving the problem or by reducing the harm it causes you.

47) Problem-focused coping is taking action to deal with the stressor or solve the problem. Emotion-focused coping is trying to regulate one's own emotional responses to the stressor.

48) emotion, problem

49) Psychological coping strategies do not include defending, which is reducing one's symptoms of stress, or rumination, which is when one dwells on negative thoughts. Psychological coping strategies include cognitive restructuring, which is especially helpful for people with chronic stress. Cognitive restructuring includes making social comparisons, which can be upward or downward. Problem-focused coping involves clarifying the stressor and taking action. Emotion-focused coping involves regulating feelings.

50) A) both options are correct, B) sense-making, C) benefit-finding, D) both options are correct, E) prolong, F) has not, G) both options are correct

51) It is the psychological and physical resources other people (usually friends and family, but could be other people and even strangers) provide to help a person cope with adversity. A) Emotional support, B) Tangible assistance (physical tasks, etc.), C) Informational support (help someone understand by providing accurate information)

52) Physical contact with a trusted partner increases oxytocin levels, which helps decrease anxiety and stress. Physical affection by one's partner, such as hand-holding and hugs, can reduce stress. This ties in with the tend-and-befriend model of stress.

53) A) T, B) T, C) F (both increase), D) F, E) T, F) T, G) T,

54) A) a need to feel competent, B) a need to have social connections, C) a need for autonomy or a sense of control

55) A) Satisfaction with one's current life is a component of SWB. People who like their work, are satisfied with their personal relationships, like themselves, have good health, have a high sense of control, have high self-esteem, are sociable, and are outgoing are high in SWB. B) Frequently feeling positive emotions is a part of SWB. People who are optimistic and generally expect success have high SWB. C) A relative absence of negative emotions is a

component of SWB. Negative emotions are fewer and are experienced less severely in people with high SWB.

56) A) F, B) F, C) F

58) Behavioral medicine is a medical field and has to do with the link between lifestyle factors and disease. Health psychology is a psychological field and has to do with the same thing. Health psychology often emphasizes emotions and cognitions, and has incorporated those topics into behavioral medicine. Both fields cover health promotion and maintenance, prevention and treatment of illness, psychological factors involved in health and illness, the interaction of body and mind, causes of illness and dysfunction, and the improvement of the health care system and policy.

59) SRRS scores are correlated with physical and behavioral symptoms, but that doesn't mean that life changes have caused stress and illness. It could be that stress and illness cause people to experience many life changes on the scale. It could also be that a third variable, such as social class or hostility, could be the cause of both life changes and illness.

Practice Tests

Item Number	Practice Test 1	Practice Test 2	Practice Test 3	Comprehensive Test
1	B	B	C	C
2	D	C	D	A
3	C	B	D	B
4	B	B	B	B
5	D	D	C	D
6	A	B	D	C
7	B	A	A	D
8	D	C	C	A
9	B	B	A	C
10	C	A	B	C
11				D
12				B
13				D
14				B
15				C

Critical Thinking Essays

1) You'll need to talk about Type A and Type B personality and the components of Type A, such as competitiveness, impatience, perfectionism, and hostility. Type A is related to anxiety and depression, as well as allergies, stomach problems, and head colds. Then you'll need to tell them that hostility that is particularly associated with heart disease. You can also tell them about protective personality factors such as hardiness, optimism, and resilience. You can tell them about the three Cs of hardiness (control, challenge, and commitment) and explain that resilience incorporates the idea of hardiness, but is even broader. Resilient people also tend to be conscientious, optimistic, and extraverted.

2) Locus of control research shows that internals believe they can take action and be effective, unlike people with learned helplessness. Nursing home studies show that giving residents even a small amount of control over their lives resulted in increased health, satisfaction, and longevity. Primary control involves taking action to control external events. Secondary control involves controlling one's reactions or cognitive appraisals. Both improve health.